Ladies-in-Waiting

Other books by Dulcie M. Ashdown

Over the Teacups
Queen Victoria's Mother
Queen Victoria's Family

DULCIE M. ASHDOWN

Ladies-in-Waiting

Arthur Barker Limited London
A subsidiary of Weidenfeld (Publishers) Limited

Arthur Barker Limited
11 St John's Hill, London SW11

ISBN 0 213 16567 8

Printed in Great Britain by
Bristol Typesetting Co Ltd
Barton Manor, St Philips, Bristol

Illustrations

Between pages 116 and 117

Acknowledgments

The author of this book wishes to acknowledge with thanks the valuable assistance given to her by the Press Secretary of Her Majesty the Queen, by the Features Editor of the magazine *Woman's Weekly* and by Miss Helen Cathcart, in her preparation of the final chapter of *Ladies-in-Waiting*. Gratitude is also due to the staff of the British Library and especially to the staff of the Chipping Barnet Public Library, whose patient attention has greatly facilitated the writing of this book.

Permission to quote from manuscripts at Blenheim has been kindly granted by His Grace the Duke of Marlborough, and from the Marlborough Manuscripts at Althorp by the late seventh Earl Spencer.

Use of other quotations in copyright has been authorized by the following publishers:

George Allen & Unwin Ltd, *Helena, Marchioness of Northampton*, C. A. Bradford (1936).

W. H. Allen & Co. Ltd, *A Queen at Home*, V. Watson (1952).

G. Bell & Sons Ltd, *The Diary of Samuel Pepys*, ed. R. C. Latham and W. Matthews (1970–).

Benn Brothers, *Letters of Princess Charlotte*, ed. A. Aspinall (Home & van Thal, 1949).

The Bodley Head, *The Diary of a Lady-in-Waiting*, Lady

Charlotte Bury (1908) and *Letters of Lady Augusta Stanley, 1849–63*, ed. H. Bolitho and W. Baillie (Howe, 1927).

Clarendon Press, *The Diary of John Evelyn*, ed. E. S. de Beer (1955) and *Walpole's Reminiscences*, ed. E. Paget Toynbee (1924).

Constable, *Queen Alexandra*, Georgina Battiscombe (1969).

Eyre & Spottiswoode Ltd, *James II*, F. Turner (1948) and *Some Materials for a History of the reign of George II*, ed. R. Sedgwick (1931).

Granada Publishing Ltd, *Lady Lytton's Court Diary*, M. Lutyens (Rupert Hart Davis, 1961).

William Heinemann Ltd, *The King my Brother*, C. H. Hartmann (1954).

Hodder & Stoughton Ltd, *Henrietta Maria* (1936) and *Mary of Modena* (1962), C. Oman.

Longman Group Ltd, *Caroline the Illustrious*, W. H. Wilkins (1901).

Macmillan (Basingstoke) Ltd, *The Youthful Queen Victoria*, D. Creston (1952) and *Fanny Burney's Diary and Letters, 1768–1840*, ed. A. Dobson (1904).

Frederick Muller Ltd, *Lady of the Sun*, F. G. Gay (1966).

John Murray, *Life with Queen Victoria*, V. Mallet (1968), *Queen Charlotte* (1974) and *Letters of Sarah Spencer, Lady Lyttelton, 1787–1871*, ed. H. Wyndham (1912).

Oxford University Press, *English Historical Literature of the Fifteenth Century*, ed. C. L. Kingsford (1913).

Routledge & Kegan Paul Ltd, *Memoirs of Count Gramont*, ed. C. H. Hartmann and P. Quennell (1930–2).

Martin Secker & Warburg Ltd, John Aubrey's *Brief Lives*, ed. O. L. Dick (1949).

Society for Promoting Christian Knowledge, *Four Margarets*, M. E. Tabor (The Sheldon Press, 1929).

University of Pennsylvania Press, USA, *Letters and Epigrams of Sir John Harington*, ed. N. E. McClure (1930).

Weidenfeld & Nicolson, *Victoria R.I.*, E. Longford (1964) and *Henry VIII and his Court* (1971) and *All the Queen's Men* (1972), N. Williams.

COURTS are strange, mysterious places: those who pretend most to despise them seek to gain admittance within their precincts; those who once obtain an entrance there generally lament their fate and yet, somehow or other, cannot break their chains. I believe, also, that it makes little difference whether those circles of society, which stand apart from the rest of the world, exist under one form of government or under another; whether under Emperors, Kings, Protectors or Consuls. They may vary as to modes and designations, but Courts are Courts still, and have been so from the earliest times. Intrigues, jealousies, heart-burnings, lies, dissimulations, thrive in them as mushrooms in a hot-bed. Nevertheless, they are necessary evils, and they afford a great school both for the heart and head. It is utterly impossible, so long as the world exists, that similar societies should not exist also; and one may as well declaim against every other defect attendant upon human institutions, and endeavour to extirpate crime from the world, as pretend to put down Courts and their concomitant evils.

Lady Charlotte Bury,
The Diary of a Lady-in-Waiting, ed. A. F. Steuart
(John Lane, The Bodley Head, 1908), volume 1, p. 1

Introduction

It is surely impossible to study the history of England, or to read the lives of English monarchs, without the realization that certain ladies-in-waiting of various queens have played a large and important part in the nation's political history. In so many cases, a lady-in-waiting of unusual intellect and ability – or of great beauty and charm – could, in past centuries, leave her seat in the background to take a firm stance on the centre of the nation's political stage.

Immediately the name of Anne Boleyn springs to mind: from the earliest history lessons of childhood, we learn that King Henry VIII cast aside his wife Queen Catherine for love of her lady-in-waiting, Anne, and that he later numbered two more ladies-in-waiting among his six wives. And then there is the maid-of-honour Anne Hyde, who converted her husband, the future King James II, to Catholicism, with disastrous consequences for the Stuart dynasty. And Sarah Churchill, who so captured the affections of Queen Anne that for years she was the *éminence grise* behind the British throne. Throughout English history there have been ladies-in-waiting who have become the mistresses of kings, and mistresses of kings who have become ladies-in-waiting to their long-suffering queens; there have been ladies who have intrigued in politics, who have amassed fortunes by their influence and who have infuriated or beguiled the women they have served.

Yet the term 'in-waiting', meaning 'in attendance', implies a background role. Ladies-in-waiting were generally background figures in the great events of history which they witnessed at the royal Courts. Only the exceptional personalities of a few outstanding ladies-in-waiting appear on the pages of formal histories of England; there were many more who did their duty quietly and patiently – yet here too there are fascinating stories to be found.

Perhaps the role and individual characters of ladies-in-waiting in English history are not the most important or the most serious study one could choose to make. Yet the formal historians who would have us concentrate on the 'significant trends' in social development and 'landmarks' in constitutional evolution are surely denying the universal love of history's 'stories'. When the causes of the Industrial Revolution, so painstakingly learned at school, are forgotten, the stories of the Tolpuddle Martyrs and the 'climbing boys' are remembered; the exploits of 'Bonnie Prince Charlie' take a far greater grip on the imagination than the terms of constitutional restrictions imposed on the Hanoverian kings whom he sought to dethrone. When the stories of our history are ignored, who can blame us for disliking the plain substance?

So here are a few good stories from English history, some well known, others salvaged from obscurity, offered unashamedly for your amusement.

I

'LOST in the mists of antiquity' was a phrase which historians once found very useful when they could find little or no evidence on their particular subjects. In the past century, painstaking research among original documents has largely removed such inadequacies from medieval scholarship. In the case of the history of the lady-in-waiting in the Middle Ages however the old cliché is still applicable – not for want of research but from lack of contemporary sources. The duties of the kings' servants, from his chamberlain down to his carvers and cutlers, are listed in various medieval manuscripts, and it is possible also to trace the routine of the queens' household officials, the men who served as treasurer, attorney, steward etc. But no medieval commentator thought it necessary to examine the role of the queens' ladies-in-waiting.

At best, one may find the names of the queens' ladies in royal exchequer rolls, and there are plenty of vague references in chronicles to the public activities of 'the queen and her ladies'. It is easier to describe the work of a medieval peasant-farmer than to recount the duties and life-style of one of these women at Court. Of course, a few powerful personalities made their mark – such as the fourteenth-century Alice Perrers, a lady-in-waiting to Queen Philippa, who in her day caused something of a national scandal by becoming mistress to King Edward III and who was reviled for her greed and her meddling in affairs of state. But in the main, medieval ladies-in-waiting are what used to be called ' shadowy figures ' in history.

In the early Middle Ages there was no regular royal Court such as there was under the Tudors, with its brilliant ceremonial and leadership of fashion. The men in day-to-day contact with the king were all functional – councillors, military leaders and the great nobles who served as royal representatives throughout the country but who gathered occasionally for consultation. Indeed, the word ' Court ' itself comes from a confusion of ' cohort ' or assembly, and the Latin *Curia*, meaning the king's council. Such a royal Court was a far cry from the Hampton Court of the Tudors or St James's under the Stuarts, with their gatherings for royal pleasure and entertainment as much as for the execution of business.

But most medieval kings were married, and their wives needed companions from ranks higher than those of their essential menial servants. So, from the earliest times, if a lord resided in the household of the king, for business, as often as not his lady would go with him and spend her hours in the queen's bower. At the same time, a queen would have more permanent companions, daughters, wives and widows from the knightly class or peerage, who would be paid for their attendance on her. So much is evidenced quite plainly from account rolls and registers.

It is in the records of such payments to ladies-in-waiting that we find our first references to them. Even here, though, there is some confusion: some ladies were paid a salary per annum, others received only occasional gifts. From this it is reasonable to speculate that there were ladies in residence with the various queens all the year round – unmarried women and widows, with no duties at home to divide their loyalty, and married women who would spend part of their year ' at Court ' and part at home on their manors in the shires. In the later Middle Ages it is possible to trace the lineage of ' Court families ', where ladies-in-waiting married officials of the king's or the queen's household, or where children followed their parents in office.* For example, in the fifteenth century, Queen Margaret of Anjou's lady Rose Merston was the wife of the Treasurer of the King's Chamber, and Catherine Whittingham was the wife of the Keeper of the Queen's Great Wardrobe. These were the women with whom the queen would have had daily contact – not duchesses and countesses, for the most part, but ladies of 'gentle birth' merely.

One of the most interesting facts to emerge from the dry lists of names in royal exchequer rolls is the incidence of foreign names among the queens' ladies. Of course, the Norman conquest of England and the consequent virtual extinction of the ancient Saxon nobility meant that French names predominated in the 'ruling class'. Joanna and Isabella de Camville who served Eleanor of Castile in the thirteenth century (as had their mother before them) were probably English-born for all their French surname, though their family may still have owned lands on the Continent as well as in England.

However, medieval queens consort of England were mainly foreign princesses married to the kings of England for reasons of international diplomacy, and they would naturally bring with them from home a small retinue of ladies who would remain in England for some time, often for the rest of their lives. Marguerite of France, the second wife of Edward I, brought seven French ladies with her; the child Isabelle of France, second wife of Richard II, had a French chamberlain, Monsieur de Vache, whose wife had a place in her household, and two chambermaids, Simonette and Marianne, who remained with the Queen throughout her five-year stay in England. Margaret of Anjou had a lady in her household named 'Barbalina Herberquyne', described by a contemporary as a German, who was naturalized English in 1449. Throughout the whole history of ladies-in-waiting, these foreigners came in for a good deal

* Sir Michael Adeane, Private Secretary to H.M. the Queen, is a descendant of a family which figured largely at Court in the nineteenth century (see Chapter 10), giving a modern analogy.

of ridicule in xenophobic England: Anne of Bohemia's ladies caused as much mirth by their horned head-dresses in the late fourteenth century as did Catherine of Braganza's Portuguese ladies with their stiff farthingales in the seventeenth.

Of course, it is the medieval chroniclers who provide the main clues as to the duties of the ladies-in-waiting. 'The Queen and her ladies' is a phrase so frequently used as to be tantalizing in its inadequacy. 'The Queen and her ladies' are present when the King receives his subject nobles; they grace banquets and church ceremonies and tournaments. Numerous illuminations in medieval manuscripts depict a crowned lady with splendidly attired attendants. As display and ceremonial came to play an increasing part in royal life, and as the royal household gradually shed its exclusively functional role, naturally the female element was called more into play. By the mid-thirteenth century there was a continual coming and going of ladies up from the shires, for Court festivals, who would follow in the train of a queen on great occasions.

In the two or three centuries after the Norman conquest, just as there was no regular Court life, so there was no permanent centre for the royal family. Windsor and Westminster were the main royal residences, but for most of the year the household was on the move. In peacetime a king would travel from one royal manor to another, moving on when he had exhausted the local supply of provisions, or when he had finished his business in the locality – and of course his council and his generals and the civil servants and priests and menials went with him. The itinerant life can have been no easy one for the medieval lady-in-waiting. If she could not ride horse-back, or was too old or too infirm to do so, she must needs take a seat in a cart. Although her conveyance was brightly painted and a much grander cousin of those used by the peasants, it was similarly without springs or comfort. In the reign of Richard II, the ladies-in-waiting of his wife Anne of Bohemia, travelling in one of these *chars* over London bridge, were tipped out onto the ground when their wagon overturned – to the delight of the Cockneys, who cheered as the Bohemian ladies went tumbling to the ground, squashing their outlandish foreign head-dresses in the fall.

But the queen did not necessarily follow her husband in his 'progresses'. At her marriage she would be endowed with manors of her own, which contributed money and produce for her support, and to which she would often retire during pregnancy or in her husband's absence abroad. In state marriages there was rarely such love between husband and wife as to keep them together continually. However, there were exceptions to the rule: Edward I and his wife Eleanor of Castile were very much attached to each other, and Queen Eleanor accompanied her husband on crusade; Edward III actually chose his wife, Philippa of Hainault, through affection, as a teenager, and the names of their children bear witness to the Queen's journeys in her husband's company: their eldest son was known as 'Edward of Woodstock', from his birthplace at one of the royal manors; Lionel 'of Antwerp' and John 'of Gaunt' (Ghent) were born during the King's military campaigns in the Netherlands; Edward 'of Langley' and Thomas 'of Woodstock' were born at home in more peaceful years. Since a queen had always to be suitably attended, her ladies would travel with her on her land and sea journeys. Often her retinue would be swelled to extraordinary proportions, as in 1346 when, as the chronicler Froissart recorded, Queen Philippa travelled to her husband's war-camp: 'The Queen brought many ladies and damsels with her, as well to accompany her [that is, to be her companions] as to see their husbands, fathers, brothers and other friends that lay at siege there before Calais.'[1]

On that occasion there was little danger for the ladies, who would be kept well away from the dangerous areas of the campaign, but often they went in peril of their lives for the privilege of 'accompanying' a queen. Eleanor of Aquitaine was the wife of King Louis VII of France before divorcing him to become the wife of the future Henry II of England, and as Queen of France encountered considerable danger on crusade with her husband. The ladies were, naturally enough, only an encumbrance on the crusade, especially on the long, dangerous journey through hostile territory to the Holy Land. But Eleanor insisted on taking part in the adventure and when Louis took the cross in 1147, she vowed to follow him. In the general zeal, many French ladies volunteered to go too and appeared in public as a sort of bodyguard for the Queen. But, tradition has it, it was the ladies, or more particularly Eleanor, who put the whole French contingent of crusaders in jeopardy.

All went well in the early stages of the journey, but in Asia Minor the Queen refused to accept the authority of the protector whom her husband had put in charge of her party, which formed the vanguard of the army. Instead of camping for the night on safe, flat, open ground, she insisted on a site in a more pleasant valley. By the time the King and his men reached the encampment, they found the Queen and her retinue open to attack, with no guards posted on the surrounding heights. A sharp skirmish between Louis and the enemy Arabs, which resulted in the death of reputedly some seven thousand Frenchmen and the capture of the baggage-train, proved the folly of Eleanor's choice of resting-place. The ladies were lucky that it was only their clothes which paid the price of Eleanor's caprice.

However, the life of the lady-in-waiting was not all foreign adventure and ceremonial display. Medieval queens had no part to play in government, no duties beyond public appearances and the bearing of heirs to the kingdom. There would be long, probably tedious hours spent in needlework and gossip in draughty and smoky castle chambers.

No chronicler of the Middle Ages ever thought it worth his while to detail the duties of the lady-in-waiting, and it is not until the fifteenth century that we are allowed an authentic glimpse of the daily round of even one of their mistresses. But there is a document which tells of the routine of the Lady Cecily, Duchess of York, the widowed mother of King Edward IV. As a young woman, she was one of the great ladies of the Court of Margaret of Anjou, wife of King Henry VI; but when her husband, Richard of York, challenged for the crown, unsuccessfully, she was forced to flee abroad with her younger children, for safety. In old age, however, she returned, to the honoured place of mother to the King, after her son Edward had wrested the crown from King Henry. As a sort of Queen Mother, Cecily had her place at Court, but after the exertions of her youth, she preferred retirement and a chance to indulge her natural piety.

Rising at seven in the morning, she heard a Mass before breakfast and three more during the morning. During dinner, she listened to a lecture 'of holy matter'. In the afternoon, the Duchess held a public audience for an hour, and then had a nap, but 'at the first peal of evening' went again to her prayers. It was only after evensong and supper that she found time 'to be familiar with her gentlewomen' in 'honest mirth'.[2]

Cecily's daughter-in-law, Queen Elizabeth Woodville, similarly turned to religion to comfort her old age, but in her prime her Court was as gay as any. A foreign visitor to her Court, impressed by the formal ritual of the Queen's public life, was allowed to see her ladies in their leisure. In Elizabeth's chamber 'she had there her ladies playing at morteaulx [marbles, or bowls], and some of her ladies were playing at closheys of ivory [ninepins], and dancing. And some at diverse games ...'.[3]

Out of the plethora of lists of names of ladies-in-waiting and of their salaries or occasional fees in royal account rolls and registers of the Middle Ages, only a few characters come to life. In 1128, in the reign of Henry I, for example, there is a writ sent out for a priory to be built at Kilburn, north of London, 'for the reception of ... three virgins of God, sacred damsels who had belonged to the chamber of Matilda, the good queen consort of Henry I'.[4] These ladies, who retired to the religious life after their mistress's death, were Emma, Gunilda and Christina. Their Saxon names highlight the factor of the Queen's own choice of their service, for at an almost totally Norman Court, they were probably members of the conquered English aristocracy. Matilda herself, a princess of Scotland, was Saxon on her mother's side, and would probably prefer women of her own race to serve her.

Throughout the Middle Ages, ladies-in-waiting were well provided for after their mistresses' deaths. On her deathbed

Philippa of Hainault, who kept a large, well-regulated household composed of English and Flemish courtiers, begged her husband to take care of her servants, and an Exchequer account proves that he discharged her wishes faithfully: 'first, to the beloved damsel Alicia de Preston [a lady generally identified as the King's mistress Alice Perrers, who had been in Philippa's service about three years], ten marks yearly, at Pasche [Easter] and Michaelmas; likewise to Matilda Fisher, to Elizabeth Pershore, to Johanna Kawley, ten marks yearly; to Johanna Cosin, to Philippa the Picard [thought to be the wife of the poet Chaucer] and to Agatha Liergin, a hundred shillings yearly; and to Matilda Radscroft and Agnes de Saxilby, five marks yearly'.[5] Queen Philippa had always been generous to her ladies (so generous in her charities and so extravagant in her personal expenditure, that she died deep in debt): Emma Priour, a lady-in-waiting in Philippa's early years in England, was awarded a life pension of her whole support to be paid by the convent of Selby; another, Joan de Carru, received the gift of six tuns of wine a year for life; and Alice de Bedingfeld received £20 and a tun of Gascon wine a year for life. In many of the account rolls of the queens, and most notably in Philippa's well-kept records, gifts of cloth or clothes to ladies are listed – for those appearing daily in the limelight of the Court frequent changes of costume would have been a great expense.

From the reign of Edward III to the mid-sixteenth century, royal tournaments were a prime feature of Court entertainment, incorporating not only a chance for the display of knightly skills in combat but also the ceremonial which was a lady's place in the chivalric convention. Edward III was the first English king to make a regular event of such tournaments, and it was he who chose the site of Smithfield in London to stage them. There would be a colourful procession out to the field from the Tower – on one occasion the King and his knights, dressed all in fur, were led through the streets by ladies dressed in crimson velvet, their faces masked. (In the reign of Edward's grandson Richard II, ladies led their champions to the fray by silver chains.) At the field, the gentry would sit or stand in wooden galleries, with the populace clamouring in pens below. Ladies whose knights were taking part in the tournament would have a special front seat in the lists, from which they could dispense their 'favours' of scarves and ribbons.

In 1374 Edward III held a seven-day tournament at the end of Lent, in honour of his mistress Alice Perrers. This former lady-in-waiting to the late Queen was herself treated as a queen for the period of the festival. This was one of the rare occasions in the Middle Ages when the chroniclers (all men) thought fit to describe a lady's costume: Alice wore a russet and white gown, with an ermine border and a trimming of pearls; over it was a gold tissue cloak, lined with red taffeta; on her head was a leather cap embroidered with jewels. Usually, the knights' ladies would ride in procession on palfreys; on this occasion all walked, to make a contrast with Alice, who rode to Smithfield from the Tower alone in a chariot. As 'Lady of the Sun', she presided throughout the festival, and no one could have been left in any doubt but that the King's mistress was the focal point of the entertainment. It was unprecedented for so 'low-born' a woman to take on such a role.

Alice Perrers, then, was the first lady-in-waiting to make her mark on English history, and she did so in no small measure. Her origins are a matter of much scholarly dispute: rumour, legend and controversial research argue that she was a niece of the great churchman William of Wykeham, or the daughter of a Devon weaver or an Essex tiler, or a member of the Perrers family, gentry of Hertfordshire. Only a guess puts her birthdate at about 1348, and her arrival at Court only probably pre-dated 1366 when the first royal gift to her, of wine, is recorded. Nor is it known when Alice became Edward III's mistress though it was probably still in the lifetime of Queen Philippa, for at the latter's death in 1369 Edward made over to Alice – beyond the pension granted to her among others of the Queen's ladies – much of his late wife's property: 'Know all,' he proclaimed, 'that we give and concede to our beloved Alice Perrers, damsel of the chamber to our most dear consort Philippa, now dead, and to her heirs and executors, all the jewels, goods and chattels that the said Queen left in the hands of Euphemia, wife of Sir William de Heserlarton, Knight; and the said Euphemia is to deliver them to the said Alice on the receipt of this our command.'[6]

This was the beginning of Alice's rapacious collection of possessions: manors, that is landed estates, were her main object, for they meant quarterly cash payments from rents, but she had other sources of income too. In 1376, with Edward III in his dotage, and with Parliament flexing its muscles to test royal resistance to its powers, Alice was brought to court. She was accused by the Commons of having taken a seat on the justices' benches in the courts in cases where her interests, or those of her protégés, were involved and of having used influence to have them decided in her favour. She would have gained a good deal of money in such bribes for the use of her influence. With fine moral indignation, the Commons declared that Alice had 'been preferred in the King's love even before the Queen', and that she had received through him vast sums from the Exchequer, beyond even her meddling in justice. No Parliament, however bold, would take such proceedings against a royal favourite lightly: Alice Perrers must have been making herself conspicuous indeed to have been so arraigned.

The King, feeble and overcome by the recent death of his eldest son, made no attempt to save his mistress. He gave his name to the warrant by which she was banished from the realm. Submitting to her sentence, Alice kissed the crucifix.

But Parliament could not long sustain its triumphs. Within weeks, the King's eldest surviving son, John of Gaunt, had overturned all the statutes of the so-called Good Parliament, including that against Alice. For all the token act of submission to her punishment, she had not left England and soon joined Edward at Eltham, remaining with him until his death in June the following year, with all her possessions restored and reaffirmed by royal writ. The King died on 21 June 1377, reputedly with Alice beside him until his last breath – at which moment, scurrilous chroniclers averred, she tore the rings from his fingers and fled from Court.

Nevertheless, Alice Perrers does not then disappear from history. She was again brought before Parliament in December 1377 and deprived of all the lands which she had gained by fraud and deceit. She fled to Essex, apparently to Sir William de Windsor, the man she had married some years earlier, and by whom, it was recorded, she had three children – though, significantly, she was always called by her maiden name in her trials and in the royal grants. De Windsor may have agreed to marry Alice, partly to give her a measure of protection but also to gain the King's favour for himself, for he received state office in the last years of Edward's reign, and he was subsequently appointed as a baron to sit in the Parliaments up to his death in 1384. Alice lived on to the then ripe age of about fifty-two, dying in 1400, having for many years contended at law for the property she claimed to be hers. In her will, she divided her bequest between her two daughters and left some provision for road repairs and for the poor of Upminster.

Alice Perrers is thus the first example of a lady-in-waiting who became a king's mistress – the first of so many. But of course it was natural that if a king's eyes strayed beyond his wife, he would look at the women whom he saw daily in his own household. Nor were kings the only philanderers at Court.

Robert de Vere, Duke of Ireland, was the favourite of King Richard II (Edward III's grandson and successor). He was married to Richard's cousin Philippa de Coucy, but fell 'in such love with one of the Queen's damsels, called "Lancegrove" that in no wise could he leave the sight of her; she was a fair and pleasant damsel, and was come with the Queen out of the realm of Bohemia. The Duke loved her so entirely that he would gladly be divorced from his own wife ... and did send for that intent to Rome to Pope Urban', apparently with the goodwill of Queen Anne who supported his request, 'and all the good people of the realm had marvel thereof, and dispraised him'.[7] De Vere's escapade aroused much ill-feeling between his friend King Richard and the rest of the royal family.

Not long after the affair, King Richard's uncle John of Gaunt, Duke of Lancaster, married his long-time mistress, Catherine

Swynford. There is no evidence that Catherine was ever a lady-in-waiting but she was formerly governess of Lancaster's daughters by his first marriage. Although Catherine was a knight's widow, her low birth and ill fame were such as to make the ladies of the Court despise her. Even though the new Duchess ranked the first lady in the realm between the death of Queen Anne and the King's remarriage, duchesses and countesses declared 'how surely they would not come into no place where she should be present; and moreover, they said, it should be a great shame for them that such a duchess, come of so base a blood, and concubine to the Duke in his other wives' days, should go and have the pre-eminence before them'.[8]

Catherine Swynford has been tentatively identified as the daughter of a member of Queen Philippa's Flemish retinue, Sir Payn Roet, the Guienne Herald, and much research has been done to prove that she was the sister of 'Philippa the Picard', one of Queen Philippa's ladies, pantrywoman to the Duchess of Chaucers figure largely in household rolls of grants of pensions Lancaster. This Philippa is also reputed to have been the wife of the poet Geoffrey Chaucer, himself a royal servant for most of his life, in the households of various sons of Edward III. Both Chaucers figure largely in household rolls of grants of pensions and salaries.

The rejected wife of the Duke of Ireland, Philippa de Coucy, has always been linked in reputed kinship with a certain Françoise de Pagnel, Dame de Coucy, who became chief lady-in-waiting to the second wife of Richard II, the child-Queen Isabelle of France. Since Isabelle was only seven years old at the time of her wedding, far too young to consummate the union with Richard or even to live at Court, Madame de Coucy ruled the Queen's household, which was generally separate from the Court. But in 1399, some two years after the wedding, Richard received the disturbing report that his wife's chief lady was living as if she were Queen Mother: 'for she has eighteen horses at her command. But this does not suffice; she has a large train belonging to her husband, and in his livery, whenever she comes and goes. She keeps two or three goldsmiths, two or three cutlers, and two or three furriers constantly employed, as much as you and your queen. She is also building a chapel that will cost 1400 nobles.'[9] Richard wasted no time in dispensing with her services. It was one of his last acts before political disaster overtook him, and he lost his throne to his cousin Henry of Lancaster, who became king as Henry IV in the same year, 1399.

The former King's disparagement of his cousin the Duchess of Ireland in her marital troubles, and his rejection of Philippa de Coucy, redounded on his widow, Queen Isabelle, who was innocent of any crime against the ladies. For, in the years between the deposition of her husband and her return home to France, aged twelve, in 1408, she was put into the custody of the Duchess of Ireland and Françoise de Coucy, at Leeds Castle in Kent, which cannot have been at all pleasant. But it was not long before the former Queen's retinue was broken up and replaced with men and women under firm instructions never to mention the name of Richard II in her presence. Yet they, in the pay of Isabelle's enemy Henry IV, became so attached to the child that when the time came for them to leave her in France, according to the chronicler, they made 'sore lamentations':

> ... before the parties separated, they all wept most piteously, and when they came to quit the Chapel of Our Lady at Leulinghen, Queen Isabelle, whose young heart is full of tenderness and kindliness, brought all her English ladies, who were making sore lamentations, unto the French tents, where she made them dine with her. And after dinner, Queen Isabelle took all the jewels she had remaining [few enough after years as a neglected widow], and divided them among the lords and ladies of England who had accompanied her, who all, nevertheless, wept mightily with sorrow at parting with their young Queen. Yet still she sweetly bade them 'be of good cheer', though weeping herself; nevertheless, at the parting, all renewed their lamentations.[10]

It was not many years before another lady-in-waiting aspired to regularize her illicit union with a member of the royal family.

Eleanor Cobham served Jacqueline of Holland, wife of Humphrey, Duke of Gloucester, an uncle of the infant King Henry VI. The match between Jacqueline and Humphrey was a mistake, both politically and personally, and in 1425 Eleanor became the Duke's mistress, living openly with him while he was awaiting his divorce from Jacqueline. The couple already had two children before their marriage in 1428, to which contemporary chroniclers attributed 'shame and more disgrace and inconvenience to the whole kingdom than can be expressed'.[11] Eleanor's rise to rank from the station of lady-in-waiting would in itself be noteworthy, but even more dramatic was her arrest in 1441 on charges of witchcraft and plotting the death of the King. Already, the second wife of Henry IV, Joanna of Navarre, had been arraigned as a witch in 1419 and put quietly away to spend the rest of her life in penitence. But Eleanor's case was made public. A priest, already convicted on both charges, had accused her of inciting him to the 'craft of necromancy' and of 'asking him to divine to what estate of life she should come', that is, to predict whether she would ever become queen, an obvious pointer to nefarious plans. Eleanor sought sanctuary at Westminster but discovered that it was a law of the Church that no protection should be afforded to suspected witches. She was put on trial and found guilty.

The Duchess of Gloucester had to do humiliating penance in public – walking through the streets of London bareheaded and carrying a large candle, on several occasions. Then, for the rest of her life, she had to endure close – though comfortable – confinement.

Farewell, damask and clothes of gold;
Farewell, velvet and clothes in grain;
Farewell, robes in many a fold;
Farewell, I see you never again. . . .[12]

So intoned a set of contemporary verses on Eleanor's disgrace, with numerous warnings to women not to follow her example.

The mid-fifteenth century was renowned for its 'unequal' marriages between aristocrats and commoners. Henry VI's mother, Catherine of France, took as her second husband a Welsh gentleman, Owen Tudor (and became, by him, the ancestress of the royal Tudor dynasty); Jacquetta of Luxembourg, widow of Henry VI's uncle the Duke of Bedford, married Sir Richard Woodville, a former member of her late husband's staff. One of the Woodville daughters, Elizabeth, was sent as a maid-of-honour to Henry VI's queen, Margaret of Anjou, and, after her marriage to the Lancastrian knight Sir John Grey, gained the more senior post of lady-in-waiting to the Queen. Later, as a widow, Elizabeth Woodville caught the eye of King Edward IV, the Yorkist who overthrew the Lancastrian dynasty. 'She was a woman more of formal countenance than of excellent beauty,' wrote the chronicler Hall, 'but yet of such beauty and favour with her sober demeanour, lovely looking and feminine smiling (neither too wanton nor too humble), beside her tongue so eloquent and her wit so pregnant.'[13]

Elizabeth was too clever to become the mistress of the King, easily taken and as easily discarded. Edward was a bachelor ripe for marriage and the foundation of a dynasty, and by her wits Elizabeth Woodville became the first lady-in-waiting to marry a king of England.

2

THE first half of the sixteenth century is the rival of the second half of the seventeenth to be deemed the heyday of the lady-in-waiting in English history. For it was in this period that King Henry VIII took former ladies-in-waiting to number among his six wives.

Henry's first wife, however, was of true royal birth: Catherine of Aragon, daughter of Ferdinand and Isabella, the joint monarchs of Spain. Catherine had arrived in England in 1501 to become the wife of Henry's elder brother, Arthur, Prince of Wales, but the Prince's early death widowed her within fifteen months of the wedding.

Catherine was subsequently betrothed to Prince Henry, now advanced by his brother's death to become heir to his father King Henry VII; but the fluctuations in Anglo-Spanish diplomacy prevented their marriage, even after Henry reached the prescribed age in 1506. Throughout the years of her widowhood, Princess Catherine could never be sure if she would ever become Prince Henry's wife. Immediately after her husband's death, she was given an independent establishment, Durham House, in the Strand in London, to be staffed by the considerable number of Spanish attendants whom she had brought to England. It was not long, however, before Spanish relations with England fell to such a low ebb, on matters of politics and trade, that King Henry began to try to extricate his son from his promise to marry Catherine. In the consequent bad relations between her father, King Ferdinand, and her father-in-law, King Henry, the Princess found herself as much a shuttle-cock as a pawn in the royal games of diplomacy.

Amid all the intrigues of the Court, there was only one person whom Catherine felt she could trust implicitly: Doña Elvira Manuel, her chief lady and duenna, whom her own mother, Queen Isabella, had chosen for her support in the foreign land to which she was sent while still only a teenager. When Catherine set up her own household, as a widow, Doña Elvira was its real ruler. Between her and her husband, Don Pedro Manrique, the Princess's major domo, the whole of the household management was divided – all the other Spanish servants had to obey their authority, and even Catherine would not gainsay those to whom her mother had entrusted her welfare. It was some years before she realized how misplaced was that trust.

Doña Elvira was the sister of Don Juan Manuel, an official high in the service of Catherine's brother-in-law Philip of Burgundy who, after the death of his mother-in-law Queen Isabella, claimed the kingdom of Castile in the right of his wife Juana, against the interests of King Ferdinand, father of both Juana and Catherine. Don Juan attempted, through his sister and her mistress, to bring King Henry VII to side with Philip against Ferdinand, with, of course, his own self-interest as his spur. Doña Elvira stood well with the King of England, and was a fierce enemy of King Ferdinand's ambassador at Henry's Court, who opposed Philip of Burgundy's influence there. She attempted to set Catherine against him too, telling her that the ambassador, de Puebla, was failing to plead her cause with her father for prompt ratification of her new betrothal, and to persuade her to write to her father-in-law to arrange a meeting between him and Philip and Juana. Catherine had already written her letter when de Puebla came to her in great consternation and revealed to her all the self-seeking of which her duenna was guilty. For all the Princess's respect for Doña Elvira, her strong sense of duty – then, as in later years, always the governing emotion in Catherine – forced her to see the truth. The duenna and her family hastily left England.

This was by no means the end of Catherine's troubles. Since the death of Prince Arthur, the later instalments of her dowry had not been paid into English coffers, and in the period since her future marriage to Prince Henry had come into doubt, it had become increasingly obvious that King Ferdinand would send no more money in the future. King Henry, on the other hand, similarly refused to continue paying the upkeep of a young woman who had almost ceased to figure in his plans (but whom he would not allow to return home, just in case she could prove useful to him at some future date). In June 1505 he stopped Catherine's allowance. Thus, when Doña Elvira departed, leaving Catherine without a chaperone and as mistress of a household whom she could not pay, needing food and clothing for which she must go into debt, it was natural for King Henry to close Durham House and take her into his own Court. There she lived for over three years, dependent on the spasmodic dole of the King and the even rarer gifts of money from her father, which invariably went towards paying her ever-mounting debts.

Yet throughout these years, many of Catherine's Spanish servants remained to share her poverty and neglect. Ines de Venega, Maria de Salinas and their fellows among Catherine's maids-of-honour might have expected, under normal circumstances, to have made grand matches with members of the English aristocracy, or to have been sent home to Spain when suitable marriages had been arranged for them through their mistress's intercession with her family. But as it was, they were dowerless and without the prospect of any future assistance. In 1504–5 Catherine had been assiduous on behalf of her maid-of-honour Maria de Rojas, whose hand had been solicited by a grandson of the Earl of Derby. But all her letters to her father to beg him to send Maria a dowry had been ignored. It was only later that Catherine found out that the mischievous Doña Elvira had advised King Ferdinand against the match, since she had hopes of Maria's marrying her own son, Don Iñigo, master of Catherine's pages. With the disgrace of the Manrique family and the obvious disinclination of King Ferdinand to send a dowry to the Derby family, Maria de Rojas was left unmarried.

In 1508, however, one of the maids-of-honour, Francesca de Carceres, could stand her plight no longer. She intrigued with the new Spanish ambassador, Fuensalida, to have the whole of Catherine's staff shipped back to Spain, and accused the Princess's confessor, Fray Diego, of persuading Catherine to remain in England in hopes of a future marriage to Prince Henry when her firm insistence on returning home might have delivered her – and her servants – from penury. But when Francesca found that she could make no headway with her plans, she turned instead to furthering her own interests by a marriage with Fuensalida's landlord, the Italian banker Grimaldi. Although Grimaldi was one of the wealthiest men in Europe, the creditor of kings, he was by no means of the rank expected for the husband of a noble Spanish lady. Nevertheless, after an open, bitter quarrel with Catherine over her interference in the Princess's affairs, Francesca left her household secretly and married her lover.

Had she waited only a few months longer, she might have been married more highly and honourably with the turn in her mistress's fortunes. In April 1509, Henry VII died, and only six weeks later his son, now Henry VIII, married Princess Catherine. Whether Henry had long been in love with his former sister-in-law, or whether, as he averred, he was merely carrying out his father's death-bed wish, is unknown. But nevertheless, he did marry Catherine, and she was transported from her former friendless state to the eminence of queen of England. Those of her staff who wished, returned to Spain; but one of them, Maria de Salinas, chose to remain in England and received as large a dowry as anyone could wish, when she was married to Lord Willoughby. She remained in England for the rest of her life, the most trusted of the Queen's friends, and for the first few years of Catherine's marriage, while the Queen held the King's love, Maria figured largely at Court. A royal ship was even named in her honour.

But this business of ladies' travelling abroad to serve queens and princesses was a two-way affair. Foreign queens brought their entourage with them but English princesses marrying abroad took Englishwomen to their new Courts. And there were troubles in that direction too. . . .

In 1514 Henry VIII's cherished younger sister was despatched to France to marry King Louis XII. She was eighteen to his fifty-two, and the French King was ailing and exhausted by his fifteen-year reign. But, as in the case of her sister-in-law Catherine, Mary of England was left no choice in her fate, for all her pleas to be allowed to remain at home. She was married by proxy to Louis at Greenwich in August 1514 and in October arrived in France to meet her husband.

The new Queen of France took with her a large and brilliant train of notables. Among the great ladies who were to convey her to Louis were the Duchess of Norfolk, her daughter the Countess of Oxford, the Marchioness of Dorset and Lady Monteagle – but their presence in the Queen's retinue was only for show; they intended to return home once the welcoming festivities in France were over. Mary's choice of her own permanent ladies was subject to the approval of King Henry's great councillor Wolsey and that of her as yet unseen husband. Louis made objection to only one name on Mary's list, that of a Frenchwoman, Jane Popincourt, who had been at the English Court for many years, for Jane was formerly the mistress of the Duc de Longueville, a French nobleman who had been a prisoner of the English for several years. It was she who had taught Mary that perfect French which was soon to charm her new Court. But King Louis would have none of her: 'As you love me', he declared to King Henry's envoy, 'speak of her no more, I would she were burned!'[1]

The ladies who finally accompanied Mary were of irreproachable character. They were of the highest birth, daughters of the great families of Grey, Devereux, Ferrers and Dacre. And the 'mother of the maids' was Mary's former governess, Lady Guildford, a courtier of long standing and the widow of the Household Controller of the late Henry VII.

It did not take King Louis long to realize that his young wife pined for England. On her arrival in France, Mary was fêted and admired as no woman before her, it was reported, and yet she was dreadfully homesick. Perhaps it was because his wife spent so much of her time mourning with her English servants that the King decided, almost immediately after their wedding at St Denis, to dismiss her whole train.

Mary was devastated. She wrote to her brother on 12 October, pouring out her grievance and begging his help:

My good Brother,

As heartily as I can, I recommend me unto your Grace, marvelling much that I never heard from you since our departing, so often as I have sent and written unto you.

And now I am left most alone in effect, for on the morn after marriage my chamberlain and all other men servants were discharged, and in likewise my mother Guildford with other [of] my women and maidens, except such as never had experience nor knowledge how to adv[ert]ise or give me counsel in any time of need, which is to be feared more shortly than your Grace thought at [the] time of my departing, as my mother Guildford can more plainly show your Grace than I can write, to whom I beseech you to give credence.

And if it may be by any means possible, I humbly require you to cause my said mother Guildford to repair hither once again. For else if any chance hap other than well I shall not know where nor by whom to ask any good counsel to your pleasure nor yet to mine own profit. I marvel much that my lord of Norfolk [the King's representative at the wedding] would at all times so lightly grant everything at their request here [in giving in to Louis's demands]. I am well assured that when you know the truth of everything as my mother Guildford can shew you, ye would full little have thought I should have been thus intreated; that would God my lord of

> York [Wolsey] had come with me in the room of Norfolk; for then I am sure I should have been left much more at my heartsease than I am now.[2]

Left without an answer, Mary wrote then to Wolsey:

> I have not yet seen in France any lady or gentlewoman so necessary for me as she [Lady Guildford] is, nor yet so meet to do the King my brother service as she is. And for my part, my lord, as you love the King, my brother, and me, find the means that she may in all haste come hither again, for I had lief lose the winning I shall have in France to lose her counsel when I shall lack it, which is not like long to be required as I am sure the noblemen and gentlemen can shew you more than becometh me to write in this matter.[3]

Wolsey took pity on Mary – or realized how great the loss of such a useful advocate as Lady Guildford would be whenever English interests conflicted with French at Louis XII's Court. He wrote to the French King:

> . . . I have no doubt, Sire, that when you will have known her [Lady Guildford] well, you will find the lady wise, honourable and discreet, very anxious and quick to pursue and accomplish in all things possible to her your wishes and desires, in all that you will order and commend to her, whatsoever, it would profit you, or may be done to the contrary; as I have written more fully to monseigneur, your chamberlain, in order to explain it to you for my part. . . .[4]

Lady Guildford waited at Boulogne for her summons to return to the French Court, trusting in Wolsey's persuasiveness and in Louis's reputed willingness to indulge his wife. But she was to be disappointed. The King completely refused to have in his wife's confidence a woman who would continually remind her of her English duty to the detriment of her new loyalty to France. As Lord Worcester reported home, Louis 'swore that there was never man that better loved his wife than he did, but rather than have such a woman about her, he had liefer be without her'.[5]

As a palliative, the King allowed Mary to keep a few of the serving-men she had brought with her, and some of her younger, unmarried ladies. Indeed, some of them may still have been children, for among their number was Anne Boleyn, the daughter of Sir Thomas Boleyn, an envoy to France, who can have been little more than seven at the time (if the uncertainty of her birthdate, generally placed at 1507, can be trusted).

Queen Mary of France had not long to endure her exile from her home. On the last day of 1514 King Louis died, leaving her a widow after less than three months as a wife. Within weeks, she secretly remarried – to the Duke of Suffolk whom, reputedly, she had long loved, and once she had turned her brother's anger into grudging forgiveness (on payment of a large fine), returned to England to spend the rest of her life quite peaceably and happily.

Of Mary Tudor's ladies-in-waiting in France, it is naturally Anne Boleyn who is the most interesting, for in the years ahead her rise to become Queen of England, and its consequent scandals, marked her out beyond all women of her era.

Anne owed her place in Mary's entourage to the growing power of her father at Court, and to the influence of her uncle the Duke of Norfolk. When Mary left France, Anne remained to enter first the household of the new Queen Claude and then that of Marguerite of Alençon, later Queen of Navarre. From her early youth, Anne distinguished herself. A contemporary at the Court of Francis I of France wrote of her:

> She possessed a great talent for poetry, and when she sang, like a second Orpheus, she would have made bears and wolves attentive. She likewise danced the English dances, leaping and jumping with infinite grace and agility. Moreover, she invented many new figures and steps which are yet known by her name, or by those of the gallant partners with whom she danced them. She was well skilled in all games fashionable at Courts. Besides singing like a siren, accompanying herself on the lute, she harped better than King David, and handled

> cleverly both flute and rebec. She dressed with marvellous taste and devised new modes, which were followed by the fairest ladies of the French Court; but none wore them with her gracefulness, in which she rivalled Venus.[6]

Though she was no beauty, Anne could make men believe that she was, by the sheer power of her attractions, and no one could have been better schooled than she had been in France to catch the eye of a king.

Anne Boleyn was not the first seductress to woo Henry VIII away from his wife, Catherine of Aragon. Henry had been brought up very strictly, always in the company of sober and discreet old men of Henry VII's council; at first he was delighted with his wife and never seemed to tire of her company, but as he grew more accustomed to being with ladies, and frolicking with them in the robust masques which he delighted to stage – in which Catherine was always audience, never actress – he lost that single-minded fidelity which he had at first led the Queen to expect. It was only a year after their wedding, in May 1510, when Catherine was pregnant with their first child, that Henry began his first flirtation with a lady-in-waiting. She was Anne Hastings, one of the Stafford family high in favour at Court and the wife of one of the King's esquires. Lady Anne was also 'free' with one Sir William Compton, another courtier, and so openly that her brother the Duke of Buckingham, having discovered the couple together, reported her to her husband. Hastings took his wife away from Court, whereupon the aggrieved Compton complained to the King. Henry, with his own penchant for Anne, raved in anger at Buckingham, who refused to stay a night longer at Court. Then it was the turn of Lady Fitzwalter, another of the Stafford family, who, it was believed, had first told Buckingham tales of their sister's misconduct. The King ordered his wife to turn her out and would have dismissed others of the Queen's ladies too, 'such as go about the palace insidiously spying out every unwatched movement in order to tell the Queen stories', but that it would have caused a scandal. However, 'almost all the Court knew the Queen had been vexed with the King, and the King with her, and thus the storm continued.'[7]

Henry and Catherine's marriage staggered on for some years after this incident with no more open infidelities. But twice again, in the years before the breach over Anne Boleyn opened, Henry took mistresses from among the Queen's ladies. The most notable was Elizabeth Blount, a cousin of Lord Mountjoy, who had been a maid-of-honour since 1513 and soon after became his mistress. In 1519 she gave the King a son, later created Duke of Richmond. Two years later, the royal favourite was Mary Boleyn. She had been at the French Court with her sister Anne, and had made herself so notorious by her sexual promiscuity that King Francis himself called her 'a hackney'. Mary became the King's mistress in 1521 – the same year in which she married William Carey, a gentleman of Henry's Privy Chamber, and she was still in Henry's affections in 1525 when her father, now Treasurer of the Household, was created Viscount Rochford as a mark of favour.

By that date Anne Boleyn was herself at the English Court, having returned home in 1522. In that same year, in March, she had appeared in a Court masque as one of the maidens rescued by the King, as 'Ardent Desire', from the 'Château Vert'. But it was not until about 1525 or 1526 that Anne won the King away from her sister. By 1527 Henry was writing the most ardent of love-letters to her, begging Anne that

> you will expressly certify me of your whole mind concerning the love between us two. For of necessity I must ensure me of this answer, having been now above one whole year struck with the dart of love, not being assured whether of failure or of finding place in your heart and grounded affection. Which last point has kept me for some little time from calling you my mistress, since if you love me in none other sort save that of common affection, that name in no wise belongs to you, for it denotes a singular love, far removed from the common. But if it shall please you to do me the office of a true mistress and loyal friend, and to give yourself up, body and soul, to

me ... I will take you for my only mistress, rejecting from thought and affection, all others save yourself, to serve you only.[8]

But Anne was wiser than her sister. She had seen, from Mary's fate, how easy it was for Henry to cast off one to whom he had sworn love. She also took account of the current political tenor and realized that it was within her power to become Henry's wife rather than his mistress. For by then it was obvious that Queen Catherine would never give her husband a son. The Tudors had been on the throne of England for only two generations and, should there be no male heir to King Henry, there could well, at his death, be yet another civil war for the crown of England. For years this thought had worried the King, and by 1527 he had managed to convince himself that he lacked an heir as God's punishment for his marriage with Catherine, his late brother's wife. He found scriptural texts to prove that such a marriage was damned and determined to win a papal bill of divorce on the grounds that his marriage with Catherine had been illegal.

So far, Catherine had suffered in silence. By that time she was well innured to her husband's infidelity. But she would not allow that her marriage was invalid. She continued to aver for the rest of her life that her marriage with Henry's brother had never been consummated, and that she was thus the King's true wife. But with Anne Boleyn still nominally a member of her household, and with the King and his ministers daily importuning Catherine for her agreement to a divorce, it was impossible to be blind to her eventual fate. After protracted divorce proceedings, which at length had to be carried through without papal approval – thereby unleashing the Protestant Reformation of England, guided by the King through a complaisant Parliament – Catherine's marriage was declared void.

In January 1533 Henry and Anne were secretly married. At Easter, with Anne already pregnant, the new Queen was proclaimed. In September she gave birth to a child – not the longed-for son, but a daughter, named Elizabeth.

Meanwhile the rejected Catherine had been sent off to her lonely exile from Court into the country, to stay in a series of strongholds where she was treated as a prisoner. Her refusal to accept the decision on her divorce, and to sign herself merely Princess Dowager, as the widow of Prince Arthur, had completed her alienation from Henry. She was refused permission to see her daughter Mary, the only survivor of her numerous pregnancies, and was shut away until such time as she should conveniently die. Henry and Anne had not long to wait. In January 1536 Queen Catherine died at Kimbolton Castle – of neglect and heart-break.

Of all those who had served her in the years of her happiness, only one came to Catherine in those last days of her life. Maria de Salinas, now the widowed Baroness Willoughby, was resolute in her championship of her former mistress. There were many at Court who hated Anne – including the King's own sister Mary, who had died in 1533 – but no one dared to speak out for Catherine at the climax of her misfortunes. But as the former Queen lay dying, Lady Willoughby rode up to the gate of Kimbolton Castle and demanded entrance. At first she was refused, since she did not carry the royal permit necessary for access to the Queen. But arguing that it was a bitter night and that she could find no shelter elsewhere, Maria was at last allowed in. She went straight to the Queen and remained with her until the end came.

At the end of the last century, the grave of Catherine of Aragon in Peterborough Cathedral was opened up. But two bodies, instead of the one expected, were found there. Beside Queen Catherine lay Maria de Salinas. No record of her burial can be traced. It can only be concluded that on her death she had been buried secretly, without permission, next to Catherine. Her loyalty extended even beyond her life.

Anne Boleyn called forth no such devotion from those who served her. When her time of trial came, in the spring of 1536, on charges of adultery, there was no woman to speak in her defence. Lady Rochford, her own sister-in-law, one of the several members of the Boleyn and Howard families who had been advanced by Anne's marriage, was foremost among her accusers, charging Anne with incest with her brother, Lord Rochford. And it was another Boleyn, the wife of Anne's uncle, who was set in charge of the Queen in her Tower prison, to report back to the Council any of Anne's words which might reinforce the charges against her.

Furthermore, it was yet another lady-in-waiting, Jane Seymour, who had won King Henry away from his second wife, to become his third. But Jane Seymour was no schemer on the pattern of Anne Boleyn. She was a modest and virtuous young woman, of the minor gentry, who had first come to Court in the days of Catherine of Aragon. While other women, even Anne's cousin Madge Shelton, had realized that Henry was ripe for another wife and thrown themselves in his way, Jane had been retiring and prudent. Henry had 'made the running'. Nevertheless, so low was the reputation of Court ladies in the 1530s, that the imperial ambassador could not believe in Jane's vaunted purity: 'You may imagine', he wrote, 'whether being an Englishwoman, and having been long at Court, she would not hold it a sin to be still a maid.'[9] But this worldly-wise courtier was wrong. There was never one word of scandal to soil Queen Jane's name.

Whether from such virtue or from the promptings of her ambitious family, Jane preserved her modesty. When Henry wrote to her and sent her money, she refused to accept either letter or purse, and vowed that she would never meet him alone. So, in the last days of Queen Anne, Jane was brought to Court with her brother and sister-in-law to chaperone her meetings with the King. Such caution had its reward. On 19 May Anne Boleyn went bravely to the block, and on the 30th Henry and Jane were married.

An adjunct to Ambassador Chapuys's remark casting doubt on Jane Seymour's virginity was his speculation that should Henry ever desire to cast her off, he had only to bring against her charges of her pre-marital incontinence. In the event, Henry was given no time to tire of his third wife, for only a few days after giving him that expensive son, the future King Edward VI, she died.

For more than two years after the death of Jane Seymour, there was no Queen of England. For that space of time all the ladies who could expect to fill interesting and lucrative positions in the royal household were disappointed.

Thus, when Henry VIII married Anne of Cleves, in 1539, there was a rush and a scramble, with much vying for favour and no little jealousy among the aristocratic familes, to obtain positions for ladies in her train. Although it was the Protestant faction at Court which had, with the consummate skill of Thomas Cromwell, engineered the King's marriage with Anne of Cleves (in the hopes of alliance with the Protestant states of the Empire), the Catholic Howard family was already in the ascendant by the time the wedding was celebrated. The Duke of Norfolk managed to gain positions in the Queen's household for several of his relations, putting in Lady Rochford (now restored to grace) as a Lady of the Bedchamber, as well as his protégée Lady Rutland, née Paston, and winning posts as maids-of-honour for his nieces Catherine Howard and Mary Norris.

But the most triumphant of all the proud mothers of maids-of-honour was surely Lady Lisle, whose whole end in life was, it seems, to place her daughters at Court.

Honor, Viscountess Lisle, was born a Grenville, with no more status than that of gentlewoman, but she had married as her first husband one Sir John Basset and after his death, Arthur Plantagenet, Viscount Lisle (an illegitimate son of King Edward IV). The new Lady Lisle had three sons and four daughters by her first marriage, the latter scarcely more than children when she accompanied her second husband to Calais, in 1535, when he was made constable of the English garrison there.

The two younger girls, Anne and Mary, were sent into France (for Calais was still then an English possession) for their education. Their training was by no means formal, or even much devoted to book-learning, but more oriented towards their acquisition of accomplishments and social graces. The two girls mixed freely in the social life of their guardians' neighbourhood, and were forever troubling their mother with requests for money and clothes. Thus Anne Basset to Lady Lisle in 1536:

Madam, I would earnestly entreat you, if I spend the winter in France, that I may have some dress to spend it in, for I have none to put on for every day. Madam, I know well that I cost you a great deal of money; but it is impossible to do otherwise, for there are many little trifles wanted here which are not needed in England: for one must do like other people.

Madam, I have received some shoes and stockings, which are too small for me; I entreat you to have the goodness to send me others, and with this I conclude, entreating God to give you in health a good and long life.[10]

Meanwhile, Lady Lisle had yet more expense over her daughter Catherine, in trying to gain her a post in Anne Boleyn's household. First she made good use of her 'contacts' among the nobility at Court, sending pleading letters to Lady Salisbury, Lord Montague, the Countess of Rutland and her own niece the Countess of Sussex to use their influence with the Queen. When this ploy failed, she began bombarding Anne with gifts of birds and dogs, reputedly the quickest way to the Queen's heart, but with no success.

Lady Lisle had more luck with Anne's successor, Jane Seymour. One happy day in July 1537 she received a letter from her agent in England, John Husee, which at last seemed hopeful:

Upon Thursday last, the Queen, being at dinner, my lady Rutland and my Lady Sussex being waiters on her Grace, her Grace chanced, eating of the quails [Lady Lisle's gift], to commune of your ladyship and of your daughters, so that such communication was uttered by the said two ladies that her Grace made grant to have one of your daughters; and the matter is thus concluded that your ladyship shall send them both over, for her Grace will first see them, and know their manners, fashions and conditions, and take which of them shall ... her Grace [like] best; and your ladyship shall not be in need to do much cost on them till time when you know which of them her Grace will have: but two honest changes they must have, the one of satin, the other of damask. And at their coming, the one shall be in my lady of Rutland's chamber, and the other in my lady of Sussex's chamber, and once known which the Queen will have, the other to be with the Duchess of Suffolk, and then to be apparrelled according to their degrees: but madam, the Queen will be at no more cost with her but wages and livery, and so I am commanded to write unto your ladyship.

And forasmuch as they shall now go upon making and marrying, it shall please your ladyship to exhort them to be sober, sad, wise, and discreet, and lowly above all things, and to be obedient, and governed and ruled by my lady Rutland, and my lady Sussex, and Mrs Margery, and such others as be your ladyship's friends here: and to serve God and be virtuous, for that is much regarded here to serve God well and to be sober of tongue. I trust your ladyship will not take this my meaning, that I should presume to learn your ladyship what is to be done, neither that I do see any likelihood of ill-appearance in them, but I do it only of pure and sincere zeal that I bear to them for your ladyship's sake, to the end I would they should so use themselves that it may sound to your ladyship's honour and their worship time coming; for your ladyship knoweth the Court is full of pride, envy, indignation, mocking, scorning and derision. Therefore I would be sorry but they would use themselves according to their birth and state that God hath called them unto.[11]

Despite the definite terms of the royal summons, it was six weeks before the Basset girls were ready to leave Calais – doubtless being outfitted for the venture. They arrived only days before Queen Jane was confined for the birth of her child. There was time only for her to choose the younger, Anne, for her maid-of-honour, and to have her sworn in, on 17 September (on the understanding that she provide her own wardrobe and pay her own maid), before, having given Henry VIII his son, Queen Jane died.

Catherine Basset had, during September, stayed in the house

of the Countess of Rutland, and the Countess had become so attached to her that there she stayed. Anne, at the death of the Queen, was sent to Lady Sussex. She was evidently the more promising of the two sisters, as witness Queen Jane's preference for her, and by the evidence of Elizabeth, Lady Wallop, in a letter to her friend Lady Lisle:

> I have not seen Mistress Catherine since we came from Court; but Mistress Anne I have seen divers times, and is as fair a gentlewoman, and as well made, as any I know, and as gentle, and as well she behaveth herself that everybody praiseth her that seeth her; and there is no doubt but she shall come to some great marriage. You are much bound to my lord of Sussex, and my lady, for they make not a little of her. My lady told me, at my last being with her, that she would do for her as much as she would for her own sister.[12]

But two years was a long time for Anne to keep her patroness's favour, and on one occasion the two women fell out quite seriously – though over the most trivial matter. Lady Lisle had sent her daughter more than a hundred little pearls to trim a girdle, and Anne took it upon herself, without permission, to share them with her cousin Catherine Stradling. Both Lady Lisle and Lady Sussex were angry at this show of independence and reckless generosity, and it took some time for tempers to cool. After all, Anne Basset was dependent on Lady Sussex for her keep, and on her mother for all her clothes and pocket-money.

It must have come as some relief to Lady Lisle to receive the following letter from her daughter Catherine towards the end of 1539:

> Madam,
>
> The cause of my writing to your ladyship is, that we hear say that the King's Grace shall be married. ... Wherefore I desire your ladyship that you will be so good a lady and mother unto me as to speak that I may be one of the Queen's maids; for I have no trust in none other but your ladyship to speak for me in that cause.[13]

Anne Basset, probably on the strength of her brief service to Queen Jane, was given her post, but nothing was said about Catherine. Lady Lisle had a good chance to make her request on her elder daughter's behalf personally to the new Queen, Anne of Cleves, for she had to pass through Calais on her way into England. But Queen Anne had little say in the composition of her own household, apart from bringing with her a dozen or so Flemish maids (reputedly 'even inferior in beauty to their mistress', the plain 'Flanders mare', and 'dressed after a fashion so heavy and tasteless, that it would make them appear frightful even if they were belles'[14]). Still, in February of the following year, Catherine was urging her mother to help her, and advising her to send to Mistress Lowe, the Flemish 'mother of the maids', a 'good token' – meaning a sizeable bribe, 'that she may better remember me'[15].

> ... I perceive right well the King's pleasure to be such that no more maids shall be taken until such time as some of them that by now with the Queen's Grace be preferred [that is, married]. Albeit, if you will make some means to Mother Lowe, who can do as much good in this matter as any one woman here, that she may make some means to set your daughter with the Queen's said Grace; and in so doing I think you shall obtain your purpose in every behalf.[16]

Finally, Lady Lisle used her daughter already at Court, Anne, to mediate for Catherine, as the bearer of presents to the King himself. Either Anne was embarrassed at such open suing for favour or she feared to lose her own place by such importuning, for on 19 February 1540 she wrote a very touchy letter to her mother:

> Madam,
>
> I have presented your codiniac [quince marmalade] to the King's Highness, and his Grace does like it wondrous well, and gave your ladyship hearty thanks for it. And whereas I perceive by your ladyship's letter 'that when the King's Highness had tasted of your codiniac, you would have me to move his

Grace for to send you some token of remembrance, that you might know the better that his Grace doth like your codiniac', by my troth, madam, I told his Grace 'that your ladyship was glad that you could make anything that his Grace did like'; and his Grace made me answer, 'that he did thank you with all his heart'; ... Whether he will send your ladyship any token by [the Calais messenger] or no, I cannot tell; for, madam, I durst not be so bold as to move his Grace for it in no wise, for fear lest how his Grace would have taken it; therefore I beseech your ladyship be not discontented with me.

And whereas you do write to me that I should remember my sister, I have spoken to the King's Highness for her; and his Grace made me answer, 'that Master Bryan and divers other hath spoken to his Grace for their friends'. But he said 'he would not grant me nor them yet'; for his Grace said 'that he would have them that should be fair and as he thought meet for the room'.[17]

Was this last a sneer at the sister who was causing Anne Basset so much trouble?

In fact, there was to be no more said on the subject of Catherine's appointment, for in March 1540, only a month after the above exchange of letters, a royal commission arrived at Calais, charged to enquire into the government there. Lord Lisle was found guilty of having kept the garrison carelessly, with raw troops who could have done little if the town were attacked; even worse, it was proved that he was conducting a correspondence with Cardinal Pole, the King's cousin who so firmly opposed his attempts at rebutting the power of Rome in the English Church, and – worst of all – that Lord Lisle had actually communicated with the Pope.

Lisle was recalled to England and, as soon as he landed taken into the Tower of London. Left behind in Calais, Lady Lisle did her best to help her husband by burning incriminating papers, but she and her daughters Philippa and Mary were closely questioned about what they knew of Lord Lisle's activities. Two years Lisle stayed in the Tower, without any trial at which he might make his stand, but at length, in March 1542, the King showed some signs of forgiving his unproven crimes, by sending his former servant a few negligible presents. It was too much for Lisle. He was not a young man and the suspense had taken its toll. On 3 March 1542 he died.

Anne, meanwhile, had remained at Court, transferring allegiance and service to her former fellow maid-of-honour Catherine Howard when she succeeded Anne of Cleves as Henry's Queen. When Queen Catherine too fell into disgrace, and her household was disbanded, Anne Basset, alone of all the maids and ladies, was kept at Court, with the King providing for her since with her father's imprisonment she had no home to go to. At this point, the Basset maids-of-honour disappear from history.

A few papers survive from the reign of Henry VIII to show the diet of such maids-of-honour as Anne Basset. While Catherine of Aragon was still queen, Henry issued an order regulating his steward's provisioning of her retinue:

> First, every morning at breakfast, one chine of beef at our kitchen, one chete loaf, and one manchet at our pantry bar, and a gallon of ale at our buttery bar.
>
> Item, at dinner, a piece of beef, a stroke of roast, and a reward, at our said kitchen, a cast of chete bread at our pantry bar, and a gallon of ale at our buttery bar.
>
> Item, at afternoon a manchet of bread at our pantry bar and half a gallon of ale at our buttery bar.
>
> Item, at supper, a mess of porridge, a piece of mutton, and a reward at our said kitchen, a cast of chete bread at our pantry bar and half a gallon of ale at our buttery.
>
> Item, at after supper, a chete loaf and a manchet at our pantry bar, and half a gallon of wine at our cellar bar.
>
> Item, every morning at our woodyard, four tallshyds and two faggots.
>
> Item, at our chandlery bar, in winter, every night one pricket, and four sises of wax, with eight candles, white lights

and one torch.

Item, at our pitcher house, six white cups.

Item, at every time of our moving, one whole cart for the carriage of her stuff.[18]

This tedious and scarcely wholesome diet was not for the girl alone; it had also to feed the maximum of three servants she was allowed to have with her – if she paid them herself.

To return to the mainstream of the history of the lady-in-waiting: we have already noted that Catherine Howard was a maid-of-honour to Anne of Cleves when she attracted Henry VIII, subsequently becoming his fifth wife. But even before she came to Court, at the age of about sixteen, Catherine was already well-versed in serving a lady. Since childhood, she had lived, a neglected and dependent orphan, in the household of her step-grandmother the Dowager Duchess of Norfolk. It was there that the laxity of the Duchess's oversight of her women gave Catherine the chance to begin that career of promiscuity which ultimately caused her ruin. At the Duchess's country-house at Horsham, she had taken as her lover a young music teacher, Henry Mannox, and at Lambeth House, the Norfolks' mansion near Westminster, one Francis Derham of the Duke's household.

Only eight months after joining Anne of Cleves's household, through the influence of her uncle Norfolk, Catherine Howard fulfilled his plan of wooing Henry from the Protestant to the Norfolk-led Catholic party at Court. Henry's distaste for the unfortunate Anne of Cleves – and his increasing dislike of Cromwell's proposed alliance with the Protestant German states through Anne – made him eager both for a new wife and for a change in the balance of power among his councillors. Thus the beauty, youth and vivacity of Catherine Howard was Norfolk's stepping-stone to power.

Never before had a queen's household been so flooded with her relations and protégées. Elizabeth Woodville, Anne Boleyn and Jane Seymour had all introduced their kin into their retinues, but never on the scale of Catherine Howard's appointments. Two of her aunts, Lady Bridgewater and Lady Margaret Howard were among her grander ladies-in-waiting, her sister Lady Baynton and her cousin by marriage Lady Rochford (the same who had so betrayed Anne Boleyn) became Ladies of the Privy Chamber; another sister, Lady Arundel, was a 'lady attendant'. More important in the long run, however, was the appointment of former gentlewomen attendant on the Dowager Duchess of Norfolk, as women of the new Queen's Chamber: Catherine Tilney and Margaret Morton.

When evidence was brought to King Henry toward the end of 1541 of his wife's infidelities, it was Mistress Morton and Mistress Tilney who figured largest in the witnesses against Queen Catherine. They were able to supply evidence against her on charges both of her promiscuity before her marriage (when they shared a dormitory with Catherine and witnessed her familiarities with Derham and Mannox), and of her infidelity on numerous occasions after her marriage with the King. Others of her former companions, Mary Lassels, Alice Restwold and Joan Bulmer, who were now in Catherine's service, could substantiate some of the charges. It is even possible that Catherine as Queen employed these women in such coveted posts to buy their silence on her earlier 'crimes' – if that were so, the bribe was a singular failure.

However, when Catherine was brought to trial, her marital infidelities were accounted far more serious than her early escapades. Her household was induced to make the fullest possible depositions in which it came to light that the infamous Lady Rochford had connived at Catherine's *affaires*. Two men, Derham and a certain Culpepper (a cousin of Catherine's on her mother's side) had to the certain knowledge of the Queen's gentlewomen, been her lovers since her marriage. Catherine's main opportunities for meeting them had come during a royal progress to the north in 1541 when, according to Catherine Tilney, at Lincoln:

> the Queen went two nights out of her chamber, when it was late, to Lady Rochford's chamber. ... And the first night this

> deponent [Catherine Tilney] and Margaret [Morton], her colleague, went up with her; and the Queen made them both go down again, but Margaret went up again eftsoons, and this deponent went to bed with Mrs Fryswith [another chamberer]. As far as she remembereth, when it was late, about two of the clock, Margaret came up to bed with them; and she [Tilney] said to Margaret, 'Jesus! Is not the Queen abed yet?' and Margaret said, 'Yes, even now.'[19]

From this, and much more, even though Catherine Tilney never saw the Queen with a man, Sir Thomas Wriothesley, in charge of the investigation, was able to come to the conclusion that 'the Queen went into Lady Rochford's chamber to meet some person whom the deponent could not see'. This was backed up by the frequent charges in the depositions that, during the progress, Catherine 'would seek for the back doors and backstairs herself'[20] in every house in which the royal entourage stayed for a night. Under torture Culpepper admitted everything.

Several members of the Howard family were attainted by a Parliamentary bill of January 1542, including the Dowager Duchess of Norfolk, Lady Rochford, Lady Bridgewater and Lady Anne Howard. But though many members of the family were fined and imprisoned, only Catherine Howard and Lady Rochford were to die. Catherine died bravely; Lady Rochford had to be dragged, screaming, to the block.

King Henry had had enough of beautiful, young, perfidious wives. He was ageing and ill, more in need of a nurse and companion than of a sweetheart or a mistress. Thus, in 1543, he married the respectable widow Catherine Parr, who had already buried two husbands herself.

This new Queen Catherine had a long acquaintance with Courts and their pitfalls. As a child, she had been brought up in the household of Catherine of Aragon. Her mother, Maud Parr, had been a resident lady-in-waiting to Queen Catherine from 1517 until her death in 1529 and, as a widow (of Sir Thomas Parr, controller of Henry VIII's household), was in permanent residence, keeping her two daughters, Catherine and Anne, with her. The Court of that time was divided between the Queen's sober, blue-stockinged elder ladies, such as Lady Parr, the Countess of Salisbury and Lady Guildford, and those younger ladies who continued, sometimes successfully – to make a play for the King. But there was a third group, the one to which the child Catherine Parr belonged: this was comprised of the children of the Queen and her elder ladies – the Princess Mary, the two Parr girls, Jane Seymour, Joan Guildford and Joan Champernowne, of a well-known Devonshire family (an aunt of the future Sir Walter Raleigh). They were brought up together, enjoying the highest advantages of education and training in courtly manners, and with good opportunities for making advantageous marriages.

Catherine was away from Court from 1529, when she married the elderly Sir Edward Burrough, but as the wife of John Neville, Lord Latymer, returned as a Gentlewoman of the Chamber to Catherine Howard – though probably only for a very short period, since she was never implicated, as were so many of her fellows, in the proceedings against the Queen in 1541–2.

In March 1543, Catherine Parr's second husband died. She was still childless, at the age of thirty, so it is obvious that King Henry did not marry her in the expectation of begetting more heirs; nor did anyone reckon her beautiful. But if Henry was winning in marriage no outstanding prize, Catherine herself was not overjoyed at the prospect of such a husband. It was even rumoured that she offered to become the King's mistress rather than hazard her neck as his wife. However, in July 1543 Henry and Catherine *were* married.

It was not infidelity to her husband which put Catherine Parr at risk but her adherence to extremist Protestantism. For all his break with Rome, Henry had remained faithful to many of the tenets of the Church which contemporary Protestants, in England as abroad, were denouncing. For example, he had refused to have the Bible translated into English lest 'that precious jewel of the Word of God' should come to be shouted blasphemously in every ale-house and tavern. Catherine, however, was one of the many of his subjects who had come under the influence of Protestant doctrine, and in the months after she became Queen, her proclivities became ever more pronounced.

The new Queen gathered around her several ladies of similar beliefs – her sister, Lady Herbert, the Duchess of Suffolk, the Countess of Hertford, Lady Lisle and others. And she introduced to the Court an old friend of earlier days, one Anne Ayscough or Askew, who was renowned for her fervent beliefs and fearless expression of them. Nor did she attempt to hide her sympathies but indeed, after she became Queen, wrote and circulated her religious apologia, *Lamentations of a Sinner*.

Despite the downfall of the Howard family with the ruin of Catherine Howard, the Catholic party at Court, led by Bishop Gardiner and the Duke of Norfolk (more timorous since his near escape from death in 1542 but no less ambitious for power), was still strong. Within a year of Catherine Parr's marriage to the King, the Catholics came to see in her and her Protestantism a threat to their control of Church policy. Moreover, the Queen and her ladies seemed secure in their influence with the King: the Duchess of Suffolk named her pet spaniel 'Gardiner' and called him to heel with malicious satisfaction.

Gardiner opened his campaign against Queen Catherine by repeatedly drawing to the King's attention the publications circulated in his realm by the Protestant extremists, advocating stern measures to curb their infiltration of the Anglican Church. The Bishop pointed out that many of their treatises could be found at Court. It was not until 1546, however, that the first blow was struck. It fell on Anne Ayscough who, in June 1546, was brought before the Privy Council as a self-confessed non-subscriber to the Six Articles, the doctrinal cornerstone of the Anglican Church.

At this point, Gardiner was emboldened by the King's sudden irritation with his wife. Henry's suppurating leg was particularly painful, and Catherine's religious discussions with him, which had once taken his mind off his pain, now irked him. Gardiner took his chance and made discreet suggestions that the Queen's doctrines were unorthodox. Henry's agreement on that point prompted Gardiner's next step: proceedings against a few of the Queen's lesser-ranking ladies which could sooner or later be stepped up to encompass such as the Duchess of Suffolk and finally reach the Queen herself. Anne Ayscough was tortured to provide evidence against the Queen's ladies, but would – or could – reveal nothing really damaging.

By now, Catherine was on her guard. She would not allow herself to be drawn into a doctrinal argument with the King that might provide him with proof of her unorthodoxy. Instead she turned the situation to her own advantage, claiming that she spoke of religion with her husband only to learn from his greater wisdom. In fact, Catherine had only just managed to save herself. While she was still speaking with the King, Sir Thomas Wriothesley, the Lord Chancellor, approached with an armed guard 'on purpose to take the Queen and her ladies'. It was only minutes since Catherine had made her submission to Henry but her pleas had been so effective that the King turned on Wriothesley, calling him 'Knave! Arrant knave! Beast! Fool!' and ordering him away. The plot against Catherine had failed.

For all her restoration to favour, however, the Queen could not save her friend Anne. She went to the stake on 16 July, only two days after the royal reconciliation, to be burned as a heretic.

Six months later Henry died. For most historians his reign is important for the political and religious issues which it comprised; in this study, however, it is an important landmark in the history of the lady-in-waiting. Of his six wives, Henry had chosen four from the royal household.

3

At the death of King Henry VIII in 1547, his only son, Edward, became King. But Edward VI was a boy of nine, under the tutelage of Council and Protector, and his Court had none of the verve and panoply of his father's day. Nor, of course, was there a queen to share his throne. For the six years of his reign there were no posts for ladies-in-waiting.

Nor, when Edward's cousin Jane Grey briefly succeeded him on the throne in 1553 (the pawn of the ambitious Duke of Northumberland) was there time in her nine days' reign for the appointment of her retinue. When she was brought from Chelsea to the Tower to take her place as nominal head of state, there was only her young sister-in-law Mary Sidney to attend her. In procession there was only her mother, Frances, Duchess of Suffolk, to bear her train.

But with Henry VIII's elder daughter Mary enthroned, once Jane Grey's usurpation had been successfully overthrown, the royal Court was restored with all its Tudor glories. The first Queen Regnant of England, for all that she was no longer youthful and had been kept on a modest income in the country for most of her life, was as fond of display as any of her family, and if her Court had neither the gaiety nor the licentiousness of her father's early years, it had a magnificent dignity.

Mary was 'a woman's woman'. Men had been kept from her in her youth, as a precaution against her affections being allied with their ambition, which might have overturned the succession to the crown. At the same time, to those men who sought to make their way in politics and government, the quiet household of this princess offered no chances of advancement. Nor was Mary an intellectual of the stamp of her half-sister Elizabeth or her cousin Jane Grey to gather about her learned men as her tutors. For the most part, her companions were her ladies-in-waiting, and these not the butterflies of the royal Court but daughters of the solid country gentry. One such was Susan White who was with Mary from her teens to the end of her life. She married Thomas Tonge, the Clarencieux King-of-Arms in the College of Heralds, and, as 'Mrs Clarencieux', at Mary's accession she was rewarded for her long service with the lucrative and prestigious posts of Lady Almoner (no sinecure, in view of the Queen's many charities) and First Lady of the Bedchamber.

Jane Dormer was another intimate of Mary's circle. Born in 1538, and thus twenty years the Queen's junior, she was known to the royal family from childhood. Her aunts Mabel and Elizabeth were long among Mary's ladies-in-waiting, and her maternal grandfather, Sir William Sidney, was for some years 'governor' or guardian of Mary's half-brother, Edward, before he came to the throne. Jane was frequently sent to play with the little prince, so close to her in age, when he was staying at Ashridge in Hertfordshire, near her home. In later years she delighted to tell the story of his remark to her, on an occasion when she lost a game of chess to him: 'Now, Jane, your king is gone, I shall be good enough for you.'[1]

All Mary's ladies were staunch Catholics, even during the years when they were forbidden to hear Mass in her house. Jane Dormer was especially regarded, as having a great-uncle, Sebastian Newdigate, who was one of the Carthusians who suffered martyrdom under Henry VIII.

Along with the fervent religious tone of the new Court, there was a moral climate in direct contrast to the lax days of Henry

VIII. Mary's Court was hailed as 'a school of virtue, a nursery of purity, a mansion of piety'.[2] Mary herself was innocent in the extreme – both by inclination and by the effects of her years of isolation. On one occasion she saw her Lord Chamberlain, the notorious profligate Lord William Howard, chuck one of her maids-of-honour, pretty Frances Neville, under the chin, and enquire, 'My pretty whore, how dost thou?' Not to be outdone in a display of affection for one of her favourites, but totally ignorant of the meaning of the word 'whore', Mary repeated the gesture and words to Frances sometime later:

'Madam, what says your Majesty?' cried Frances Neville in amazement.

'What is the matter? Have I said or done more than the Lord Chamberlain did? And may not I be as bold with thee as he?'

'My Lord Chamberlain is an idle gentleman, and we respect not what he saith or doth,' declared the maid-of-honour, 'but Your Majesty, from whom I think never any heard such a word, doth amaze me either in jest or earnest, to be called so by you. A whore is a wicked, misliving woman.'

Thus informed and corrected, Mary could reply nothing but: 'Thou must forgive me; for I meant thee no harm.'[3]

The arrival of the Spaniards for Mary's marriage to her cousin Philip caused some of the innocence to go out of the Court. King Philip himself, scarcely enamoured of his ageing, plain wife, took a fancy to one of the young ladies in her retinue, the statuesque Madgalen Dacre. But he had chosen the wrong woman for any dalliance: Magdalen Dacre was a paragon close to the Queen's heart, renowned for her modesty. 'She never in her life dressed her head or adorned herself by a glass, which in a woman, especially noble and a courtier, may be esteemed a miracle.'[4] One day Philip saw Magdalen washing her face by a window on the ground floor of the palace. 'Sportively' putting his arm through the window, he made as if to touch her. But she, with brave *insouciance*, picked up a handy stick and caught him a blow on the offending arm.

The Spanish marriage brought more heart-ache than happiness to Mary, but it resulted in Jane Dormer's happier match with one of Philip's retinue. Her bridegroom was Don Gomez de Figueroa y Cordova, Duke of Feria, one of the foremost diplomats on Philip's staff. Though she was no heiress, and certainly not of the first rank of nobility, she was such a confidante of the Queen that she was a matrimonial prize even for a duke of Spain. Jane and de Feria became engaged during Mary's lifetime, but were not married until a month after her death, in December 1558. The new Duchess took a large train of English ladies with her to Spain and among them was Susan Clarencieux, who spent the rest of her life with her former colleague from Mary's household.

Among the 'great ladies' of Mary's Court – that is, those ladies whose high rank made their duties ceremonial rather than practical, there was one notable absentee. There were two good reasons why Catherine, Dowager Duchess of Suffolk, should have occupied a high place in Queen Mary's favour: first, she was the widow of Charles Brandon, Duke of Suffolk, having married him soon – some said indecently soon – after the death of his wife Mary Tudor, Queen Mary's aunt; secondly, Catherine was the daughter of Maria de Salinas, the most faithful of Catherine of Aragon's Spanish attendants, and her mother's devotion to Queen Catherine should have made her a natural object of Mary's affections. But Duchess Catherine not only did not frequent the Court but actually fled the realm: she was the most fervent, extreme Protestant. In the last years of Henry VIII's life, she had been the constant companion of Catherine Parr and her mainstay during the period when the Queen's neck felt insecure with the threat of proceedings against her on a charge of heresy. Thus, with the accession to the throne of the loyally Catholic Mary, Catherine deemed it wise to hasten abroad, and wait out the years of the Queen's reign in safety.

Had Catherine ever been a friend to Queen Mary, however, she would now have enjoyed the sweets of royal favour to the full, for the new queen was extremely generous to all who had ever befriended her in her earlier lonely days. Anne, Duchess of Somerset, widow of Edward VI's first Lord Protector, was released from the Tower and picked up the threads of friendship with Mary, who always called her 'my good gossip Nan'. Of the first companions of the Queen's youth, Mary, Duchess of Richmond, stood in good stead. Daughter of the Duke of Norfolk, she had married Mary's bastard half-brother Henry Fitzroy, Duke of Richmond, and after his death she never remarried, frequently sharing house-room with Mary at Syon and Hatfield. The Duchess had been the Catholic party's candidate as seventh wife for Henry VIII, at such time as they could engineer the ruin of Catherine Parr. Failing this, they intended that she should become the King's mistress. On hearing her fate, Duchess Mary 'defied her brother [the Earl of Surrey who formulated the plan], and said that they all [the Howard family] should perish, and she would cut her own throat rather than she would consent to such villainy.'[5] As time went on, it transpired that neither sacrifice was required of her.

A third member of the trio of ladies sheltering together during Henry VIII's reign was Margaret Douglas, since 1547 Countess of Lennox. She was Mary's cousin, as the daughter of the second marriage of King Henry's sister Margaret. Margaret Douglas had been a gay figure at the Courts of Henry's queens, but had twice nearly lost her head – and did in fact lose her liberty – by falling in love with two scions of the Howard family, the first during Anne Boleyn's brief triumph, the second under Catherine Howard. The hasty disappearance of both queens saw Margaret deprived of her lovers. During Edward VI's reign, 'my cousin Marget', as the boy called her, was one of the leading figures of the Court.

With the accession of Mary, there were not a few who speculated that the Queen would make her cousin Margaret her heir, should she fail to provide an heir to England herself. Apart from the Princess Elizabeth, Anne Boleyn's child, whom Mary feared was illegitimate, there was only the Scottish Queen Mary with a better claim to the English throne than Margaret Douglas, and it would be no light matter to decide to leave the English throne to Scotland in view of the uneasiness of the relations between the two kingdoms. On many state occasions Queen Mary had

Margaret Douglas take precedence of all the ladies at Court, including the Lady Elizabeth, which was reckoned to be a sure sign that Margaret would be the next Queen of England.

Scarcely less likely an heir was Mary's cousin Frances, Duchess of Suffolk, daughter of Henry VIII's younger sister Mary. The fact that she was the mother of Lady Jane Grey, at that time still confined to the Tower for having dared usurp Mary's throne at the death of Edward VI, seemed not to matter to the new Queen. She could not free Jane, but she could release the Duke of Suffolk, Frances's husband, and until the Wyatt rebellion of 1554 raised a new threat to her security, Mary might have offered him a pardon. As it was, she was forced by circumstances to have both Suffolk and Jane beheaded. But it by no means lessened her attachment to her cousin Frances who continued at Court for some time, and who was, like Margaret Douglas, marked out as a possible inheritor of the crown.

Frances's younger daughters, Catherine and Mary, the sisters of the unfortunate Lady Jane Grey, were brought to the Queen's Court as Ladies of the Bedchamber, the highest rank that could be given them. Again there was speculation, especially in Spain (where no one wished to see the pro-French Queen Mary of Scotland succeed Mary Tudor), that Catherine Grey would be Mary's successor.

However, when the Queen died, in November 1558 the accession of her half-sister Elizabeth was peacefully accomplished. There remained, of course, the problem of who would rule after the death of this last surviving child of Henry VIII, but at twenty-eight, Elizabeth could afford to stave off the unpleasant decision. She knew that once she named her successor, the great men of her Court, and the foreign ambassadors, would start courting the heir as they had courted her in the last months of her sister's life.

It was to discourage speculation on the subject that Queen Elizabeth demoted the Grey sisters from posts in the Bedchamber to the Privy Chamber. Catherine Grey, a forthrightly ambitious young woman, complained bitterly at being set aside. She was a protégée of the Spanish ambassador de Feria, who had plans to marry her off to a Spanish prince, help her to the English throne and thus accomplish the uniting of England and Spain which the late Queen Mary's death had thwarted once already. De Feria charged Catherine Grey not to change her religion – that is, not to become a Protestant (for despite the most liberal Protestant upbringing, she had so successfully feigned adherence to Catholicism in Mary's reign that Spain believed her to be more amenable to the restoration of English allegiance to Rome than Queen Elizabeth was proving); nor was Catherine to marry, but to remain free in order to wed her Spaniard when the time was ripe.

What de Feria did not know was that Catherine was planning to marry Edward Seymour, Earl of Hertford. He was the eldest son of the late Protector Somerset and Queen Mary's 'good gossip Nan', with whom Catherine had frequently stayed during Mary's reign. It was at the Duchess's house at Hanworth that Catherine had met, and fallen in love with, Hertford. Their marriage, however, could prove as dangerous to Queen Elizabeth as that of Catherine with a Spaniard, for over the last twenty years the Seymour family had come to the very forefront of English politics, and there were many who still held the late Protector in reverence: Catherine and Hertford together would provide a formidable rival to Elizabeth for the hearts of the English, especially should the Queen name them her heirs.

Catherine's mother the Duchess Frances was enthusiastic about the match. She had had a nasty shock when she saw her plans for her eldest daughter end in failure and death, but she had speedily comforted herself for the loss of her husband by marrying again (to a gay young spark half her age) and now renewed her ambition with schemes for her second daughter. Frances must have known when she put to Catherine the case for a marriage with Hertford in March 1559, that her daughter loved the young man, an excellent adjunct to her plan. She promised that as soon as possible she would write to the Queen, begging her favour on the couple. But the Duchess was ill throughout the summer of 1559, and in November she died without the vital petition's having been sent.

Rumours of Spain's intentions for Catherine were flying round the Court, with such noise as to prevent any general whispers of her love for Hertford. But William Cecil, the Queen's wily chief councillor, had a sharp ear. He thoroughly approved the match, reasoning that the Queen was likely to marry Robert Dudley, and thus offend the country, and so the uniting of two such pleasing young people, of such popular birth, would provide a new focus for national loyalty. The marriage would also prevent one with Spain, which he justifiably feared. While the whole Court was speculating as to whether Catherine would be 'enticed' to Spain, there came an even more disturbing rumour: that Catherine would marry the Earl of Arran, at that time the heir of Mary, Queen of Scots. The consequent uniting of England and Scotland would be even more advantageous to her claim.

Elizabeth played her usual canny game. She took no action but determined to prevent her cousin from becoming more disaffected than she was already. Some months back there had been some hasty words between the two women, and though Catherine continued at Court, she was uneasy with the Queen. Now Elizabeth promoted Catherine to her old post as Lady of the Bedchamber and made much of her, 'to keep her quiet', wrote the Spanish envoy Bishop de Quadra. 'She even talks about formally adopting her.'[6] The Bishop also reported home that Catherine might marry yet another suitable young Englishman, the Earl of Huntingdon, who had quite a good claim to the throne as a descendant of the Yorkish Plantagenets.

Catherine was not as clever intellectually as her sister Jane, but she had a good measure of the Tudor shrewdness. Even while she was playing her part of dutiful lady-in-waiting and 'daughter' to the Queen, she was meeting Hertford secretly. In Hertford's sister, who bore the illustrious name of Jane Seymour, she had an able and sympathetic co-conspirator. This Lady Jane was the main instrument by which the marriage was at length effected.

On several occasions Lady Jane, also a maid-of-honour in Elizabeth's Court, accompanied her friend on excursions from the palace to Hertford's lodgings in Cannon Row, in the City of

London. She also arranged for them to be alone together when Hertford came to Westminster or Whitehall. It was in Jane's closet, off the Maidens' Chamber at Whitehall, that Hertford proposed to Catherine.

'I have borne you goodwill of long time,' he said, 'and because you should not think I intend to mock you, I am content, if you will, to marry you.'

'I like both you and your offer,' she replied, 'and am content to marry with you.'[7]

Easier said than done. Without her mother to act as intermediary with the Queen, there could be no risking a direct appeal for Elizabeth's blessing. If Catherine and Hertford were to marry, it would needs be secretly. Here again Lady Jane Seymour was the mainspring of the action. This pale and serious young woman, who had once been tipped as the future wife of Edward VI, burned with ambition for her family and was prepared to risk anything to see her brother marry the probable heiress to the throne.

One day in December 1560, when the Queen left London early in the morning to go hunting at Eltham, Jane and Catherine slipped away to make the walk east along the River Thames to Cannon Row. Hertford, who was awaiting them, had sent his servants off on a day's holiday. There was a slight delay when the priest whom Jane had commissioned failed to arrive, but she quickly found another. With Jane as their only witness, Catherine and Edward Seymour, Lord Hertford, were duly wed. Once the priest had gone, Jane left the newly-married couple alone for two hours, 'perceiving them ready to go to bed'.[8] Then Catherine joined her and they returned to Whitehall, to go straight in to their dinner as though nothing unusual had happened.

Four months later, in March 1651, Catherine knew that she was pregnant. But Hertford was just off an a diplomatic mission to France, and on the 23rd of the same month Jane Seymour died (probably of tuberculosis). The only other accessory to the illicit marriage, Jane's maid Mrs Leigh, who had connived at Hertford and Catherine's meetings after their wedding, took fright. She could not face the responsibility of being the only one to know of Catherine's 'crime' if it should come to light. On the plea that her mother was dying in the country, Mrs Leigh left Court, to disappear completely. Catherine was left alone to face the consequences of her daring and duplicity.

In July she wrote to her husband: 'I am quick with child, I pray you therefore to return, and declare how the matter standeth between us.'[9] But she waited in vain for a reply. Most likely, William Cecil was intercepting the letters, holding them back for his own reasons.

Catherine could not bear the strain. She had to go on appearing at Court, serving the Queen in her bedchamber daily, even parrying an offer of marriage from Lord Pembroke's son. At the end of the month, she was one of the ladies attendant on the Queen on a progress through Suffolk. One night, as the courtiers lodged at Ipswich, Catherine stole into the bedroom of Robert Dudley, her former brother-in-law and the man closest to the Queen. She poured out all her troubles to him, calling for his aid. Dudley felt himself unequal to such a risk, and quickly sent her packing. In panic the girl went straight to Mrs St Looe, an old friend of her family, and repeated her tale. But Mrs St Looe was that formidable woman Bess of Hardwick, who would risk nothing for anyone's gain but her own; she turned on Catherine in fury.

The next morning Dudley told all to the Queen. Immediately on the Court's return to Westminster, Elizabeth had her cousin thrown into the Tower, and called a Privy Council to examine Catherine's actions. There was no prospect of attainting Catherine and her husband for any crime, since it was no longer illegal, as it had earlier been, for a member of the royal family to marry without the sovereign's permission. Elizabeth could only maintain that the marriage was invalid by lack of evidence of its legality.

This proved remarkably easy, due to the haste and secrecy of the wedding. With the only independent witness, Jane Seymour, dead, and with the impossibility of tracing the priest who had performed the ceremony – whose name Catherine had never known, there remained only Catherine and Hertford's word that the wedding had ever taken place. Catherine had lost a vital document in which Hertford named her as his wife, when he made over some property to her, the only proof she had that he regarded her as his wife.

Hertford, meanwhile, was still in France. Rumour had come to him of Catherine's imprisonment, and he hesitated whether to obey the royal summons to return home or to flee. In September, however, he landed at Dover, was immediately arrested and was taken to the Tower – to a cell separate from that of Catherine. They were not allowed to meet throughout the whole lengthy examination of their stories. The fullest depositions were taken from everyone even remotely connected with the couple's former meetings and on 12 May 1562, the Royal Commission found their marriage to be invalid.

By that time, however, Catherine had been the mother of Hertford's child for some eight months. Her son Edward was born in the Tower on 24 September 1561. Thus there was no question of a royal pardon. Catherine and Hertford remained in the Tower, but it was easy enough to bribe gaolers for their meetings, and by July Catherine was pregnant again. She kept her secret well, and it was only on the birth of her second son, Thomas, in February 1563 that her further folly came to light.

An oubreak of plague in the Tower caused the Queen's prisoners to be allowed to leave – but only under the closest guard, separately, to strongholds in the country.

Catherine Grey and the Earl of Hertford never met again. On 22 January 1568 she died. Hertford was later set free, to live into a comfortable old age and to remarry twice.

In 1610 Catherine's son Edward married Arbella Stuart (the grand-daughter of Margaret Douglas, Countess of Lennox), a young woman who was then a very feasible heir to the thrones of England and Scotland. The uniting of their two claims was as dangerous as that of Catherine and Seymour's. And they too went to the Tower.

Throughout the tribulations of Catherine Grey, her sister Mary had remained with Elizabeth as a lady-in-waiting. She was small and mis-shapen, known to the Court as 'crookback Mary'. She had neither Jane's intellect nor Catherine's beauty, vitality and ambition. But she had a will of her own, in true Tudor fashion.

In August 1565, when she was nineteen, realizing that her royal birth would always be a bar, in the Queen's eyes, to her contracting a regular marriage, Mary secretly married Thomas Keyes, a sergeant porter of the Palace. It was an incongruous match between this dwarf of a woman and a man reputedly the biggest in London. But Keyes had no rank, no pretensions to the crown. Whatever Mary's motives for marrying him, ambition was not one of them.

Only a few weeks passed before Mary revealed her secret; obviously she had less courage, or less guile, than her sister. Inevitably the consequence was her imprisonment. She was sent to the country, Keyes to the Fleet prison. But such a match had no smack of ambition or treason, and the Queen's anger soon abated. Mary was soon released into the custody of her step-grandmother, Catherine, Duchess of Suffolk, who found her frightened and guilt-ridden: 'Lady Mary is so ashamed of her fault', wrote Duchess Catherine to the Queen's chief minister, Cecil, 'that I can scarcely get her to eat anything. In the two days she has been with me, she hath not eaten so much as a chicken's leg, and I fear me, she will die of her grief. A little comfort would do her good.'[10]

There was to be no comfort for Mary, for she was never allowed to see her husband. On the other hand, neither did she die of grief, but lived comfortably in the country, with occasional visits to the Court, until her death in 1578.

Mary and Catherine Grey were exceptional cases among the ladies-in-waiting of Elizabeth's Court. Their royal birth set them apart from the others, and made their marriages matters of national importance. But they, or at least Catherine, had proved that it was possible for a lady-in-waiting, presenting a bland face to the Queen, to hide an illicit marriage. It was a precedent which many of their fellows were to follow during Elizabeth I's long reign.

4

ELIZABETH I's long reign saw the apogee of the glories of English Court life. It was a continuous pageant in which men and women of beauty, wealth and high birth took supporting roles around the star Elizabeth. Never before had places at Court been so eagerly sought; never before had the rewards of proximity to a sovereign been so great: for young men there was the chance to take the Queen's fancy, with the ever-tantalizing but never-fulfilled prospect of marriage to Elizabeth – or at least lucrative office to pay for their hedonistic pleasures; for young women there was the opportunity to satisfy the most fantastic dreams of female vanity, in fine clothes, in luxurious settings, and always the chance of a rich marriage.

Surely no woman was ever so enthralled with her own power as was Elizabeth, nor anyone so fitted to occupy the centre of so brilliant a stage. In her childhood she had known the bleakness of poverty as the discarded daughter of the reviled Anne Boleyn. As a young girl she had come early to the intrigues and plots of Tudor England, as the pawn of the treacherous Sir Thomas Seymour, her suspected lover. In the most recent years before her accession, she had entered the dread Tower as the prisoner of her suspicious sister Queen Mary, and had gone in fear for her very life. Now she emerged from all this into the bright world of her own reign, in full knowledge that she must firmly rule both Court and government to survive and to be held great.

There were rich rewards to mete out to those who had proved themselves loyal to her in her trials. First, there was Catherine Ashley, long her governess, who for all her weak confessions of Elizabeth's youthful indiscretions with Thomas Seymour, had borne patiently the rages and tempests of the Princess's frustrations and, apart from that one lapse, had never swerved from her devotion. There was Isabella Markham, Elizabeth's companion in imprisonment, who, for her mistress and for the Protestant religion, had suffered even rejection by her family. There were Elizabeth's maternal relations: the Knollys and Carey families, descendants of her aunt Mary Boleyn, and the whole huge tribe of the Howards, who throughout the reign occupied key posts in all spheres of English life.

For all that the Queen was happiest in the company of men, revelling in flattery and flirtation and in her power to overrule even the most obdurate statesman, she had still charm and energy to spare to hold women also in thrall. There was Blanche Parry, already in her late twenties when Elizabeth was born, who served her until her death, aged eighty-one, in 1589. Thus part of the verse on her memorial tablet in Bacton Church, Herefordshire:

I lived always as handmaide to a Queen,
In chamber chiefe my tyme did overpasse,
Uncareful of my welthe there was I sene,
Whylst I abode the runnynge of my glasse,
Not doubtynge wante that whylst my mystresse lyvde,
In woman's state whose cradell saw I rockte,
Her servant then, as when she her crown atcheeved,
And so remayned till death he my doore had knockte:
Preferrynge still the causes of each wyghte,
As far as I doorste move her grace's eare
For to reward decerts by course of ryghte
As needs resyte of sarvys done each wheare.

So that my time I thus did passe awaye
A maed in court, and never no man's wyfe,
Sworne of Queene Ellsbeths hedd chamber allways
With Maeden Queene a mayde did end my lyfe.

Blanche's nearest rival for the accolade of long service was one Mary Radcliffe, who was with Elizabeth for forty years. She had come to Court one New Year's Day early in the reign, standing among the lesser guests to watch the Queen receive her gifts from her courtiers. Last of them all, her father stepped forward and boldly presented Mary herself as his gift to Elizabeth. He was counting on this original ploy to have his daughter accepted as one of Elizabeth's maids-of-honour, overriding the better and more formal claims of others. His gamble was rewarded. Mary repaid her advancement in future years by rejecting all offers of marriage to remain with her mistress – a sure way to keep the Queen's affection.

From the outset of Elizabeth's reign, it was clear that one man was favoured above all others: Robert Dudley, one of the sons of that Lord Protector and would-be 'Queenmaker' who had lost his life for his engineering of the *coup* designed to set Jane Grey on the throne in 1553. The female counterpart of the royal favourite was Dudley's own sister, Lady Mary Sidney, the Queen's closest confidante until her death in 1586. It was she who nursed Elizabeth through her near-fatal attack of smallpox in 1562, and in the process contracted the disease herself. The Queen emerged unscathed, but Lady Mary bore the scars and pits of smallpox for the rest of her life. As her husband wrote at the time: 'When I went to Newhaven, I left her a full fair lady, in mine eyes at least the fairest, and when I returned I found her as foul a lady as the smallpox could make her; which she did take by continual attendance on Her Majesty's most precious person.'[1] Thereafter, Mary Sidney was rarely at Court, and then keeping to her rooms, where she was frequently visited by the Queen. She and her husband were accorded almost viceregal state during Sidney's term of office in the principality of Wales.

It was while they were there that their daughter Ambrosia died in February 1575. The Queen sent them one of the kindest letters ever to come from her eloquent pen, remarking on the unsearchable will of God, and then adding:

> He hath left you the comfort of one daughter of very good hope [another Mary], whom, if you shall think good to remove from those parts of unpleasant air [Ludlow], if it be so, into better in these parts, and will send her unto us before Easter, or when you shall think good, assure yourself that we will have a special care of her, not doubting but, as you are well persuaded of our favour towards yourself, so will we make further demonstration thereof in her; if you will send her unto us, and so comforting you for the one, and leaving this our offer of goodwill in your consideration for the other, we commit you to Almighty God.[2]

This girl, Mary Sidney the younger, was only fourteen when she arrived at Court, to be made much of by the Queen; but it was little more than a year before she was transferred from her post among the maids-of-honour to the more senior position of Lady of the Bedchamber, by reason of her new marital status. The Queen contrived her match with Lord Herbert, later Earl of Pembroke – but Mary's uncle, Robert Dudley, Earl of Leicester, found her dowry.

It was Mary's brother who most demonstrated the ideal of the sixteenth-century nobleman: Philip Sidney, poet and soldier, the ' veray parfit gentil knight' of his age. Mary was his perfect complement, as learned as any woman of her time, herself fêted by poets. Edmund Spenser, who gave Queen Elizabeth her eternal rôle of 'Gloriana', hailed Mary as 'Urania, sister unto Astrophel', writing of her:

> Into whose brave mind, as in a golden coffer,
> All heavenly gifts and riches locked are,
> More rich than pearls of Ind or gold of Ophir,
> And in her sex more wonderful and rare.

Mary herself was a versifier, working with her brother on a

translation of the Psalms into English verse and after his death, undertaking the publication of his poems.

Another member of the Dudley family, this time by marriage, was Anne, Countess of Warwick. As Anne Russell, daughter of the Earl of Bedford, she had married Robert Dudley's brother Ambrose in November 1565. She too had been a maid-of-honour, and her wedding was provided at the Queen's expense at Whitehall, with a banquet and a three-day tournament. Again, she too was lauded in poetry, this time by the Italian Pietro Bozzari, in his epithalamion:

> O to how blest a lot is he commended
> Who, winning thee, with virtue will embrace
> A form like Helen's, by delight attended,
> And tender love, and every virgin grace;
> Thee, o'er whose cheek ingenuous honour throws
> Her exquisite rose!
>
> Though thine be genius, thou dost deign to cherish
> Genius with care – with many-languaged powers
> Reaping the spoils of deed that ne'er shall perish,
> Speeding with lyre or lute th'enchanted hours,
> Or broidering webs whose beauty well might dare
> Arachne to despair.
>
> Why should I say that refined discreetness
> Thy converse teems? Why speak thy charming voice?
> Thy gaze – thy steps – thy smile so full of sweetness –
> Or thrilling dance, if dancing be thy choice?
> Why speak of aught, when all thou say'st and dost
> Is beautiful and just.

A somewhat later favourite of the Queen was the Marchioness of Northampton, one of the most senior peeresses of the realm. She was Helena Ulfsdotter Snakenborg, a Swedish girl, born in 1549, who came to England in 1565 as a maid-of-honour to the Queen's guest Cecilia of Sweden, Margravine of Baden. But when Cecilia left in April 1566 (having long outstayed her welcome) Helena stayed behind. For all that she had no money of her own, she was sought in marriage by the Marquess of Northampton. Admitted, he was nearly forty years her senior, but he was so besotted by her that, as Helena wrote home, 'if only God would give him the happiness of my loving heart, he would ask no other wealth. Even if I brought nothing but my shift and gave him happiness, it would be a dowry from God.'[3] Pleading with her 'heart's dearest mother dear', Helena won permission to stay in England. However, it was not until 1571 that the couple were married and then Northampton lived only six months after the wedding. She later married Sir Thomas Gorges, a gentleman usher of the Queen's Privy Chamber, but continued to rejoice in the title of Marchioness, and was frequently in attendance on Elizabeth at Court, where she also retained her rank's precedence. As senior peeress at the Queen's death in 1603, she was chief mourner at the funeral.

It was no sinecure, serving Queen Elizabeth. The Queen Bee was at the centre of an ever-moving, ever-busy hive. Or rather she lived at the centre of a labyrinth: the Court passed its time in the galleries of the palace, but to penetrate to the Queen at her leisure, one had to pass through the Presence Chamber, then the Privy Chamber, to the *sanctum sanctorum*, the royal Bedchamber. It was here that the Queen was attended by the closest and most senior of her ladies, with the lesser ranks in waiting in the Privy Chamber and the maids-of-honour darting hither and thither on their errands.

Elizabeth's ceremonial was nothing compared with the later etiquette of Louis XIV's Versailles, but it nevertheless had its own rituals. A contemporary traveller, Hentzner, once observed the preparations for the Queen's dinner, noting carefully the details of the guards who accompanied her food and chattels, and the gentlemen who danced attendance, but more especially the duties of the ladies who, under a female sovereign, performed the duties that had formerly belonged to the gentlemen of the Court. After the Queen's table had been set up and her cloth laid,

> At last came an unmarried lady [a maid-of-honour] ... and along with her a married one, bearing a tasting fork; the former was dressed in white silk, who, when she had prostrated herself three times in the most graceful manner, approached the table and rubbed the platters with bread and salt with as much awe as if the Queen had been present. ...

After she had given each guard a taste from each dish of food, a precaution traditionally observed against poison, 'At the end of all this ceremonial, a number of unmarried ladies appeared, who, with particular solemnity, lifted the meat off the table, and conveyed it into the Queen's inner and more private Chamber, where after she had chosen for herself, the rest goes to the ladies of the Court.'[4]

The old system of the 'bouche of Court' was thus kept up in supplying the courtiers. At the same time, the ladies were still allowed stabling for their horses too, and the maids-of-honour, who were often short of money and unable to provide for themselves, had the use of horses from the Queen's stables. 'Roan Howard', 'Bay Dormer', 'Grey Fitton', 'White Smithfield', 'White Howard' and 'Bay Compton' were the names of the maids' mares towards the end of the century.

There were, of course, many other 'perks' for the ladies. As the Queen's godson John Harington reported in July 1602, 'My Lady Ambassador of France was entertained by the Queen yesterday very graciously, and gave among the Queen's maids French purses, fans and masks, very bountifully.'[5] Nor was Elizabeth herself mean with her wealth, but frequently gave gifts of clothes – and not only her cast-offs – to her ladies.

But the most desirable perquisite of the ladies close to the Queen was their vaunted influence in gaining posts and pensions for their friends – an influence which was the envy of all, not always with reason. Although there are instances of the ladies' obtaining their suits, such as when Mistress Russell obtained the Lord Wardenship of the Cinque Ports for Lord Cobham, over Lady Scudamore's nominee the Earl of Essex, there were numerous other cases when they failed. This by no means prevented their attempts, so that their wrangling and jealousies prompted Sir Walter Raleigh to say that the ladies were 'like witches, capable of doing great harm, but no good'.[6]

Places at Court, for such supposed influence, for the chance of a good marriage for a young girl or for a pension for an older woman, were the subject of great rivalry, and not a little expense to the suitor. First there was a petition to be written, then the bribing and favour-currying with established courtiers for their aid in bringing the matter repeatedly to the Queen's ear – Lady Denny's father paid out some £1,300 for her advancement. When, in the 1580s, Lady Leighton threatened to resign from her post in the Bedchamber if a certain suit in which she had an interest were denied, there were at least a dozen applications for her place on the spot.

It is safe enough to presume that most of the young girls who went up to Court to become maids-of-honour went with the intention of giving useful service to the Queen, as well as of forwarding their own careers. One of their number, at least, was left in no doubt of her duty. When Bridget Manners arrived at Court in 1595, she soon received a letter from her great-uncle Roger, full of charges and warnings:

> First and above all things that you forget not to use daily prayers to Almighty God to endue you with His grace; then that you apply yourself wholly to the service of Her Majesty with all meekness, love and obedience; wherein you must be diligent, secret and faithful. To your elders and superiors, of reverent behaviour, to your equals and fellow-servants civil and courteous; to your inferiors you must show all favour and gentleness. Generally that you be no meddler in the causes of others. That you use much silence, for that becometh maids, especially of your calling. That your speech and endeavours ever tend to the good of all and to the hurt of none. Thus in brief madam have you these rules: which, if you have grace to follow you shall find the benefit, and your friends shall rejoice of your well-doing.[7]

It is also clear, however, that the first awe at being so close to the Queen soon wore off. So many teenaged girls together, with so many restraints on their public conduct, were naturally high-spirited when left to themselves, as a contemporary noted:

> The Lord Knollys, in Queen Elizabeth's time, had his lodging at Court where some of the ladies and maids-of-honour used to frisk and hey about in the next room, to his extreme disquiet a nights, though he had often warned them of it; at last he gets one to bolt their own back door, when they were all in one night at their revels, strips off his shirt, and so with a pair of spectacles on his nose and Aretine in his hand, comes marching in at a postern door of his own chamber, reading very gravely, full upon the faces of them. Now let the reader judge what a sad spectacle and pitiful sight these poor creatures endured, for he faced them and often traversed the room in this posture above an hour.[8]

There was even one young woman, Lady Mary Howard, who evinced no fear of the Queen, going so far as to make herself Elizabeth's rival for the Earl of Essex. No one would have dared so much in Elizabeth's heyday, but now, in the 1590s, even though the Queen's temper was more uncertain than it had ever been, there was more freedom to misbehave. To attract Essex (by then a married man), Lady Mary bought herself one of the finest of dresses ever seen at that Court renowned for its high fashion, flounced with gold and pearls on velvet. Elizabeth was furious to be so out-done by Mary Howard and, in her absence one day, stole the dress. In Mary's presence she paraded in it and asked her if it were not becoming. Sulkily, the girl replied that the dress was too short. 'Why then,' retorted Elizabeth, 'if it become not me as being too short, I am minded it shall never become you as being too fine, so it fitteth neither well.'[9] Mary put away her dress and it was taken out only after the Queen was safely dead.

But Mary nursed her grudge against Elizabeth. When she even refused to carry the Queen's cloak, or to bring her cup at meals, her friends began to be alarmed for Mary, and warned her:

> to be more dutiful, and not to absent herself at meals, or prayers, to bear her Highness's mantle and other furniture, even more than all the rest of her servants, to make ample amends by future diligence; and always to go first in the morning to her Highness's chamber, forasmuch as such kindness will much prevail to turn away all former displeasure. She must not entertain my lord the Earl in any conversation, but shun his company; and moreover be less careful in attiring her person, for this seemeth she has done more to win the Earl than her mistress's goodwill.[10]

Mary must surely have reformed, for no more is heard of her misconduct.

Elizabeth had always been a difficult mistress. Even as a child, she had had her right royal rages, and as a woman she was feared as much as loved. During her worries about the war in the Netherlands (when her beloved Leicester was in the thick of it), the Queen was sleepless, quick to anger and beat 'one or two' of her ladies. 'When she smiled, it was pure sunshine', wrote Elizbeth's godson John Harington, 'but anon came a storm from a sudden gathering of clouds, and the thunder fell in wondrous manner on all alike.'[11] Another wrote that 'she was subject to be vehemently transported with anger; and when she was so, she would show it by her voice, her countenance and her hand. She would chide her familiar servants so loud that they who stood afar off might sometimes hear her voice. And it was reported that for small offences she would strike her maids-of-honour with her hand.'[12]

One of the maids-of-honour so chastised was Mary Shelton who secretly married one James Scudamore. Elizabeth was 'liberal in blows and words', so that 'no one ever bought her husband more dearly.'[13] In fact, the Queen broke one of Mary's fingers with her blows. Later, Elizabeth repented her anger and made Mary one of the Gentlewomen of her Privy Chamber.

Mary Shelton was not the only maid-of-honour to marry without the Queen's knowledge or permission. Towards the end of the reign there were so many illicit weddings as to become almost a commonplace. When Frances Vavasour was secretly married to Sir Henry Shirley and broke the news to the Queen after the ceremony, Elizabeth railed angrily at her, declaring that 'She hath always furthered any honest and honourable purposes of marriage or preferment to any of hers when, without scandal and infamy, they have been orderly broke to her.'[14] To be just to Elizabeth, who always had the reputation of harshness to her ladies in the matter of their marriage, there is no record of her ever refusing any suitable proposal for the hands of her maids. Her reputed antipathy to their marriages rests on remarks quoted by her godson Sir John Harington that 'she did oft ask the ladies around her chamber if they loved to think of marriage. And the wise ones did conceal well their liking thereto, as knowing the Queen's judgment.'[15]

An imprudent young woman, one of the several girls of the Arundel family who had places at Court, admitted to Elizabeth that 'She had thought much about marriage, if her father did consent to the man she loved.'

'You seem honest, i'faith. I will sue for you to your father,' replied the Queen.

On hearing of his daughter's wishes, Sir Robert Arundel was surprised: 'He never had heard his daughter had liking to any man; but he would give free consent to what was most pleasing to her Highness's will and advice.'

'Then I will do the rest,' said Elizabeth.

She called the girl, and told her the news. 'Then I shall be happy, an please your Grace.'

'So thou shalt; but not to be a fool, and marry. I have his consent given to me, and I vow thou shalt never get it in thy possession. So, go to thy business. I see thou art a bold one, to own thy foolishness so readily.'[16]

From all the female members of the Arundel family at Court, it is impossible to trace which one this might be. Certainly many of the Arundel maids-of-honour married, so perhaps Elizabeth later relented.

The key to her antipathy to her maids' marriages lay in her words to Frances Vavasour, that she disliked underhand business, 'scandal and infamy'. If one may dare hazard an analysis of this, in view of the many psychological analyses of the Queen by eminent writers, it would be that Elizabeth herself never dared place trust in any man to the extent of putting her honour, and her crown, in his care. As a girl she had nearly lost all by her trust in Sir Thomas Seymour; throughout the difficult years of Mary's reign she had trusted her own judgment, making no man her sole mentor. As Queen, she balanced the opposing parties at Court, in her government and in the Church, never wholly trusting anyone. After the death of Robert Dudley's wife (a murder, many suspected), which many supposed to be a step towards her own marriage with him, Elizabeth balanced his claim on her with plans for a foreign marriage (which never took root) and scattered her favours more widely in her Court. So, when she saw one of her ladies risk all for love, she both despised and perhaps envied her, with emotional rages resulting. Certainly there were more than enough honourable marriages among her ladies to prove that she had no immovable antipathy to the estate. It was natural that she should prefer to be served by unmarried women and widows who could attend her without home-cares to divide them, but married women were also numbered among her friends.

At the same time, whatever Elizabeth's reasons for remaining unmarried – and, so she claimed, a virgin – she loved to be in love. Until she was an ugly old woman, painted and wigged, hunched in her gorgeous robes, she could still fancy that every man who saw her loved her. And the evidence also points to the fact that she could not bear to think that her lovers could also love elsewhere.

First there was Robert Dudley, Earl of Leicester, her 'bonny sweet Robin', to whom she would give anything but herself and her kingdom. His affair with Douglas Sheffield was bad enough, but his marriage with her own cousin Lettice Knollys, the widowed Countess of Essex, was miserable treachery. When the new Countess of Leicester appeared at Court, adorned with all her finery and with an immense retinue, Elizabeth boxed her ears and declared that 'as but one sun lighted the east, so she would have but one queen in England.'[17] It was many days before the Countess dared show her face at Court again, and then it was to be received with coldness and spite, though 'Robin' was soon back in his mistress's favour.

Already we have observed Elizabeth's conduct to Mary Howard, when the latter tried to catch the attention of Elizabeth's later favourite, the young Earl of Essex (actually Lettice's son by her first marriage). He was already married to Frances Walsingham (a chivalrous gesture to the widow of his great friend the late Philip Sidney), but that did not prevent the Court ladies from vying for his smiles. Catherine Bridges and Elizabeth Russell were once caught watching the Earl in a ball game, whereupon the Queen struck Mistress Bridges, and put both the ladies out of her Court. They stayed away three days before returning to brave the Queen's sour looks.

Catherine Bridges, daughter of Lord Chandos, was altogether a bold, saucy girl. Although she was a great heiress, she was kept short of money and was reduced to pawning her diamonds. One of her suitors, Charles Lister, gave her money and more jewels, on the condition that she agree to marry him. Catherine gave her promise, but kept postponing the wedding day until Lister was forced to sue her.

Like so many of the maids-of-honour, Catherine Bridges is remembered in verse, this time by George Gascoigne in his 'In Praise of Bridges':

In Court who so demands
What dame doth most excel,
For my conceit I needs must say,
Fair Bridges bears the bell.

Upon whose lively cheek, to prove
My judgment true,
The rose and lily seem to strive for
Equal change of hue.

And there withall so well her

Graces all agree,
No frowning cheer dare once
Presume in her sweet face to be.

Although some lavish lips
Which like some other best
Will say the blemish on her brow
Disgraceth all the rest.

That 'blemish on her brow' was the scar of a cut: Gascoigne claimed that it was the stroke of Cupid himself, lest Mistress Bridges's beauty 'break him of his rest'. More likely, it was from the force of Elizabeth's ringed hands in her anger.

Apart from Mary Shelton, in the 1560s, and one Anne Vavasour (Frances's sister), a 'drab' who gave birth to a child in the 'Maidens' Chamber' in 1581 (by Lord Oxford, who refused to marry her, but made a monetary settlement of £2,000), most of the scandals of Elizabeth's Court occurred in the 1590s.

There was Bess Throckmorton, who dared to fall for Elizabeth's current favourite Walter Raleigh, the poet, historian and famous explorer. He was a notorious womanizer, and Bess was not the first maid who had lost her honour to him. Aubrey tells the tale of Raleigh's 'getting one of the maids-of-honour against a tree in a wood'. "Nay, sweet Sir Walter. Oh, sweet Sir Walter," she first cried in protest. Then, as she yielded, and 'as the danger and the pleasure at the same time grew higher, she cried in the ecstasy, "Swisser Swatter! Swisser Swatter." She proved with child.'[18] Raleigh had been at Court more than ten years before he met Bess, and she was the only one of the ladies who managed to bring him to marriage. When, Bess being pregnant, rumours of the match came to the Queen's ears in July 1592, Raleigh at first denied that he had married her. Having fled from Court to the dock-yard at Chatham, he wrote to Robert Cecil:

> I mean not to come away, as they say I will, for fear of a marriage, and I know not what. If any such thing were, I

> would have imparted it to yourself, before any man living, and therefore, I pray, believe it not, and I beseech you to suppress, what you can, any such malicious report. For I protest before God there is none on the face of the earth that I would be fastened to.[19]

Later, in the Tower, Raleigh confessed his guilt. Both he and his wife were later released, but Elizabeth ceased to care for him and withdrew that generous favour which he had so long enjoyed.

The next to fall from grace was that Bridget Manners who had arrived at Court with so much good advice to guide her in 1595. She had brought with her one of her mother's waiting women, Mary Harding, who had express orders to stop Bridget from 'stooping' or slouching. The girl's *gaucherie* soon disappeared, leaving her, in the words of the poet Barnaby Barnes, 'Rose of that garland! fairest and sweetest of all those sweet and fair flowers! Pride of chaste Cynthia's rich crown!' This time, however, it was not the girl's moral frailty but her mother's ambition which brought the Queen to fury. On the plea that her daughter had been over-long from home and in ill-health, she took Bridget from Court and secretly married her to her wealthy ward, Robert Tyrwhitt. When the news came out, the Countess of Rutland panicked and swore to the Queen that it was Bridget's own doing. Elizabeth was no fool, and she knew her Lady Rutland. A friend wrote to the quaking woman:

> Her Majesty neither by the sight of your ladyship's letter nor by all the reasons they can use, will be persuaded to believe your honour could be ignorant of it. Her Majesty grounded her concept upon the opinion Her Highness hath long had of your ladyship's wisdom, and of my Lady Bridget's obedience to you, concluding thereupon that a matter of such weight could not be done without your ladyship's acquaintance, the same being no less than the marriage of your own daughter in your own house, and by your own chaplain.[20]

It took many pathetic tears from Bridget to have her surely

blameless young husband released from the Tower, whence the Queen's wrath had sent him.

Elizabeth Vernon, however, had no one but herself to blame, when she became pregnant by the Earl of Southampton. 'Some say that she hath taken a venue [a thrust, in fencing terms] under the girdle, and swells upon it,' went the gossip, 'yet she complains not of foul play but says the Earl of Southampton will justify it.'[21] He did – just in time for the birth of Elizabeth's child. Through the intercession of the Earl of Essex, Southampton had to endure only a fortnight's imprisonment in the Fleet, and Elizabeth but a few weeks at home in Shropshire, before the Queen forgave them their 'crime'.

Finally, there was the scandal to top them all: the affair of Mary Fitton and Lord Herbert. Mary had come to Court at the age of seventeen, and her prudent father had put her under the especial care of his friend Sir William Knollys, the Comptroller of the Queen's household. Knollys had promised Fitton that he would:

> in no wise fail to fulfil your desire in playing the good shepherd and will to my power defend the innocent lamb from the wolvish cruelty and foxlike subtlety of the tame beasts in this place, which when they seem to take bread at a man's hand will bite before they bark; ... I will with my counsel advise your fair daughter, with my true affection love her and with my sword defend her, if need be; her innocence will deserve it and her virtue will challenge it at my hands, and I will be as careful of her well-doing as if I were her true father.[22]

It was not long, however, before this fatherly concern became more passionate. Knollys kept up a frequent correspondence with Mary's married sister Anne Newdigate in which he frankly (and imprudently, since he was a married man) confessed his love for the girl:

> My hopes are mixed with despair [he wrote] and my desires starved with expectations, but were my enjoying assured, I could willingly endure purgatory for a season to purchase my

heaven at last. But the short warning, the distemperature of my head by reason of the toothache and your sister's going to bed without bidding me goodnight, will join in one to be a means that for this time I will only trouble you with these few lines scribbled in haste.

Knollys signed himself 'Your most assured friend, I would fain say brother'.[23]

It was in the summer of 1600 that rumour linked the names of Mary Fitton and William Herbert (son of Mary, Countess of Pembroke). It was said that the maid-of-honour had been seen creeping out of the palace to Herbert's lodgings, her gown tucked up under a big white cloak, and marching along the street 'as though she had been a man'.

Herbert, now in 1601 Earl of Pembroke, acknowledged his paternity of her child but refused to marry her. In the Fleet Prison, angry with the girl for making such trouble for him, he wrote her a taunting verse:

> Then this advice, fair creature, take from me:
> Let none pluck fruit, unless he pluck the tree.
> For if with one, with thousands thou'lt turn whore.
> Break ice in one place, and it cracks the more.

Mary had been confident that Pembroke would marry her; now she was in despair. No less distraught was Knollys, but since he was still married, there was nothing he could do for her. By the time his wife died, in 1605, he had decided against such a *mésalliance* and instead turned his attentions to the nineteen-year-old Lady Elizabeth Howard, whom he subsequently married.

Mary Fitton might have remained as obscure as any other of the maids-of-honour had it not been for years of speculation that she was Shakespeare's 'dark lady of the sonnets'. There is now agreed to be little likelihood of this, but William Knollys is still generally regarded as the model for 'Malvolio' in *Twelfth Night*. 'Mal' was a contemporary contraction for Mary, and 'Mal-voglio' – 'I desire Mal', a subtle witticism such as Shakespeare loved.

The story had a happy ending for Mary, for she married in 1607, and again a second time – though to no such title or estate as Pembroke's.

If Queen Elizabeth had frequently been unkind to her younger ladies in the matter of their stolen marriages, she had always a cheering word for widows (perhaps with the happy prospect of their undivided attentions to her). Lady Paget and Lady Norris were recipients of the kindest of letters, and one addressed to the widowed Lady Drury shows Elizabeth at her best:

> Be well aware, my Bess, you strive not with Divine ordinance, nor grudge at irremediable harms, lest you offend the highest Lord, and no whit amend your marred hap. Heap not your harms where help there is none, but since you may not that you would wish, that you can enjoy with comfort, a king for his power and a queen for her love, who leaves not now to protect you when your case requires care, and minds not to omit whatever may be best for you and yours.[24]

Nor would she sacrifice her ladies for state reasons and her own extension of power. In May 1583 an embassy was sent from the Court of Ivan the Terrible of Russia to find an English wife for him, to cement Anglo-Russian relations and trade agreements, and Mary Hastings, a distant cousin of Elizabeth's on her father's side then serving as a maid-of-honour, was elected to fill the role. Elizabeth refused to allow the terrified maid-of-honour to be sent to barbaric Russia, despite all pleas from the Tsar. For years afterwards Mary was jokingly named 'Tsarina of Muscovy', but she must frequently have shuddered to think of her near escape. In 1601 Boris Godunov sent a vast shipment of sables to woo a wife in England, and the Earl of Derby's daughter was considered, but again the plan was quashed.

That 'pure sunshine' of Elizabeth's smile had endeared her to three generations of ladies-in-waiting by the time of her death in 1603. The girls with whom she had grown up sent their daughters to her in the 1560s and their grand-daughters in the eighties and nineties. Her godchildren numbered over a hundred, and each had his or her chance of a place at Court.

But even to the end of her life, Elizabeth firmly, obstinately, irrevocably, held the reins. She could be won over by smiles and flattery, but she could turn hard and bitter if she were betrayed. When the Earl of Essex was under sentence of death in 1601, the Queen waited in vain for the arrival of a ring from him – a ring which she had once given him, and which was between them a token of his devotion to her. Had that ring ever arrived, the story goes, he would have been saved. In fact, Essex despatched the ring, with instructions to his messenger to deliver it to the Queen's chief lady, Lady Scrope. But it accidentally fell into the hands of her sister the Countess of Nottingham, whose husband was so bitter an enemy of Essex that he made her withhold it from the Queen. Essex was therefore left unpardoned, and beheaded. Not until January 1603 did Lady Nottingham confess what she had done.

It was the death-blow to Elizabeth. Two months later she died. At the end her old friends Lady Warwick and Lady Scrope were with her, and it was Lady Scrope who dropped a sapphire ring taken from the hand of the corpse from a window of the Palace to her waiting brother Robert Carey, who was deputed to take the news to Elizabeth's heir, King James of Scotland.

5

THE history of the kingdom of Scotland (from which James Stuart came in 1603 to become King of England) had no stories of ladies-in-waiting on the scale of those in England. Only one of them, Catherine Douglas, had entered the annals of Scotland, but her heroism had no parallel south of the border. In 1437 there had been an attempt on the life of King James I by his kinsman the Master of Athol. The King, his English wife Jane Beaufort and her ladies-in-waiting were all penned, without protection, into one room of the royal apartments. Realizing that the door would not hold off the assailants for long, the ladies began to tear up the floorboards to effect an escape into a lower storey. Then, seeing the lock nearly broken under the force of Athol's co-conspirators, Catherine Douglas thrust her arm into the door-bar, to gain more time. Her effort was in vain: her arm was broken as the assassins burst open the door; the King was killed and the Queen wounded.

Such violence was almost a commonplace in Scottish history, and it is scarcely surprising that James VI was always ready to smell plot and conspiracy in even the cleanest air.

Even the storms which postponed his bride's arrival in Scotland smacked to him of foul-play. The fourteen-year-old Anne of Denmark first embarked for Scotland in September 1589, but so strong were the gales of the North Sea that she was driven back to take shelter in Norway. When news of the delay reached Scotland, the King set out to meet her but was himself driven back into harbour by bad weather and only on the second attempt reached the coast of Norway. The couple were married in Denmark and remained there until the spring, when, crossing to Scotland at last, they were again troubled by high seas.

Popular opinion had it that there were witches at work in Scotland, who, 'in conjunction with their sisterhood in Norway, had brewed the storms to drown the harmless young Queen'.[1] Anne had escaped unharmed but, in Scotland, the witches claimed one victim. Jane Kennedy had been a maid-of-honour to King James's mother, Mary, Queen of Scots, one of the women who had indeed attended her to the block, and now, *en route* for the Court and the service of Queen Anne, she was drowned while crossing on the Leith ferry in stormy weather.

There were witch-hunts in Denmark and Scotland as a result of the widespread panic after the storms. King James, neurotic with fear for his own safety, sent out commissioners with powers to torture men and women to get to the root of the supposed ill-wishing. Some of the resulting evidence pointed to the implication in the plots of the Earl of Bothwell (nephew of Queen Mary Stuart's third husband), a man whom James had long feared. Bothwell was taken but escaped. Well might the King fear his intentions, for on three occasions, in 1590, 1592 and 1593 the Earl made attempts to reach the King by force – to kill him, so James feared. Bothwell evaded capture, but several of his supporters were caught.

Among them was one John Wemyss, the lover of one of Queen Anne's Danish maids, Margaret Vinster. In the summer of 1592, Wemyss was held prisoner at Dalkeith, where the King and Queen were lodging. One night, he was called from his cell on the pretext of examination before the King. He was led into the royal apartments where one of the Queen's ladies ordered his guards away. It was Margaret Vinster who had sent the message to the cells herself, once James and Anne were asleep. Now she led Wemyss silently through the King's own bedroom and lowered him by rope from the window to safety.

When the escape was discovered, James was furious (shuddering that his supposed enemy had passed within inches of him, and he defencelessly asleep). Knowing that Anne had some sympathy for Bothwell and his friends was enough to make James suspect that she had abetted the escape. The Queen refused to say one word which would harm her maid, even when the King threatened to send her home to Denmark. The incident passed and, not long after, Margaret had her reward in marrying Wemyss.

This was not the end of the Bothwell attempts against James, nor was Scotland free of other conspirators and plotters. On the other hand, however, James was so obsessed with the dangers of his position, that he was always ready to see plots where there was none. This may have been the case with the so-called 'Gowrie conspiracy' of 1600. The Ruthven family, of which the Earl of Gowrie was the head, had a history of bad terms with the House of Stuart, but the contemporary generation had nothing known against them. Indeed, the Queen had three Ruthven women among her ladies, of whom the eldest, Lady Beatrice, was her firm favourite.

Thus when James produced the dead bodies of the Earl of Gowrie and his brother Alexander, with a complicated, scarcely-credible tale of their foiled attempt to murder him, Anne had more sympathy for her friends than for her husband.

Beatrice Ruthven and her sisters were dismissed from Court, their family estates forfeited and their name execrated. James refused all Anne's pleas to have her friend, at least, forgiven. Her only weapon against him was to threaten the life of the child she was carrying: she stayed in bed, refusing to eat or speak until Beatrice was brought back. But Anne was still very young, and not yet used to her husband's temperament: where his rage could not break her resolve, his guile prevailed. She allowed herself to be lured back to Court when James hired a famous French acrobat to amuse her (at a fee of more than £300). Nevertheless,

Anne herself was not without duplicity. Finding her pleas unavailing, she arranged for Lady Paisley and Lady Angus to smuggle Beatrice Ruthven, disguised as their servant, into Holyroodhouse; they 'stowed her in a chamber prepared for her by the Queen's direction [according to an English spy or 'agent' in Scotland], where the Queen had much time and conference with her'.[2] James found out, inevitably, and, suspecting his wife of complicity in the whole plot (for so far did his neurosis go), he instituted an enquiry through all the ranks of her household. Fortunately he could find no further guilt and three years later was even brought to admit that although Beatrice's family was 'hateful on account of the abominable attempt against the King, she has shown no malicious disposition',[3] and awarded her a pension of £200.

The quarrels between Anne and James continued until the very time of her death in 1619. In the first months of their marriage, James had been infatuated with his wife, but soon his latent homosexuality became evident. This reign offered no chance for nubile maids-of-honour to make their fortunes by catching the King's eye; now it was the turn of the effeminate 'gallants' of the Court. Queen Anne was driven by her husband's neglect of her into the company of favourites, whom James never ceased to mistrust; they quarrelled over their children, and over religion – Anne became a Catholic towards the end of the 1590s, abetted by her Catholic ladies-in-waiting Jane Drummond and Henrietta, Countess of Huntley. But James and Anne quarrelled mostly over money. Even when they took on the wealth of England in 1603, Anne could still deplete her allowance at a speed horrifying to James – and a good deal of it was spent on her absorbing hobby of performing in 'masques'.

Anne of Denmark liked nothing better than to take part in the most lavish and brilliant form of Court theatricals, the masque. Coming from Italy, these entertainments combined music, dancing and fine poetry on classical themes with the most ambitious use of scenery, costume and stage-effects ever seen in Europe, their actors drawn from the ranks of the courtiers. Now ladies-in-waiting found that acting was one of their main duties.

Court theatricals had always been splendid affairs. They were first introduced under the Tudors. The earliest 'spectaculars', not yet masques in the accepted form, involved movable pieces of scenery, usually a castle, a ship or a mountain. 'Le fortresse dangereus' was the centre-piece of the entertainment for Henry VIII's Court on New Year's Eve 1512, with its six beleaguered ladies and its six knights (including the King himself) who released them from captivity and led them out to dance. In 1522 Anne Boleyn had taken part in a pageant which Cardinal Wolsey had arranged for the imperial ambassadors, and the King had played opposite her as the knight 'Ardent Desire' – surely presaging later *amours*. Already fantastic costumes had been introduced – Henry was once garbed as a Russian, his sister Mary as an 'Ethiop queen' in a black gauze mask. His daughter Mary, as Queen, had a pageant which combined the various disguises of 'Almaynes, Pilgrymes and Irishmen' and Queen Elizabeth, of course, was forever being fêted on her progresses with entertainments rustic and classical in which she was courted as Diana or Gloriana or Belphoebe or any one of several goddesses and queens of myth, history or imagination.

Elizabeth did not take part in the 'masking' or 'disguising' which was the main feature of the entertainments. She was always herself, whatever name she was addressed by. But she would condescend to dance at the end of the pageant. (On one occasion, when the main part of the play was done, one of the characters, played by her maid-of-honour Mary Fitton, approached Elizabeth on her dais and 'wooed' her to join the dance. The Queen asked what her character was. 'Affection', answered the girl. 'Affection!' exclaimed the Queen, 'Affection's false!'[4] And so, in Mary's case, did it prove.)

Anne of Denmark, however, not only took part in several masques but led the fashion for them, encouraging her courtiers to spend greater and greater sums of money on outrageous costumes and effects.

In Scotland, she had enjoyed pageantry in the old style. In

1594, for example, she was regaled with the sight of a chariot in which sat several of her ladies, attired as Ceres, Fecundity, Concord, Liberality and Perseverance, and then with a ship, eighteen feet long, steered by another of her ladies. It was not until her arrival in her husband's second kingdom, however, that Anne discovered the pleasures of the Italian-style masque, which, for the first time in England, combined poetry with music and dancing. On her progress to London in 1603, she was fêted at Althorp with Ben Jonson's *Masque of Fairies* which, on a summer evening, in the open air, with fairies, satyrs, coloured lights, music and dancing, must have been entrancing.

It was not long before Anne tried her own hand at providing such alluring entertainments. In the words of a scarcely approving contemporary, her Court became 'a continued masquerado, where the Queen and her ladies . . . appeared often in various dresses to the ravishment of the beholders, the King himself being not a little delighted with such fluent elegancies as made the night more glorious than the day'.[5]

In Ben Jonson the dramatist and Inigo Jones the stage- and costume-designer, who had learned his arts in Italy where the Court spectacle reached its zenith, Queen Anne had the perfect combination of talent. Her first masque, *The Masque of Blackness*, of 1605, found her painted black to represent the African River Niger, surrounded by her ladies representing her tributaries. They rode on an immense scallop-shell drawn by sea-horses, with sea-monsters 'swimming' around them. She repeated her success in the part in a different piece in January 1608, *The Masque of Beauty*, which had as an inset 'The Queen's Masque', in which Anne danced with her ladies-in-waiting. *The Masque of Queens*, which Jones and Jonson produced in 1609, cost some £5,000 – with, of course, the participants' extra expenditure on the hire of worthy jewels to set off their flamboyant costumes.

The English Court was becoming a by-word for extravagance, licentiousness and debauchery. 'The ladies abandon their sobriety and are seen to roll about in intoxication,'[6] wrote Sir John Harington, Queen Elizabeth's godson who was himself no stranger to rich living but who obviously found the manners of the new Court distasteful. It was Harington who provides a glimpse of a masque performed at the Hertfordshire manor of Theobalds, in 1606, which celebrated the visit of Anne's brother King Christian of Denmark, at which a lady's drunkenness nearly ruined everything:

> One day a great feast was held, and after dinner, the representation of Solomon, his temple and the coming of the Queen of Sheba was made, or (as I may better say) was meant to have been made, before their majesties, by the device of the Earl of Salisbury and others. But alas, as all earthly things do fail to poor mortals in enjoyment, so did prove our presentment thereof.
>
> The lady who did play the Queen's part did carry the most precious gifts to both their Majesties; but forgetting the steps araising to the canopy, overset her caskets into his Danish Majesty's lap, and fell at his feet though I rather think it was in his face. Much was the hurry and confusion; cloths and napkins were at hand, to make all clean. His Majesty then got up and would dance with the Queen of Sheba; but he fell down and humbled himself before her, and was carried into an inner chamber and laid on a bed of state; which was not a little defiled with the presents of the Queen, which had been bestowed on his garments, such as wine, cream, jelly, beverage, cakes, spices and other good matters.[7]

As Anne became more ambitious and more anxious to amaze her audience, so Jones rose to the challenge with ever more exotic staging. *The Masque of Tethys*, of 1610, was set on an elaborate structure of rocks, caverns and niches, with waterfalls and fountains. Anne, as Tethys, the wife of the sea-god Poseidon, was enthroned on the edifice, with her ladies around her, each representing a river associated with her birthplace or with the estates of her family: the Countess of Essex was the nymph of the Lea; Princess Elizabeth the nymph of the Thames; the Countess of Arundel, the Arun; the Countess of Derby, the Derwent; and so on. Around them cavorted a band of children, led by the little Prince Charles wearing silver wings, as Zephyrus, with eight nobly-born little girls in his train.

Queen Anne's last masque was *Love freed from Folly and Ignorance*, another Jones-Jonson extravaganza, in 1612. Only a few months later, the Prince of Wales died, Anne's elder son and partner in so many revels. She never again took part in a masque, though she continued to watch others do so.

The great collaboration of Jonson and Jones continued into the next reign, producing for Charles I's queen, the French Henrietta Maria, such masques as the fine *Chloridia*, led by the Queen as Chloris; but in 1631 the pair broke company after violent disagreements. Jonson had been jealous of Inigo Jones for some time, bitter that the trappings of the masque were overshadowing his own poetry. When Jones dared to put his name first on the title page of the published text of *Love's Triumph through Callipolis*, Jonson would tolerate him no longer. But Jones was the Court's pet, the unique deviser of their main amusement, so it was Jonson, the easily-replaceable poet, who lost patronage.

Thereafter Inigo Jones lent his magnificent skills to such poets as Aurelian Townsend, Thomas Carew and Sir William D'Avenant, the latter composing *Salmacida Spolia*, the last masque seen at the Court of Charles I before the Civil War put an end to such frivolities. The Puritans were already railing against Court theatricals: Prynne's famous *Histriomastix* was written as a condemnation of ladies, and especially the Queen, as actresses.

Masques were revived in England at the Restoration of the monarchy in 1660 but enjoyed only a brief return, for with the advent of professional actresses to the theatre and a new vogue for professional drama, amateur theatricals at Court lost favour. One of the last notable masques was *Calisto, or the Chaste nymph*, by Crowne, acted on 2 December 1674, in which two future queens, the Princess Mary and Anne of York took part. The fact that they were coached in their roles by the fashionable actress Mrs Betterton well illustrated the changing times. As usual, the maids-of-honour shared the supporting roles, and the later famous Sarah Jennings, future Duchess of Marlborough, figured largely among them. Another performer, taking the part of the goddess Diana, was the Duchess of York's former maid-of-honour Margaret Blagge, surely one of the most unwilling actresses ever to take the stage. She was extremely devout and felt unsure of the efficacy of flaunting her not-inconsiderable talents on stage, so to soothe her conscience she took with her to rehearsals a book of devotions, with which she would retire to a quiet corner whenever she was not needed. Her scruples were scarcely calmed by the fact that on the night of the performance, she lost a diamond, worth £80, which she had borrowed from the Countess of Suffolk.

The end of the seventeenth century saw the end of the masque at Court. Court ladies now relied on dancing only to reveal their graces, and all preferred a professionally mounted play, or the new Italian operas introduced by Charles II's queen, to such strenuous personal exertions as learning words and songs and new dances for masques.

Anne of Denmark's Court in England, apart from its fine ceremonial and brilliant entertainments, was scarcely an exciting place for Jacobean ladies. But even from the first months of its inception, all the age-old elements of ambition and jealousy were there. As the Queen approached London from Scotland in 1603, mothers and daughters flocked to meet her, in the hopes of gaining places. But Queen Anne preferred to retain those of her Scottish ladies whom she had long known and trusted (and her Danish maids, such as Anna Kaas who had arrived with the King's bride and who remained with her until her death). She had even the temerity to refuse positions to some of the highest-born ladies in the realm. Even when the Court was established, there was a good deal of vying for the Queen's favour, as the Earl of Worcester wrote to his friend the Earl of Shrewsbury, before the first year of the reign was out:

> We have ladies of diverse degrees of favour: some for the private chamber, some for the drawing chamber, some for the

> bedchamber and some for neither certain, and of this number is only my lady Arbella and my wife. My lady of Bedford holdeth fast to the bedchamber; my lady Hertford would fain, but her husband hath called her home. My lady of Derby the younger, and Lady Suffolk, Rich, Nottingham, Susan, Walsingham and, of late, the Lady Southwell, for the drawing chamber; all the rest for the private chamber, when they are not shut out, for many time the doors are locked; but the plotting and malice among them is such that I think envy hath tied an invisible snake about most of their necks to sting one another to death.[8]

The 'Lady Arbella' mentioned by Worcester was King James's cousin, the daughter of his father's brother. As a young woman she had had hopes that Queen Elizabeth would pass over James's claim to England and award her the crown (as the grand-daughter of Henry VIII's elder sister). Alternatively she was not loath to uniting her claim with James's in marriage. On both counts, however, she was disappointed. Nevertheless, she appeared several times at James's Court, acting, as Worcester said, as an unofficial lady to Queen Anne, with much the same position as those 'great ladies' of the early Tudor period. (In 1610 Arbella married William Seymour, grandson of that Catherine Grey whom Elizabeth I had imprisoned for her pretensions to the royal succession and for the marriage which seemed so much a threat to her own position. Like Catherine and Hertford, Arbella and Seymour were imprisoned for their presumption.)

Arbella also acted as a sort of unofficial governess to James and Anne's only daughter, Princess Elizabeth. On the transition to England, Elizabeth, then aged six, was put into the charge of the Harington family of Exton, to be brought up with several other girls of about her own age, who would thus become ideal maids-of-honour for her. In fact, several of them accompanied Elizabeth when, on her marriage to the Elector Palatine, she went to Germany, with Lady Harington herself later following her to become head of the household.

One of their number, Anne Dudley (the Haringtons' niece), in the time-honoured fashion of maids-of-honour abroad, sought permission from home to marry one Count Schomberg, one of the Elector Palatine's councillors and master of Elizabeth's household. Her family, however, did not think the Count sufficiently elevated a person for Anne, and refused to allow their marriage. Schomberg consoled himself with strenuous activities in the war in the Netherlands while Electress Elizabeth pleaded their case in her letters home. It transpired that her best ally was her father, who, always anxious to follow etiquette, believed that it was the German rule that the first lady of her household, the position then occupied by Anne, should be a married woman. Elizabeth wrote to him:

> Touching my *dame d'honneur*, I can assure this truth, which I beseech Your Majesty to believe, that she hath ever been careful for my good, and hath most faithfully served me, without ever having taken present of me, since I came into Germany, and I shall even be ungrateful when I do not witness this same; and since Your Majesty desires to know if it be the custom that the *dame d'honneur* should be married, to this I can tell Your Majesty, yes; that is the fashion, and that the Elector, his council, and all here, have often desired me to forward their marriage – Your Majesty yourself having written me word that you wished it, and should like she were married to Schomberg.[9]

King James took care of the parental objections, and in March 1615 Anne and Schomberg went to the altar.

But Anne, Countess Schomberg, lived only long enough to bear her husband a son and died in December of the same year as her wedding. It was left for time to show that the child whose life cost hers would prove to be that heroic Field-Marshal Schomberg who served William III so well, dying at the Battle of the Boyne, and whose son would prove himself a worthy successor under Marlborough.

Between the death of Anne of Denmark in 1619 and the marriage of her son Charles in 1625, there was no queen in England – James I had no interest in women other than the wives of his favourites, whom he treated as daughters, and did not marry a second time. His successor on the throne in 1625, his son Charles, had, like his father, never shown an interest in women in his youth, being more concerned with his friendship with 'Steenie' Buckingham. But it was indisputably the duty of a king to marry for the sake of begetting heirs, and marry the dutiful Charles did, and speedily.

During his father's lifetime, Charles and his bosom friend had been despatched to Spain to court an Infanta, without success. *En route*, they had taken in the Court of France incognito and there had watched a young princess, no more than a child, take part in a masque. That princess was Henrietta Maria, daughter of King Henry IV of France, and child as she was, she was piqued when she heard that Charles had gone on to Spain for a bride. 'He might have had one nearer hand,'[10] she said. However, when the Spanish marriage plans fell through, Charles looked for a wife in France.

Henrietta Maria arrived in England, aged only fifteen, in June 1625, having had nearly as rough a passage to England as her future husband's late mother. Like all foreign princesses going to their wedding, she brought with her an immense retinue, with the intention of some of them remaining with her in her new Court.

As usual, the English had a low opinion of the foreign arrivals, an observer noting that the French ladies were 'a poor lot, not one worth the looking after, save [Henrietta Maria] herself and the Duchesse de Chevreuse, who though she be fair, yet paints foully'[11] (the Duchess was later to scandalize the people of Richmond by swimming the River Thames). The English were horrified at the number of priests the new Queen brought with her, for although the late Queen Anne had been a Catholic, she had never paraded her piety as the new Queen was to do.

Chief among the ladies, in Henrietta Maria's favour, if not in rank, was one Madame de St Georges, daughter of her former governess. When Charles and his bride entered the coach which was to carry them on the first stage of their journey from the coast to London, 'Mamie' insisted on travelling with them.

This was but the first, and certainly not the most annoying, of the faults displayed by the new Queen's French entourage. The priests were, naturally enough, the worst offenders in English eyes. There was an unedifying, noisy quarrel one day between the King's Protestant chaplain and the Queen's Catholic confessor over the royal dinner-table, with each prelate urging his own claim to say grace for the meal. On another occasion the Queen and her ladies, who were allowed special facilities for the observance of their own religion, paraded noisily through the Protestant service held for the rest of the royal household.

Charles was a patient man, and though he had as yet little affection for his wife, he was determined to treat her well. He had even put on a calm face at the French refusal to allow Henrietta Maria, as a Catholic, to take part in the Protestant coronation service. But such displays as these, and Henrietta Maria's wilfulness and her championship of her French servants against the English courtiers did nothing to help him. The disagreements between the King and Queen came to a head when Charles arrived in his wife's apartment one day to find her French ladies-in-waiting 'unreverently dancing and curvetting' before the Queen. When he demanded to talk with her alone, she refused him, saying that he could speak openly. Charles insisted on privacy and, once alone with Henrietta Maria, declared that all her French servants would have to go. They gave her bad advice, he said, and made her neglect her duties.

Horror-stricken, Henrietta Maria became hysterical, throwing herself on her knees and begging him to relent. But the King would not even allow his wife to say goodbye to her friends. When she saw the French men and women standing in the courtyard below, the young Queen broke the windows with her fists, screaming and calling out to them. Charles dragged her back, her hands pouring with blood.

The Queen was not allowed to see any of her French servants again. They were confined at Denmark House until arrangements could be made for their transportation to France. By that time the news of the royal quarrel was all over London, and a crowd collected to see the hated foreigners depart. One zealous Cockney actually threw a stone at 'Mamie' St Georges, but it was an Englishman who revenged the insult by cutting down the offender with his sword.

When tempers died down, and the main body of the French were safely off the English coast, Henrietta Maria was somewhat consoled by the fact that she still had her old nurse, Madame Pantelet, left to her, and the Duchesse de Thouars (though she was a Dutch woman, by birth, and a Protestant), and that she had two priests remaining with her – though neither of them French.

The King himself superintended the replacement of the French ladies. The Queen, sulky and resentful, offered her doubts as to 'whether they were set to watch her as a prisoner or wait upon her as a princess'.[12]

However, it was not long before the French teenager who professed a dislike of everything English, including her husband, turned into the self-titled 'happiest woman in the world'. Charles I was an innocent before his marriage, blushing at every immodest word uttered in that flamboyantly vulgar Court of his father's, and in marriage he presented an unusually (to contemporaries) bland picture of fidelity and affection. At length Henrietta Maria responded to him, and from that time the royal couple became a by-word for mutual devotion.

The Queen even learned to love her English ladies, especially one of them, Lucy Hay, Countess of Carlisle. The Countess was a Percy by birth, one of the nobly-born children brought up with the King's sister Elizabeth. At seventeen she had eloped with King James's Scottish favourite James Hay, Earl of Carlisle (with the connivance of the evilly-reputed Lady Essex), which enfuriated her family (with their pride in ancient lineage and, as magnates on the Border, hatred of everything Scottish). 'Lucinda' as the Queen called her, was the closest of her friends, not even ousted by Madame de Chevreuse, who returned to England in 1638, having fled France after antagonizing the all-powerful Cardinal Richelieu. The two ladies, realizing that rivalry could only lead to trouble and probably to the loss of favour of them both, professed the closest friendship.

It soon proved, however, that the Queen's trust in her English confidante was more dangerous than even her ties with her French ladies had been. Lady Carlisle was the devoted friend of the King's trusted but immensely unpopular minister Strafford. The latter had a fine appreciation of her usefulness to him, and of her complex character: as he wrote to his colleague Archbishop Laud in 1637, 'I judge her ladyship very considerable; she is often in place and extremely well skilled how to speak with advantage and spirit for those friends she professeth unto, which will be many. There is this further in her disposition, she will not seem to be the person she is not, an ingenuity I have always observed, and honoured her for.'[13]

But King Charles allowed Strafford to fall victim to the growing might and antipathy of Parliament, and Lady Carlisle, horrified by the King's impotence in the face of his enemies and by his weakness in sacrificing his friend, turned against both King and Queen. More from spite than from conviction, she 'took up' with the Parliamentarians and proved one of their most effective spies in the royal household. It was she who forewarned the Commons of the King's approach as he went to arrest the five Members who were the ringleaders of the opposition to his policies. Henrietta Maria had confided in her friend the purpose of her husband's errand, and the Countess was able to send out the secret message to the Commons, so that the five Members fled before Charles's arrival.

That moment of triumph was Lucy Carlisle's main achievement. In later years she proved a tireless but largely ineffective intriguer, mainly in Scottish affairs, during the Commonwealth period, even spending three months in the Tower in 1649 for her meddling.

The attempted arrest of the five Members took place in January 1641. Soon after, the outbreak of the Civil War, with King *versus* Parliament, saw the end of formal Court life in England for almost twenty years.

Queen Henrietta Maria's troubles really began in February

1643 when she arrived home from taking her eldest daughter, Mary, to join her future husband William of Orange in Holland. After a year's absence, during which she settled her daughter in her new home, the Queen disembarked at Bridlington, on the Yorkshire coast, then a small village with a busy port.

During the night after her arrival, she had her first taste of being under fire in the first phase of the Civil War. As she slept, in a thatched cottage near the sea, four vessels under Parliamentarian commanders sailed into the bay, opened fire on the royal ships and began the bombardment of the shore-line. The Queen was hastily wakened and persuaded to flee to the safety of ditches behind the village. There was confusion and panic: one of the maids-of-honour 'through plain fear went stark mad',[14] as one report tells, and as the party of ladies sped towards the ditches, the sergeant escorting them was shot, only twenty paces from Henrietta Maria. She lay for two hours in a hole, with cannon-balls hurtling over her head.

The next months were safer and more comfortable for the Queen, but with the exigencies of war, her home was necessarily itinerant. Through York she journeyed south, arriving in Oxford, the Royalist headquarters, in July. There, for the last time in her life, Henrietta Maria headed a brilliant Court, its members crowded into the stately chambers of the Colleges. In the fever of war, the boisterous young Cavaliers shocked the townsfolk with their carousing, and the ladies no less scandalized the austere dons by appearing at church in fashionable *déshabille*.

The younger ladies-in-waiting were by no means sobered by the solemnity of the times in which they were living, but became over-excited by the bustle of war-making. For some cheap amusement one Lady Isabella Thynne took her companion Mistress Fanshawe on a visit to Dr Ralph Kettel, President of Trinity College and a well-known misogynist. Unabashed by the giggling young women, Dr Kettel confronted them squarely. 'Madam,' he addressed Lady Isabella, 'your husband and your father I bred up here, and I knew your grandfather; I know you to be a gentlewoman, I will not say you are a whore, but get you gone for a very woman.'[15]

Soon the time for frolics was past. The Queen found herself pregnant and lost the energy which had made her the 'generalissima' of the Royalist troops. In April 1644 she parted from King Charles – as it proved, forever – and made her way towards Exeter. In June she gave birth to a daughter and soon after, with the Roundheads advancing on the town, fled to the west. In July she took ship for her native France.

6

NOT all the Cavaliers in exile were congregated in Paris. Some of them had sought shelter in the Netherlands where the King's daughter Mary was living. In 1643, when she was aged only thirteen, she had married the seventeen-year-old Prince William of Orange, a grandson of the great Dutch patriot William the Silent who had freed the United Provinces from Spanish rule not many years earlier. Prince William died, still a young man, in November 1650, and a week later, the nineteen-year-old Mary bore his posthumous son, another William. For all that the Orange family had held the major offices in the government of the United Provinces for many years, theirs was not a hereditary status within the state. Thus, though Mary received assurances as to the future powers of her child, in her widowhood she had no state duties to perform and could keep up a comfortable and gay Court of her own on her vast fortune.

With the influx into the Netherlands of Royalists fleeing from defeat in the wars, the former Princess Royal, as the daughter of Charles I and sister of Charles II, was a natural rallying-point. She did all in her power to assist her brother and the other members of her family who were now abroad, arranging loans and even seeking to win support for Charles from the Dutch government – though without success. But she could also be of great assistance to the King's impoverished supporters, many of whom arrived on her doorsteps with little cash and no potential means of support.

One of the families to whom Mary gave succour was the Hydes. Edward Hyde was one of the principal agents of Charles II, a former Royalist in the Parliamentary disputes of the 1640s who now served on diplomatic missions for the King and who subsequently became Chancellor in the government in exile. In 1651 he took his family – his wife Frances, two sons and two daughters – over to the Continent (whither he had preceded them several years earlier). They were housed rent-free, by Mary at Breda, her barony beyond the United Provinces' borders, where she might meet her brother Charles without the States General's criticism. The Hyde family were thus frequently to be seen at the Princess's Court, and it was natural that, when Mary was seeking a new maid-of-honour in 1654, one of Hyde's daughters, Anne, should be her choice. She was called in to replace Mistress Kate Killigrew, who had recently died of smallpox.

But the appointment was not without its drawbacks. Away in France, Henrietta Maria had her eye on her daughter's affairs, and, in the midst of her bitter feud with Edward Hyde over his management of King Charles's affairs, it annoyed the Queen intensely that his daughter should seem to be favoured by Mary above the many other possible candidates for the post, of families just as deserving as the Hydes and of fathers who were more amenable to her will. But despite the pressure put on her by her mother, Mary refused to give up her choice. 'I have always paid the duty to the Queen, my mother, which was her due,' wrote Mary to Hyde, who would rather have seen his daughter lose her place than further antagonize the Queen, 'but I am mistress of my own family, and can receive what servants I please, – nay, I should wrong my mother, if I forbore to do a good and just action lest her Majesty should be offended at it. I know that some ill offices have been done you by my mother, but I doubt not that in due time she will discern that she has been mistaken.'[1] 'In due time' the quarrel was forgotten and Anne retained her position in Mary's household, but it did not ease Henrietta Maria's constraint towards Hyde, and in later years it was to have rather more serious repercussions.

So Anne, at seventeen, left her home to take up residence at Mary's Court. The troubles of her father's career, and indeed the parlous state of England, had left her more with her mother than were most girls of a similar rank at that time. Left alone by her husband for months at a time as he performed his missions, and mistress of only a small household in her comparative penury, Frances Hyde had long relied on her daughter's companionship. So reveals Anne's letter to her father, on leaving home in October 1654:

> I have received yours of the 13th and shall ever make it so much my business strictly to observe all your commands in it that when ever I transgress any of them in the least degree it shall be out of ignorance and not wilfulness so that I hope you shall never have cause to repent of the good opinion you are pleased to have of me, and which I shall daily endeavour to increase, and since you think it fit for me, shall very cheerfully submit to a life which I have not much desired but now look upon not only as the will of my Father, but of Almighty God and therefore will doubtless prove a blessing; but Sir, you cannot wonder if being happy in so excellent a Father and Mother I cannot part with them without trouble, for though as you say I have been so unfortunate as always to live from you, yet I look upon myself now as still more unlikely to be with you or see you, and though I shall often hear from my Mother, and I hope see her, yet that will be but little in respect of being continually with her.
>
> I say not this that I repine at going to the Princess for I am confident that God has made her so gracious in desiring me will make me happy in her service, but I should be the worst of children if I were not very sensible of leaving so good a Mother and leaving her so much alone; but I hope you will be together this winter, and in the meantime I beseech you

to persuade her to stay as long as she can with us at The Hague, that she may be as little as possible alone here; I humbly beg your blessing upon, Sir,

Your most dutiful and obedient daughter
Anne Hyde[2]

Most of Anne's life for the next six years was spent with Princess Mary. Her small Court, with its Dutch comfort and English manners, was renowned for its gaiety, in contrast with the austere life-style of the Dutch and with the opulent but solemn household of her mother-in-law, another widowed Princess of Orange, Amalia von Solms (herself a former lady-in-waiting to Mary's aunt, the Electress Elizabeth). Mary was not always resident in the United Provinces, or in Breda, but often toured into Germany, frequently in the company of her brothers. On one occasion, from January to November 1656, the Princess paid a visit to her mother in France.

In her years with Mary, it was, of course, inevitable that Anne Hyde should come into contact with other members of the Stuart family. She saw Charles II many times, and his brother the Duke of York, but it was not until the spring of 1659 that James, Duke of York, 'noticed' her.

Anne was no beauty, but then neither in his youth nor in later years did James's taste in women run to beauties. It was said that it was her wit which attracted him and, indeed, from the evidence of Anne's later years, it is obvious that she had an intelligence beyond that expected of women in her day. James was not the first man to fall in love with her: various scions of the English aristocracy had already been attracted to Anne, so much so, in fact, that even King Charles himself had taken part in the teasing of her suitors. And in 1660, a minor member of the Orange family, Maurits Beverweert, was almost at the point of asking for her hand when the news of her marriage to James broke on the world.

The Duke of York made a secret marriage with his sister's maid-of-honour at Hounslaerdijk in August 1659. The validity of the ceremony and the extent of his intentions to honour his promises to Anne, remains a mystery, but it is obvious from later developments that the couple found opportunities to consummate their marriage. However, it would have been against James's interests – indeed, against the interests of the monarchy – for him to declare that he was married: a match was in the wind, in 1659 and the beginning of 1660, between James and a daughter of the Parliamentarian General Lambert, with a view to co-operation between the Royalists and elements in the English government in restoring the monarchy. But it came to nothing, and later in 1660 the Stuarts were restored without the need for such a *mésalliance*.

With the Restoration came Hyde's return to England. He had left as a fugitive; he returned, knighted, as Chancellor. It was natural, of course, that he should now seek to advance his family and secure his place a couple of rungs higher up the social ladder than that on which he had started. To this end, he sent for his daughter Anne, intending to marry her into the aristocracy as soon as possible. As yet, he had no inkling that she was married already, and to one who ranked higher than any husband he could have found for her. In all the allegations and accusations which flew around Anne in the later months of 1660, there were rumours that Princess Mary had discovered her maid-of-honour's liaison with her brother and sent her packing. Whether that were true or not, the secret broke soon after Anne Hyde's arrival in England for she was obviously pregnant.

At first, James could not be brought to acknowledge Anne as his wife. (Anne had feared that this was so, for while still in Holland she had sought, unsuccessfully, to procure an abortion.) He had some thoughts of repudiating the marriage entirely, since now that he was both brother and heir to the King of England, he could expect a higher match than one with a commoner's daughter. Throughout the whole of his life, James showed a tendency to hesitate, to vacillate and then suddenly to turn stubborn. At this point, he consulted with his friends as to what to do. Lord Falmouth advised him that his marriage was invalid, since it lacked the King's consent, and that the Duke need not scruple to cast Anne off since, he claimed, she had been notoriously free with her favours to other men. There were many men at Court jealous of Edward Hyde's advancement and only too eager to help the Duke of York for their own gain. The Earl of Arran told the tale that, during his stay in Holland, he had once been playing at nine-pins with some friends, including Anne, when she had feigned illness, and that, following her out of the room, 'having cut her lace to lend probability to the pretence of the vapours, he had acquitted himself to the best of his abilities, both to assist and to console her'.[3] In the same vein of euphemism, one Killigrew 'affirmed that the great moment had come in a certain apartment built over the water, for a purpose very different from that of giving ease to the pains of love! that three or four swans had been witnesses to his happiness, and might perhaps have been witnesses to the happiness of many others, as the lady frequently visited that place and was particularly delighted with it'.[4]

Meanwhile, Chancellor Hyde was averring to all who would listen that he would rather see his daughter mistress of the Duke than his wife, if their marriage would result in *lèse-majesté* for the still shaky Crown. What he really meant was that the mild disgrace of his daughter's misconduct would be preferable to his own loss of his government post if Anne held out for recognition of her marriage in the face of royal denial of it.

Hyde had not reckoned on James's conscience – always the strongest part of his will, for good or evil. At midnight on 3 August 1660 the couple were remarried – once again with the greatest secrecy – at the Hydes' London mansion, Worcester House in the Strand, and this time according to the rites of the Church of England with regular, if unconventional witnesses. Lady Hyde connived at their subsequent meetings, since Anne's father had shut her up and refused to allow her to go to Court.

On 22 October Anne's child was born, a son, with Court ladies in attendance to witness the circumstances of his birth, as for a royal child. But all through her labour she was harassed and cross-questioned by the Bishop of Winchester (Dr Morley, once her tutor and an old friend of the family) as to the true paternity of her child and the validity of her marriage. It was counted well to Anne's credit that throughout her labour, even in the greatest pain, she never swerved from protesting that she was truly the wife of the Duke of York.

In the days that followed, her patience was rewarded. The King gave his brother permission to acknowledge Anne as his wife. The men who had spoken against her virtue were made to deny their words and come to kiss her hand in token of their apologies. Her father was created a baron to ease his fears at royal displeasure of his conduct.

Still, however, there were further difficulties. Princess Mary was in England, enjoying her brother's glory and recalling the days of her childhood before her Dutch marriage. She refused to be in the same room with the woman who had once been her servant but who was now to be treated as her sister. (She had always despised her own mother-in-law, the former maid-of-honour, for her low origins, and could not bear to give Amalia the chance of returning the sneers to her brother's wife.) But the member of the royal family most incensed by this irregular marriage (the first between royalty and commoner in England for more than a century) was Queen Henrietta Maria. Her visit to England to congratulate her eldest son on his restoration was marred by her bitterness against James and by her initial refusal to receive Anne. But she had been charged by Cardinal Mazarin, the real ruler of France in the minority of Louis XIV, that she must open no breach between herself and her sons which could lead to the failure of French influence on English royal policy. Nevertheless, it was not until after the death of Princess Mary, at Christmas-time 1660, and the Princess's death-bed forgiveness of Anne for her supposed wrongs to her, that Henrietta Maria relented. Her manner towards Hyde was no warmer, but she received the new Duchess and promised to be godmother to her son.

In the event, the child died the following May. In retrospect, it was perhaps as well that he never lived to become heir to the throne, for one conceived and born in such dubious legitimacy would have been as open to challenge as was the future 'warming-pan baby' of James's second wife. The Duke and Duchess had sworn to their marriage in February, and witnesses of the Worcester House ceremony had been brought forward to testify, but even so, there would always have been the doubt as to the young Duke of Cambridge's legitimacy.

Once the scandal had died down, Anne Hyde was readily accepted into the royal circle. Until the King's marriage in 1662, and with the absence of the Queen Mother in France for most of the year, she, the daughter of a commoner, was the first lady in England. And she bore her rank with all the more dignity for having come late to it: 'Madame the Duchess of York ... is as worthy a woman – the word "honest" is not strong enough – as I have met in my life,' wrote the French ambassador to Louis XIV, 'and she upholds with as much courage, cleverness and energy the dignity to which she has been called as if she were of the blood of kings.'[5] Less kindly critics were later to claim that Anne was more regally haughty and arrogant than if she had been born to the purple herself.

But the Duchess did not live to become Queen. When James, Duke of York, succeeded his brother Charles as King in 1685, she had been dead fourteen years and he had been remarried for twelve (this time to a suitable princess). Yet it was Anne who had brought James to take a step which affected the whole of his policy, which coloured the whole of his reign and which, in the end, resulted in his loss of the throne and its settlement, with Parliamentary restrictions, on the House of Orange. She had induced him to become a Catholic. Anne herself had been the first to take the step, arousing the ire of her father, who predicted the ruination of herself and her family. Subsequently, she had influenced her husband to his conversion, a success for her where James's long years in Catholic France and the blandishments of his Catholic mother had failed. The Duke's conversion was a turning-point in his career and in his relations with English politics. When he came to the throne and openly espoused the cause of Catholic dissenters and adopted Catholic alliances, James was seen to strike at the corner-stone of the English monarchy – its resting on the Anglican Church. Where one former lady-in-waiting, Anne Boleyn, had been instrumental in taking England out of the Catholic allegiance, another – but for the ineptitude of her husband – might have taken it back. But James had neither the strength of will, nor the political acumen, nor the chance, to take his policies through to their conclusion, for in 1688 the 'Glorious Revolution' swept him from his throne.

The leader of that Revolution was William of Orange, the son of Anne's former mistress, Princess Mary. And the wife of that Prince of Orange was Anne and James's own elder daughter, Mary, who, with her husband, would now become sovereign of England in her father's lifetime. Thus Anne Hyde, the maid-of-honour, was mother of Queen Mary II of England and of Queen Anne. Neither of those queens showed much aptitude for government, or much judgment or wisdom, but then, neither did their father, so who can blame their shortcomings on the fact that their mother was only a lady-in-waiting?

King Charles II had not married during his years of exile but within months of his return to England, at his first official meeting with the newly-elected Cavalier Parliament, he announced his intention to marry the Princess Catherine of Braganza, sister of the young King of Portugal.

A year passed before Catherine set sail for England, time enough for the nation to give full voice to its doubts of the King's wisdom in choosing so obviously Catholic a wife, for all her rich dowry. But it was obvious that the King must marry, for although he had an heir in his brother (who had not yet proved himself unsuitable, in the eyes of the English, to succeed to the throne), it was always deemed more natural for the succession to pass from father to son. And it was indeed Charles's inclination to take a wife, being a natural lover of women; though he had none of his father's single-minded domestic piety, he was always at his best in the home circle.

Catherine of Braganza arrived in England after that stormy passage traditional to the brides of the Stuart kings of England. Fortunately the Princess herself was a good sailor, but several of her Portuguese ladies had been ill on the voyage, and her first lady, the Countess of Penalva (sister of the Portuguese envoy, Catherine's godfather, who had negotiated the match), was so ill that she had to be carried ashore at Portsmouth.

'The Queen arrived with a train of Portuguese ladies in their monstrous farthingales, or *guarde-infantas*, their complexions olivaster [dark olive], and sufficiently unagreeable,'[6] wrote the diarist Evelyn. 'Six monsters who were known as maids-of honour',[7] was another's summation of the young women in Catherine's train. 'Old, ugly and proud',[8] scoffed the Duchess of York's father, Chancellor Clarendon. It was not long before the gossips were regaling each other with the tale that the Court had had to wait two days in Portsmouth for extra coaches to be brought to accommodate the Portuguese ladies with their singularly ugly, immense farthingale skirts which showed to such disadvantage against the smooth lines of the English ladies' gowns. It was rumoured also that the Portuguese ladies refused to sleep in any bed which a man might once have occupied, no matter how long ago and no matter how many times the bed-linen had been changed since. Unaccountably, to the English, they had also been heard to express horror at seeing men of high and low station relieving themselves quite openly against the walls of the palace.

At the time of Catherine's arrival, only one member of her English suite had been chosen: Lady Suffolk, her chief lady.

> No other office is yet visibly disposed of [wrote Anne Hyde's brother Lord Cornbury], though I think there are forty pretenders to every one; and they are all here [at Court], both men and women, expecting their doom, and I am sure they will not all be pleased. There are twenty little intrigues and factions stirring, but with these I do not meddle, and I will not venture to give you any account of them; only this much I will tell you, that there are great endeavours used to make – –, you know who, a lady of the Bedchamber, but it is hoped by many they will not take effect; a little time will show us a great deal, I will say no more of this for fear of burning my fingers.[9]

The mysterious 'you know who' of Cornbury's letter was in fact a niece of Lady Suffolk, one Barbara Palmer, *née* Villiers. It was not her relationship with the new Queen's chief lady which made her so likely a candidate for a post in the household but her relationship with the King. Since before the Restoration, Mrs Palmer had been Charles II's mistress, and by the time of his marriage had already borne him one child and was carrying a second. Only recently her husband (a quiescent, background figure) had been ennobled, and she was rejoicing in the euphonious title of Countess of Castlemaine.

Barbara Villiers was an extraordinary person. A member of the family which had produced that favourite of James I and Charles I, reputed lover of a queen of France, the Duke of Buckingham, she had early and willingly come to a life in which intrigue and *amour* played major parts. Just prior to the Restoration she had acquired her royal lover, at the expense of her long-time 'protector', the Earl of Chesterfield (though he later shared her 'favours' with King Charles – and others).

Catherine of Braganza may have been forewarned by her mother of the existence of her husband's mistress before her arrival in England, but in the first months of marriage she gave no sign that she knew of their continuing relationship. Thus when Charles put before her a final list of the ladies to be appointed for her service, Catherine was aghast to find among the names that of Lady Castlemaine. Immediately, she struck the name from the list. Charles was amazed and immediately on the defensive, swearing to his wife that he had broken with Barbara and that the appointment was merely a recognition of the services which her father had rendered him during the Civil War. When Catherine insisted, however, he agreed that Lady Castlemaine should not be employed.

The royal mistress, on the other hand, had a resolution to rival the Queen's. Already angered by reports of Charles's pleasure with his new wife, she was furious at being so openly overridden.

Ever one for a quiet life, where jealous women were concerned, Charles resorted to a surprise attack on his wife's prejudice. At a public reception, he led Barbara forward, and it was not until Catherine had smiled upon her and given her hand to be kissed, that she realized what was happening. She turned white; she burst into tears; blood rushed from her nose, and she fainted. While Catherine's attendants hovered around her, the King led Lady Castlemaine away.

Over the next few days, Charles avoided his wife, and it was not until she received a visit from Lord Clarendon that the Queen knew what was in her husband's mind:

> I have undone this lady [Charles claimed], and ruined her reputation, which was fair and untainted till her friendship with me [a blatant lie], and I am obliged in conscience and honour to repair her to the utmost of my power. I will always avow a great friendship for her, which I owe as well to the memory of her father as to her own person; and I shall look upon it as the highest disrespect to me in anybody who shall treat her otherwise than is due to her own birth and the dignity to which I have raised her.
>
> I like her company and conversation, from which I will not be restrained, because I know there is and will be all innocence in it. My wife shall never have cause to complain that I broke my vows to her if she will live towards me as a good wife ought to do, in rendering herself grateful and acceptable to me, which it is in her power to do. But if she continues uneasy to me I cannot answer for myself that I shall not endeavour to seek content in other company.[10]

Clarendon reasoned with the Queen to the utmost of his persuasive tongue, promising her that the King would never be unfaithful to her. But he had no success. Charles lost his temper. Like his father before him, though for a different reason, he resorted to dismissing his wife's foreign servants to bring her to obedience. There were a few more tears, more reproaches – then Queen Catherine gave in.

Lady Castlemaine was presented to the Queen formally, as a Lady of the Bedchamber.

Catherine was isolated. Before her arrival the Court had been gay and carefree, now it was becoming gloomy. All knew that it was the King who dispensed favours and whose smile on them could raise them to rank and power; the Queen had no influence on him – 'the Lady' had. As Clarendon himself wrote, servants and courtiers 'showed more respect and more diligence to the person of the Lady than towards their own mistress, who they found could do them less good'.[11]

Perhaps it was the thought of a lifetime of loneliness and of veiled insults that led Catherine to capitulate. Certainly it was not long before she ceased to gaze tearfully at her husband and to avert her eyes from the offending Lady. One day, not long after the terrible scenes which had clouded the Court, Clarendon noticed that, 'The Queen on a sudden let herself fall first into conversation and then to familiarity, and even in the same instant to a confidence with the Lady; was merry with her in public, talked kindly of her, and in private used nobody more friendly.'[12] Of course, there were ups and downs in the relationship between wife and mistress. Catherine, once she had grown in confidence in her adopted country and in its language, could not resist the occasional pointed remark to Barbara. 'I wonder your Majesty can have the patience to sit so long a-dressing,' said the Lady one day, in her office in the Queen's Bedchamber. 'I have so much reason to use patience that I can very well bear with it,'[13] replied Catherine sadly.

For all Charles's earlier protestations that he was no longer keeping Barbara as his mistress, it was clear to all that he was. At Court she was always at hand, and each evening he supped with her and a few close friends in private. He might do his marital duty with Catherine, but everyone knew that he went for his pleasure to Barbara.

For ten years she held the King in thrall. She was undeniably beautiful, undeniably clever, and she wielded no little influence over the King (Clarendon always swore that it was her enmity which caused his downfall). She also had the advantage over Catherine of the ability to give Charles children. The King was fond of his children, and besides dispensing three dukedoms among his sons by Barbara, always treated his illegitimate offspring as well as he would have any whom Catherine gave him had she not proved barren.

Inevitably, however, Charles would not remain faithful to one mistress any more than he would to his wife. On the other hand, Barbara was not averse to taking on occasional extra lovers herself, though that was partly to arouse the King's jealousy. There was Harry Jermyn, Earl of St Albans, at one end of the scale and Jacob Hall, the tightrope-walker, at the other. But perhaps the most notable of her conquests was the young John Churchill, later Duke of Marlborough but at that time still a minor official of the royal household. Legend has it that the King once surprised them, *in flagrante delicto*, but, to his mistress's pique, merely laughed and said to Churchill, 'Go; you are a rascal, but I forgive you because you do it to get a living'.[14] This was probably an apt summation, for Barbara was a useful 'contact' for an ambitious young man at Court, and a generous patron.

There were quarrels, of course. Charles would never tolerate any rudeness to his wife, and when Barbara did once offend, in 1667, he threatened to send her away. A little judicious blackmail on her part ended that notion. As the years passed, too, though the Lady lost none of her looks, she had to face the fact that her successors were all younger than herself and that they were becoming rivals to her position of *maîtresse-en-tître*. According to one courtier (Anthony Hamilton, a fascinatingly observant gossip):

> She told [Charles] once that it very ill became him to reproach the one woman in England who least deserved it; that he had never ceased to pick quarrels with her since his low tastes had first declared themselves; that to gratify his base desires he needed only stupid geese like Stuart and Wells and that little slut of an actress [Nell Gwynn] he had recently taken up with.[15]

In the early years, Barbara had actually encouraged the King to look elsewhere for occasional diversion, to facilitate her own *affaires*. While her *affaire* with Jermyn flourished, she had made quite a display of her affection for Frances Stuart, one of Queen

Catherine's maids-of-honour, who had put up a firm resistance against that generally irresistible Charles.

Frances Stuart was a distant cousin of the royal Stuart dynasty. She had come to Court at the time of the King's marriage, fresh from triumphs at the Court of Versailles, although she was still only fifteen years old. 'Had it not been for this purpose', wrote the King's sister 'Minette' who had formerly employed Frances, 'I assure you I should have been very sorry to let her go from here, for she is the prettiest girl imaginable and the most fitted to adorn a Court.'[16]

The 'prettiest girl imaginable' (Roetier's model for Britannia on the coins) was virtuous, however. From the outset she refused the advances of both the King and his brother the Duke of York, who considered the Queen's maids fair game as well as his wife's. Still sure of her own powers, however, Barbara tantalized Charles by having Frances always with her. The King even came upon them in bed together on several occasions, which only made him burn even more with unfulfilled desire.

Frances seemed always to be hinting at the possibility of giving in to the King but never came to the point of it. On one occasion, she tried her strength: the King had received the gift of a new coach, a *calèche*, from France, which all the ladies of the Court were eager to drive in. The Queen had the first honours, but after her Lady Castlemaine claimed her 'right'. She declared that, pregnant as she was, she would miscarry if she did not get her way. Frances went one better: she would never even become pregnant (by the King), she averred, unless the prize fell to her. She won. Nevertheless, there was still no news that Charles had had his way, and Frances was so obviously high in the Queen's favour that everyone said that the Queen was sure that he never would.

In Catherine's second pregnancy when, in February 1666, she miscarried for the second time, everyone was saying that Frances had played a canny game, planning to be the next Queen of England. But Catherine recovered. It was suggested to Charles that, since his wife could never have children, he should send her into a convent and marry another – again, Frances was in with a chance; but to the King's credit, for he was sincerely attached to his wife, he refused even to consider the possibility.

The maid who kept her honour was not averse to the idea of marriage. Indeed, she was said to have declared that she would marry any man (any man, that is, possessed of £1,500 a year) to rid herself of the King's relentless pursuit of her. The man whom she chose had more debts, however, than substance. He was another Charles Stuart, the Duke of Richmond and Lennox, only twenty-six to Frances's eighteen but already twice widowed and with a terrible reputation as a drunkard. However, Frances wanted him, and she persuaded Queen Catherine to help her get him.

But Catherine could not persuade the King to give his consent. Disappointed and piqued, Charles listed quite graphically all the Duke's failings. Frances was no fool; she knew them already. Still, she had hopes of reforming or at least of putting up with such a husband, whom she loved despite his drawbacks, for the sake of a safe, settled position in society. Even Barbara Castlemaine took their part, hoping by Frances's marriage to rid herself of a rival who had become tedious. 'The Lady' led the King into Frances's apartments one night and surprised her in bed with the Duke. That was the end of it, as far as Charles was concerned. In the aftermath of the recriminations, Frances eloped with her lover, leaving behind the many jewels which the King had given her in the days when his hopes had been high.

Frances had not been a duchess many months when she contracted smallpox. The King relaxed his strictures against her, which included the Richmonds' total banishment from Court, and even sent to enquire for her. On impulse, one day, he made a surprise visit to her, tormented by the dread that her beauty might have been forever marred by the scars of the smallpox. He had written to his sister in France, 'If you consider how hard a thing 'tis to swallow an injury done by a person I had so much l ... [at that point Charles crossed out the word 'love' which he had begun to write] tenderness for, you will in some degree excuse me the resentment I use towards her.'[17] Now he wrote, 'I must confess this last affliction made me pardon all that is past, and I cannot hinder myself from wishing her very well.'[18]

As soon as Frances was restored to health, she and her husband received the King and Queen at their house. Soon afterwards, the new Duchess returned to Court as a Lady of the Bedchamber. Queen Catherine was repaid for her trust in Frances and for her help to her in gaining her marriage, by keeping by her the one disinterested and exclusively loyal friend she had.

King Charles's long passion for Barbara Castlemaine and the intensity of his unrequited love for Frances Stuart by no means precluded other, more light-hearted *affaires*. Yet another maid-of-honour, one Winifred Wells, was his bed-fellow on and off for ten years. According to Hamilton, she had 'the carriage of a goddess' but at the same time 'a certain air of indecision which gave her the physiognomy of a dreamy sheep'.[19] On 8 February 1663 Samuel Pepys recorded in his diary that:

> a child was dropped by one of the ladies [at Court] in dancing, but nobody knew who, it being taken up by someone in a handkerchief. The next morning all the Ladies of Honour appeared early at Court for their vindication, so that nobody could tell whose this mischance should be. But it seems that Mistress Wells felt sick that afternoon, and hath disappeared ever since, so that it is concluded that it was her.[20]

Such a miscarriage was a mistake not to be repeated. Though Mistress Wells continued to 'pleasure' the King for years, there was no child. While other mistresses, the mothers of the King's children, gained titles and estates, Winifred was content with the lesser prizes of the profits of the sale of underwood gathered in parts of the New Forest, and the forfeitures of felons, and a pension of £200 *per annum*.

Of all the Court ladies and actresses whom King Charles 'loved' during the first ten years of his reign, there was only the elusive Frances Stuart to rival Lady Castlemaine, and by Barbara's good luck and good management she was soon put out of the running. But for Barbara this was accomplished too late.

Charles may have doted on the children she had given him, but for their mother he felt now only the kindliness of an out-worn passion. Generous in the extreme with his grants of money and property, Charles capped all by bestowing on his mistress the title of Duchess of Cleveland – as a parting gift. At last Queen Catherine was relieved of the strains of politeness to a distasteful Lady of the Bedchamber, though Barbara continued to visit the Court on occasion. Many were the tales of the unsavoury lovers with whom she comforted her middle age.

The King's new fancy arrived just as Barbara Villiers was leaving. In May 1670, only a few weeks before the Countess of Castlemaine became the Duchess of Cleveland, the King had been much occupied with negotiating the Secret Treaty of Dover with France, largely accomplished through the intermediacy of his sister 'Minette', Henrietta Anne, Duchess of Orleans, who was the wife of the King of France's younger brother. In her train she had brought with her to England a twenty-year-old Breton maid-of-honour, Louise Renée de Penancoët de Kéroualle, who had immediately caught the King's eye.

When 'Minette' was on point of departure, she had sent Louise to the King with a casket of jewels from which he might choose his own parting gift. 'I choose Louise,' said the King. Though not averse to a little romantic dalliance herself, Minette said regretfully that she must return the girl to her family and swept her off.

Two weeks later Minette was dead. The King was overwhelmed with grief for the sister whom he had always loved, but was partly comforted when Louise de Kéroualle arrived, bearing many of the late Duchess's belongings to present to him. Queen Catherine made only token objections to having the girl become one of her maids-of-honour (after all, she had only recently accepted the notoriously vulgar, low-born Nell Gwynn as a nominal Lady of the Bedchamber and could sink no lower than that). A year later, the birth of Louise's son left no doubt in anyone's mind that as the latest royal mistress she was in England to stay.

King Louis XIV of France had cleverly engineered Louise's place in Charles II's heart, Court and bed. Although England and France were closer than they had been in years (with the signing of the secret Treaty of Dover which put Charles so firmly in Louis's power), it was indubitably to France's greatest advantage to have a spokeswoman so close to the English king. For the fifteen years of life which remained to Charles, he never lost that first infatuation for Louise, and though she had not perhaps the political influence often accredited to her, there is no doubt but that her association with the Earl of Arlington, a member of the King's powerful Cabal, had its place in the politics of the day in keeping Charles true to his French commitments.

Catherine loathed Louise, yet another of the King's mistresses placed so close to her, though after so many years of insult and slight she was more disposed to acquiesce quietly in all her husband's plans. Those of the King's ministers who opposed his liaison with France (though few of them knew the extent of his commitment) used all their resources to oust Louise – the Duke of Buckingham championing the claims of Nell Gwynn as a counter-balance, though without success. The King continued to patronize 'sweet Nell of old Drury', but her status was nothing compared with that of the woman who was created Duchess of Portsmouth in 1672. Nell contented herself with frequent jibes at her rival, calling her 'Weeping Willow' and 'Squintabella', unfortunate references to the slight cast in Louise's eye which marred her beauty.

The war between France and Holland in 1672–8, with Charles II a willing supporter of France, to the horror of England, showed up his long-hidden adherence to the nation's traditional enemy. Xenophobia and ultra-Protestant feeling focused the hatred of the populace, who preferred the Dutch, Protestant cause, on the French Catholic Louise de Kéroualle. So violent was the ill-feeling against her that she dared not leave the Palace for fear of her life. It was Nell Gwynn, in fact, who caught the brunt of the people's hostility: her coach was mobbed in the streets of Oxford, mistaken for that of the hated Duchess of Portsmouth. With characteristic courage and Cockney wit, the former actress leaned from the window and shouted to her assailants: 'Pray, good people, be civil enough to let me pass. I am the Protestant whore.'

If Charles II was a gourmet in his sexual appetites, his brother James was a gourmand. 'The most reckless ogler of his day', he preferred easy conquest to the rigours of the chase which were the King's *aperitifs*. James as well as Charles went in pursuit of the elusive 'Belle Stuart', but gave up before long, realizing that his defeat was inevitable; in other cases too, maidenly modesty or jealous husbands cooled his ardours. Nor was James too particular in his choice of mistresses. One of them, Catherine Sedley, once claimed: 'We are none of us handsome, and if we had wit, he had not enough himself to discover it.' Courtiers scoffed that James's ugly mistresses were a penance imposed on him by his confessor.

Nevertheless, he was happy enough. Having discovered that a bachelor could be entrapped into marriage by a clever mistress, as a married man he would no longer go in fear of being forced to spend the rest of his life with more women he had tired of: a mistress could be discarded where a wife could not. That is not to say that Anne Hyde was any trouble to him. She went on bearing children – though only two of them survived to maturity, and as long as she could rule his public life, she was content to let his private *amours* go with a few sniping jeers – none of the wifely reproaches and tears which so clouded Charles II's extra-marital adventures.

James's *affaires* were mostly short and not altogether satisfactory. His first mistress of any note, Jane Middleton (renowned for the tedium of her conversation and her offensive body odour more than for her beauty) was quickly replaced by Lady Chesterfield. When the latter's jealous husband bore her off to the country, the Duke found consolation with Lady Denham. As Margaret Brooke, she had been one of Duchess Anne's maids-of-honour, and now James began to importune his wife to have his mistress become one of her ladies of the Bedchamber. This was very little to Anne's taste. She was no patient Catherine of

Braganza, and her tolerance of James's infidelities went only so far. Soon the whole Court was singing:

As I went by St James's, I heard a bird sing
That Denham's fair wife was a miss of the King;
But the King goes without her, or so I am told,
And the Duke does enjoy her, though Nan pout and scold.

Sir John Denham, thirty years older than his wife, was even more affronted than the Duchess of York. When James began to go openly to Margaret's apartments, and she became known as his *maîtresse-en-tître*, Denham was furious – some said he went mad. When Lady Denham became ill, she openly accused her husband of poisoning her. It was only months before she lay dead, but a post mortem showed no signs of poison in her system.

James was not inconsolable. There was Goditha Price, another of Anne's maids, and Lady Carnegie too. Yet again, a husband was an angry cuckold, but he engineered a unique and appropriate revenge – or so the gossips delightedly said. Carnegie deliberately contracted a venereal disease and made sure that his wife passed it on to the Duke.

Arabella Churchill lasted longer than most. Another of Anne's maids-of-honour, James had never taken much notice of her in her first years at Court. She had no beauty in her face, but her legs were remarkably well-made. It was only when she fell from her horse one day that that fact was discovered – enough to attract James. In 1670 she gave the Duke a son (the future Duke of Berwick, who stood loyally with his father after 1688), swiftly followed by three other children. At last James had settled down: Arabella Churchill lasted right through the 1670s.

There were of course several who thought it no honour to join the legion of James's mistresses. Frances Stuart resisted him as firmly as she did his brother, and so did several of Duchess Anne's maids-of-honour, including the fascinating Frances Jennings. Mistress Jennings was no prude – one day she was caught out masquerading in the London streets as an orange girl, the prey of all the gallants and commoners who saw her; but she saw no profit in falling like a ripe orange herself into James's lap. (Yet in later, less carefree years, as Duchess of Tyrconnel, she was one of the most ardent of the Jacobites in exile.)

Real virtue did exist in that somewhat loosely-moralled Court. There was that Mistress Blagge who so disdained theatricals, a maid-of-honour to Anne Hyde, then with the Queen. So devout was she that, it was said, in order to be out of bed in the morning in time for seven o'clock prayers, each night she tied a thread to her toe and passed it through the key-hole so that the patrolling sentry might pull it and waken her in time – but that might have been one of the joking stories that were passed off for truth in later years. By her own confession, however, Margaret Blagge was unusually modest and strait-laced; unlike so many of her companions, she made rules for herself – and kept them. 'When I go into the withdrawing room,' she wrote in her journal, 'let me consider what my calling is: to entertain the ladies, not to talk foolishly to men, more especially the King.'[21] And again, she reminds herself: 'When you are abroad [that is, merely, out of the house], talk to men as little as may be; carry your prayer book in your pocket, or anything that may decently keep you from conversing with men.'[22] Later, she denies herself any part in the latest, fashionable vice: 'I will never play [cards] this half year but at 3d ombre; I do not vow, but I will not do it – what, lose money at cards, yet not give to the poor? It is robbing God, mis-spending time and misemploying my talents: three great sins! £3 would have kept three people from starving a month: well, I will not play.'[23] And yet it was this woman who could long keep the affection of her religious mentor John Evelyn, and who could inspire ardent passion in the prosaic Sidney Godolphin, whom she later married.

Margaret Blagge was a witness of the death of the Duchess of York, in 1671, and left the last word of one maid-of-honour on another:

> The Duchess dead, a princess honoured in power, had much wit, much money, much esteem; she was full of unexpected fortune, and died (poor creature) in doubt of her religion,

> without the Sacrament, or divine by her, like a poor wretch; none remembered her after one week, none sorry for her; she was tossed and flung about, and everyone did what they would with that stately carcass. What is this world, what is greatness, what to be esteemed, or thought a wit? We shall all be stripped without sense or remembrance. But God, if we serve him in our health, will give us patience in our sickness.[24]

For all Margaret's pious words on the fate of the dead, the Duchess did leave some considerable reputation behind her. She was not really loved by her husband, having grown immensely fat and tiresomely strong-willed over the years, but as far as he was concerned, she had done him the immeasurable service of leading him into the Catholic Church. Whether that was a service to England too is a matter of controversy. Also, she had given him two daughters, and England two future queens – again, debatably for good or ill. Little as she had reproached James for his infidelities, *he* had never allowed *her* to stray into adultery. When Anne had shown some signs of fondness for one of her servants, Henry Sidney, the Duke had firmly put an end to it. Anne Hyde, having proved herself a 'natural' royal highness despite her common birth, had to be taught that she could not act in matters of the heart like other maids-of-honour.

As a widower James continued happily for two years with Arabella Churchill. Various ladies were tipped as his second wife, including Mary Bagot, yet another of Anne's maids – and yet another who had refused James's overtures. Now the widowed Countess of Falmouth, she had no such unsullied reputation, however, and she was never really in the running. Susan, Lady Bellasys, another widow, was. James went so far as to propose to her – but his brother stepped in, telling him that he had played the fool once, but he would not allow him to do so a second time. Lady Bellasys was compensated for her loss with a handsome annuity and the promise of the post of First Lady of the Bedchamber to whomever James did eventually marry.

After an arduous search through the Courts of Europe, the candidate finally selected, in 1673, to be the second Duchess of

York was a fifteen-year-old Italian girl, the Princess Mary Beatrice of Modena. Well-versed in the annoying propensities of royal brides, the Duke instructed his envoy at the Court of Modena: 'You will do your utmost to inculcate to the Princess herself, and the ministers there, the great inconvenience that would follow her being attended by a numerous train of foreigners, who are seldom so useful here as natives, and are obnoxious to censure upon any miscarriages.'[25] The Italians took the advice to heart: of the ladies who were to remain with the new Duchess in England, only her old nurse Pellegrina Turrini and the Contessa Montecuculi were advanced in age and likely to be demanding and critical; Anna Montecuculi, the Contessina Lucrezia Vezzani Prateroni and a girl surnamed Molza were all teenagers.

There were some distinguished names on the list of the Duchess's English ladies: the Duchess of Monmouth, wife of King Charles's eldest bastard son; the former Frances Stuart, now the widowed Duchess of Richmond; and, as Groom of the Stole, Lady Peterborough, wife of the man who had negotiated the match so successfully, now reaping the reward. The sprightly Sarah Jennings, sister of Frances, now Lady Hamilton, figured among the maids-of-honour, with the talented poet Anne Kingsmill (Pope's 'Ardelia') and the poet and painter Anne Killigrew of great renown.

When Sarah Jennings left the ducal household, in 1678, as the wife of the up-and-coming John Churchill (who had risen as much by the fact that his sister was Arabella, still the Duke's mistress, as by his own merits), her place was taken by one Catherine Sedley, the daughter of the popular poet (and notorious rake) Sir Charles Sedley. She had had hopes of John Churchill herself at one time, and it was only fair exchange that she should have taken his wife's place with the Duchess. In the end, she took his sister's place too, with the Duke.

The young Duchess of York had paid little attention to the fact that James was still keeping Arabella Churchill as his mistress, for that lady could be discreet, and at least, while James was occupied with her, there would be no more scandals such as there had been in the lifetime of his last Duchess.

But Catherine Sedley was another matter. Here was a maid-of-honour – and one who had not even Mary's beauty to commend her – infatuating the man whom the Duchess had come to admire and respect. And she had done so within weeks of taking up her post in April 1678. Some said that Catherine became James's mistress as direct revenge on Mary for her having championed the match between John Churchill and Sarah Jennings, thus depriving Catherine of her expected husband.

That autumn the Duchess took her younger step-daughter, Princess Anne, on a trip to Holland to see her elder step-daughter, Princess Mary. James stayed at home.

With the political situation unfavourable to the Duke of York, widely known as he was as a Catholic, and now indubitably the future king of England, since Catherine of Braganza neither had a child nor died to make way for a queen who could bear one, the Yorks spent much time out of England, now in Scotland, now in the Catholic Netherlands. It was while she was living in Brussels that Duchess Mary wrote a letter to Susan, Lady Bellasys which well illustrates her affection for one who, had her luck been better, might have been in her own place:

> You cannot imagine the pleasure I have to hear any news from dear England, let 'em be what kind they will. Them as you sent me were very pleasant ones and made me laugh which few things do at this time, being as sad and melancholy as it is possible for anybody to be, and I think I have great reason to be so. Pray don't fail, if you love me, to tell me all the silly news you know, and of all kinds.[26]

The Duchess's reasons for being 'sad and melancholy' showed no signs of disappearing. Catherine Sedley was firmly ensconced as James's acknowledged mistress, and in 1683 gave the Duke a son, while Mary herself only continued to miscarry.

When he came to the throne, on his brother Charles II's death, in February 1685, the new King James II firmly resolved to be faithful to his wife in future and made the position plain to Catherine Sedley. But his flesh was weak, and besides, he was sorry for her when their child died, that spring, so that he was soon relying on her again. If Mary was upset then, she was miserable the following January, when James created Catherine Countess of Dorchester and Baroness Darlington. Then Mary produced a master-stroke: she had James's priests, always his respected mentors, issue a concerted rebuke to him, and they forced the King to agree to sending his mistress away.

Catherine refused to go to the Continent – claiming to be afraid that once there, she would be manœuvred into entering a convent. Instead, in February she left for Ireland.

The Countess of Dorchester did not like Ireland. In April she gave notice that she was returning to England to take the waters at Tunbridge Wells, for her health. Despite a message forbidding her to enter the country, she not only disobeyed but in September forced her way into the Queen's drawing-room. 'That minx appears to have gathered a fresh stock of impudence in Ireland.'[27] muttered Lady Bellasys from her post beside her mistress. Of course, James could not long resist the temptation of Catherine's dubious charms.

It is unlikely that the Countess of Dorchester had any strong feeling for her lover. When James was forced to flee abroad from the 'Glorious Revolution' of 1688, she made no attempt to follow him to France. On the other hand, nor did she ever go whole-heartedly over to the new monarchs, James's daughter Mary and her husband William of Orange. 'Why so haughty, madam?' Catherine said to Mary II, 'For if I broke one commandment *with* your father, you have broken one *against* him.'[28]

The Court in exile was a dull place without Catherine's wit, though now Queen Mary of Modena was happy in the full attention of her husband, who became faithful and increasingly devout as his troubles weighed on him.

'The Queen over the water' could now be sure too of the devotion of the ladies who served her. There were few rewards for those who became her maids-of-honour or ladies-in-waiting, and only loyalty and affection prompted women to emigrate to France to the tedious, pointless round of the Stuart Court at St Germain.

Pellegrina Turini, Queen Mary's childhood nurse, was still with her, and it was her friend and erstwhile maid-of-honour Anna Montecuculi, now Contessa Davia, who had so successfully engineered the Queen's escape (James created her Countess of Almond as thanks). Lady Bellasys was at St Germain too, and old Lady Powis, who had been with Mary of Modena since her wedding. The Duchess of Tyrconnel, the no-longer-madcap Frances Jennings, was there to bring a sparkle of past hilarity into the sombre Court.

The merry age of the maids-of-honour was over. The new King, Dutch William, might follow his uncles' example and take a mistress from their midst, but he took his pleasures more soberly than ever they had done.

Four ladies-in-waiting who became queens. *Above left:* Elizabeth Woodville, a former lady in the household of Henry VI's queen, who, as a widow, married Edward IV. *Above right:* Anne Boleyn – the scandals surrounding her marriage to Henry VIII reverberated throughout the Continent. *Below left:* Jane Seymour, Anne Boleyn's maid-of-honour, who had attracted Henry even before her mistress's downfall. *Below right:* Catherine Howard, who supplanted Anne of Cleves to become Henry VIII's fifth wife.

Two maids-of-honour whose *amours* offended Queen Elizabeth I. *Left:* Catherine Grey, with Edward Seymour, her son by Lord Hertford, born in the Tower of London in 1561 after his parents' imprisonment. As a cousin and possible heiress of the Queen, Catherine was extremely imprudent to attempt to marry secretly. *Below left:* Mary Fitton, who was sent from Court in disgrace in 1601 after the scandal of her *affaire* with Lord Herbert.

Elizabeth I amid the panoply of her Court. She is shown (in this picture attributed to Robert Peake the Elder) on her way to the wedding of a maid-of-honour, Lady Anne Russell, to the Earl of Worcester's son in June 1600. Anne received the Queen at Blackfriars on the Thames and conducted her to her mother's house, where the Court dined and where several maids-of-honour (including Mary Fitton) performed a masque.

Two designs for costumes by Inigo Jones to be worn in masques performed by James I's wife, Anne of Denmark, and her ladies. *Left:* Penthesilea. *Below left:* Tethys.

Below: Charles I with his wife Henrietta Maria and their Court walking in Greenwich Park. His Court was immeasurably more sober and pleasant than the riotous household kept by his father, but still came under censure from the Puritans.

The heyday of the lady-in-waiting: the reigns of the last Stuarts. *Above:* Two mistresses of Charles II – Lady Castlemaine *(left)*, who was foisted on the King's bride as her chief lady, and Louise de Kéroualle, her rival after 1670. *Below left:* Anne Hyde, the maid-of-honour who married the future King James II. *Below right:* Sarah Churchill, the 'power behind the throne' in the early years of Queen Anne's reign.

THE PROSPECT BEFORE US.

Above: 'The Prospect before Us', a Rowlandson cartoon of 1788 satirizing Queen Charlotte and her German 'dresser' Mrs Schwellenberg. The influence attributed to the latter was much over-rated, for the Queen disdained to meddle in politics.

Below left: Baroness Lehzen, Victoria's former governess who ruled her Court and her affections in the first years of her reign.
Below right: Lady Flora Hastings, a lady-in-waiting to Queen Victoria's mother. The Queen's wrongful accusation of this unmarried lady of pregnancy caused a national scandal.

Her Majesty Queen Elizabeth II enthroned at a State Opening of Parliament. On her left stand the Mistress of the Robes and the Lady and Woman of the Bedchamber, their offices the last vestiges of the great *entourages* of former queens.

7

WHILE the male members of the Stuart family enjoyed amorous adventures with total licence, the women of the family were both more self-restrained and under more restraint. Neither Queen Catherine of Braganza nor either of the two Duchesses of York ever figured in any sort of scandal. The Portuguese Catherine and the Italian Mary of Modena had been brought up in the most confined of households and had been rigorously inculcated with high ideals of marital fidelity.

The York princesses, daughters of James and Anne Hyde, were similarly protected from temptation. At an early age they were sent from Court to the more homely atmosphere of Richmond Palace. True, their guardians were members of the Villiers family which had long provided royal favourites of easy virtue, but Colonel Edward and Lady Frances Villiers were of more sterling quality.

In the main, it was a household of women and young girls, with the six Villiers daughters and selected royal *protégées* as companions to the Princesses. Even on their visits to Court, Mary and Anne of York were kept in female society. It was natural, therefore, that they should develop ' schoolgirl crushes ' for other young women; what was unusual was that they did not later pass on to any fervent admiration for young men. Apart from their husbands, whom, dutifully and sincerely, both would come to love, the Princesses remained devoted all their lives to certain women who responded to their affectionate cravings. There is no evidence that either of them ever had lesbian relationships in the physical sense, and, in view of the Stuart family's propensity for illicit sexual relations, it was probably just as well – for their reputations and for the legitimate succession of the crown – that they never indulged in the heterosexual promiscuity of their male relations. It was only in the political nature of Anne's favourites' power that any evil accrued by the Queens' proclivities.

By the early 1670s, in the years soon after their mother's death, both Mary and Anne began their love-affairs with their Court and country companions. Anne's first love was one Cicely Cornwallis to whom, it was said, she wrote some thousand letters before one was discovered by her step-mother, who was appalled at the passionate outpourings of the teenaged girl and put a stop to the correspondence.

Mary had already shown her partiality for Frances Apsley, a girl some nine years older than herself who had been, for some time, an inmate of Richmond under the tutelage of the Villiers.

Again, she wrote frequently and ardently to her friend, this time employing romantic *noms-de-plume*: Mary was 'Clorine', a character from a fashionable play, Frances 'Aurelia'. Frequently the Princess addressed Frances Apsley as her 'husband' and made great play on her fidelity within the 'marriage'.

All sorts of stratagems were used to keep the correspondence secret (for Frances Apsley was rarely at Court for the Princesses to enjoy her company) but it continued up to and far beyond Mary's marriage to William of Orange in 1687, and for many years the Princess would find difficulty in writing to one 'husband', Frances, of the other, William, without complication.

At the time of Mary's marriage, when her English household was being prepared for her removal to the Netherlands, she had little choice in her ladies-in-waiting. There was no chance for her to nominate Frances as one of their number. And there was no shortage of applicants for the coveted posts. 'It were worth your while', wrote one courtier to another, 'to see the old ladies and the young beggarly bitches . . . suing for places about the Princess.'[1]

In the end, however, Mary's entourage was composed mainly of old friends. Lady Frances Villiers was nominated as her chief lady – only to die of smallpox at the eleventh hour, just as the newly-wed Princess was setting forth. But two of that lady's daughters, Elizabeth and Anne, and a cousin, Lady Inchiquin, did go to the Netherlands, with the Princess's old nurse and two of her Richmond friends, Anne Trelawny and Jane Wroth.

For all Mary's initial reluctance to marry her Dutch cousin William and leave her family, she soon found her position as first lady of Holland pleasant enough. Though her husband was indifferent to her despite her developing adoration of him, Dutch domestic comforts and her Court's well-regulated society were exactly to her taste. She soon overcame her aversion to William's close friend Hans Bentinck when Anne Villers married him soon after her arrival in the Netherlands, and added several Dutch ladies to her own circle of intimates.

It was only some two years after her marriage that Mary discovered that one of her ladies-in-waiting, in time-honoured fashion, had become her husband's mistress. This was Elizabeth Villiers, the companion of her childhood. 'Squinting Betty', as the lady was called, was no beauty, but she had sensitivity and wit – and consummate duplicity in hiding her treachery from Mary.

The situation might have continued unobserved by the Princess, though many of her household knew of it – had not a complicated chain of events occurred which led to certain of her 'friends' enlightening her. It began with the revelation that one of her maids-of-honour, Jane Wroth, was pregnant, having been seduced by a paternal cousin of the Prince's, Count Zuylestein. The Count had administered 'potions' to his mistress to induce her abortion, but without success. When the shocking facts came to Mary's ears – as fate would have it, in the absence of her husband – she insisted that the Count should marry Jane. On his return, William was furious that a man of whom he had always been fond (and, it should be remembered, the Prince was always suspected of homosexual tendencies) and who was, if remotely, a member of the princely House of Nassau, should have been forced by Mary into marriage with a nonentity.

With William's coldness to her, and bereft of the undivided affection of Frances Apsley by the latter's marriage, Mary turned increasingly for comfort to old Mrs Langford and to Anne Trelawny, with whom she could remember the balmier days of her childhood. But she was unwise in placing her trust in these women who, as spies and reporters to Mary's father, were only too ready to promote the disaffection between the Prince and Princess. The Duke of York, who became King in 1685, had little love for the dour Protestant Dutchman who must, if James had no son by his second wife, overturn his Catholic policy for England if the royal succession took its due course to Mary. Thus his minions in Mary's household fed her fears that her husband did not care for her and at last revealed to her that her own lady-in-waiting was his mistress. Mary was at her lowest ebb. After several years of marriage, she had given William no child; all her blandishments and coaxing could spark no warmth in her husband's treatment of her. So she resolved on confrontation.

One night, as he left the apartments of Elizabeth Villiers at about 2 am, the Prince found his wife shivering on the stairs. She had been waiting for him to emerge and was ready with her accusations and complaints. But she was quite unable to shame her husband into renunciation of his Betty. Instead, the Prince turned the tables on Mary, showing her that her household was a hotbed of spies. Mrs Langford and Anne Trelawny were sent packing.

Despite her lifelong gentleness and complaisance, in this one instance Mary stood resolute. While William was away, she dispatched his mistress to England, on the pretext of carrying a letter to her father. When Elizabeth Villiers tried to return to her post in Holland, Mary refused to receive her. However, in the face of William's authority, she was later forced to have the woman she hated about her once more.

Another of Mary's ladies who left her at this time – though not through any fault of her own, was the lively Lady Mary Forester, to whom Mary subsequently wrote a letter in her most tranquil strain of friendship – with none of the extravagant professions which once characterized her correspondence with Frances Apsley:

> I had been very glad your concerns and your condition would have permitted you to stay longer since I have learned to know you too well to be willing to lose you quite, and I could now chide you for being so good humoured while you were here, but that your grave letter makes me think I am writing to that sober Lady Mary Forester I once knew at the Hague. If you had always been seen at the basset table making al pios and wanting an interpreter to ask for what you won, you might have gone away almost without being missed, but since you have been at Loo working, walking and romping, you must not wonder if I should have been very glad to have found you still at the Hague for all you deceived me so much as you really did when we played at hide-and-seek in the little wood; if I had then known your condition, you would have never got the reputation of as good a walker as myself, at least we had never passed ditches as we did together, but I am very glad it has succeeded so well and hope you will get into England and have a good deliverance which I think is the best wish can be made you now ... I hope you have learned to know me enough to believe though I can make no compliments that nobody can wish you better ... than I, Marie.[2]

Even without Mrs Langford, Anne Trelawny and Lady Mary, there were women enough in the Netherlands whom Mary found sympathetic. There was the English maid-of-honour Mistress Jesson, who made her swain prove his love for her by wading into the River Vyver, until he was shoulder-high, with the jeering Court looking on. There was the pious Mademoiselle Obdan who assisted Mary in planning her works of charity. Countess Zuylestein remained with her, a favourite to the end. And there was Lady Derby, a Dutchwoman and member of the Beverwaert family which claimed kinship with the House of Nassau. Great events were stirring. In England King James had estranged himself from that Parliament which had offered him unprecedented loyalty at his accession. The furore which his Catholicizing polices created and his alienation of powerful men from his government led directly to a summons to William of Orange to set the kingdom of England to rights. Such limited aims soon broadened, however, once William had landed his army in England and attracted overwhelming support – and once the unhappy James had fled abroad. William and Mary were proclaimed joint sovereigns and, after a decade on the Continent, the Princess returned home as Queen.

Anne Bentinck (*née* Villiers), Countess of Portland, died soon after the return to England. As Mary's chief confidante, she had always stood as the Princess's firm champion against her own sister Elizabeth. But in November 1688, as she lay dying, it was the wronged wife herself who brought about the reconciliation between the sisters. Mary was leaning solicitously over her friend on her deathbed; Elizabeth, in formal attendance on her, stood apart by a window. With a gesture of that almost sanctity for which she was long renowned, Mary led her greatest enemy over to Anne, and urged them to make their peace.

But there was no peace between Mary and Elizabeth themselves. Mary once confided to her journal:

> I must confess and set it down here, that it may keep me from the like again, I own then to my shame, that there was one among my ladies who had been sick, and whom I not only could have spared but came near to wishing she might make room for Lady Nottingham, of whom I had heard so much good and liked so well, that I thought my set could not be more mended than by the change. But it pleased God to make room for her in another way, by removing Lady Dorset, who was really grown very dear to me.[3]

Mary could not bring herself to write that she wished that Betty Villiers might die, but, with her strong conscience and well-settled religious convictions, came as near to it as she dared.

In fact, it was Mary's own death, in 1694, which ended King William III's fourteen-year attachment to Betty Villiers. After years of slighting and neglecting his wife – though never publicly, for he knew that he owed his established position in England as much to her hereditary right as to his might – after her death, he was compelled by remorse to avow how deeply he felt her loss. Betty Villiers was pensioned off (in princely fashion), and consoled herself for the loss of a position which, by reason of William's discretion, had never been one of grandeur comparable with that of the Stuart *maîtresses-en-tître*, by marrying the Duke of Hamilton.

When Mary II arrived in England, it might well have been expected that she would shower honours upon her old 'husband', Frances Apsley, now Lady Bathurst. But she did not. Frances's husband, Sir Benjamin, became Treasurer of the household of the new Queen's sister, the Princess Anne. In the following years, as a breach opened between the royal sisters, their quarrels precluded close association. Only Barbara, Lady Fitzharding, another of the Villiers sisters who served Anne as lady-in-waiting, retained Mary's favour, but only by carrying tales to the Queen of Anne's 'misdeeds'. With Lady Fitzharding blackening the Princess's character with the Queen, and Betty Villiers doing the same with the King, it was no wonder that not long after the 'Glorious Revolution' of 1688 the Princess came to feel herself an outcast from the royal circle.

After her elder sister had married and left home in 1678, Princess Anne had leaned ever more on the young women whom she admired. In particular, she took up with one Sarah Jennings, a maid-of-honour to the Duchess of York. Sarah was almost a charity case, the daughter of an impoverished widow, who, with her elder, more beautiful sister Frances ('la belle Jennings' of Charles II's Court), had been granted a place at Court to earn her living.

Sarah was a young woman of extraordinary intelligence, with a strong will, a commanding manner and enough charm to give herself a consequence among her peers. She made herself agreeable to Anne, helping her to conceal her illicit correspondence with Frances Apsley from her governess, but she had a sharp tongue and a biting wit which made her no few enemies. It was Sarah who described Anne's governess, the successor of Lady Frances Villiers, with so sarcastic but so amusing a turn of phrase. Flower, Lady Clarendon, belied her romantic name: she 'looked like a madman and talked like a scholar, which the Princess thought agreed very well together [no doubt at Sarah's instigation, for Anne was more patient with fools, being not very astute herself]. She was very passionate, but they called her a good woman, I suppose because her lord made a great rout with prayers; but she never did anything in her office that looked as if she had common sense.'[4] In addition, Sarah was a tale-bearer, who lost the popularity which her wit won her among her fellow maids-of-honour by her spite against anyone who crossed her.

In about 1678 or 1679 (the actual date has never been established) Sarah Jennings married John Churchill, a page of the Duke of York (brother of James's mistress Arabella and himself formerly one of the lovers of Lady Castlemaine). In 1683 Anne was married to Prince George of Denmark, a heavy, ponderous, slow-witted young man who never gave anyone any trouble, but who did his duty by giving his wife numerous pregnancies. With the dignity of her independence, the Princess could now advance her friend Sarah to the rank of her first lady-in-waiting and could command her assiduous attendance and almost constant company. So enthralled was Anne by the woman who sparkled where she, the Princess, scarcely gleamed, so intoxicated was she by Sarah's liveliness and amusing ways, that she gave herself up to what must surely count as a love-affair comparable in its dog-like devotion with that of Henry VIII in his first passion for Anne Boleyn.

While Sarah was pregnant and away from Court, Anne would write her the most humble, yearning epistles. Screeds of professions of devotion poured from the Princess's pen with little regard for spelling and grammar. To close the gap in their rank, Anne suggested that they should name themselves Mrs Morley and Mrs Freeman, and with characteristic generosity left the choice between the two to Sarah. 'My frank open temper', wrote that lady in later years, 'naturally led me to pitch upon Freeman.'[5]

During the bewildering events of James II's brief reign, Sarah was Princess Anne's mentor. Anne was an affectionate daughter, but she had a deep mistrust of her father's religion, having herself been inculcated with the most entrenched adherence to the Church of England. When King James took arms against the invading William of Orange, both George of Denmark and John Churchill rode out with his army. Churchill, however, had long before thrown in his lot with William's adherents in England, and it was not long before both he and George went over to the Dutch side. But at the time, Anne was still in London, which was held by the Jacobites. It was Sarah, with her genius for decisive action, who master-minded the Princess's flight to the Orangist town of Northampton. So well and so secretly did she accomplish the manœuvre that not even the Princess's servants knew of her 'moonlight flit' until the next morning, by which time she was well away from the capital.

With the establishment of the childless William and Mary on the throne of England, and with James II and his putative son in exile abroad, it was clear to Sarah Churchill that it was only a matter of time before Anne should succeed to the throne of England. In the years that followed that great political upheaval, she clung fiercely to the Princess and put herself out to strengthen the bond which would one day prove so much to her advantage. Many years later, Sarah wrote an account of her endeavours with Anne (writing of herself in the third person):

> ... they were shut up together for many hours daily. Every moment of absence she [Anne] counted a sort of tedious lifeless state. To see [Sarah] was a constant joy and to part with her for never so short a time a constant uneasiness, as the Princess's own frequent expressions were. This worked even to the jealousy of a lover. She used to say she desired to possess her wholly and could hardly bear that she should

ever escape from this confinement into any other company. All who knew the tempers of them both knew it to be a confinement indeed for one who had a very great sprightliness and cheerfulness of nature joined with a true taste of conversation, to be perpetually chained as it were to a person whose other accomplishments had not cured the sullenness of her temper nor wholly freed her conversation from an insipid heaviness. ... [Sarah] had too great a sense of her favour not to submit to all such inconveniences to oblige one who she saw loved her to excess. ... But though there was this passionate love on the one side and as I verily believe the sincerest friendship on the other, yet their tempers were not more different than their principles and notions on many occasions appeared to be.[6]

Anne's dependence on Sarah, and her involvement with the political stance of John Churchill and his colleague Sidney Godolphin, which was at variance with King William's policies, soon caused a breach between the Princess and her sister the Queen. The mistrust which Mary II felt for Sarah Churchill came to a head early in January 1692 when she reproved Anne for giving Sarah the then outrageously high wage of £1,000 a year. Only some twelve days later, John Churchill, now Lord Marlborough, was accused of having Jacobite sympathies and was sent from Court in disgrace. Protocol demanded that Anne should dispense with Sarah's services immediately, but such was her devotion to her that she not only kept her in her service but actually took her to Court with her.

Mary remonstrated with her sister, kindly enough but in such a way as to bring out that stubborn streak which always exists in unreasonable and unimaginative people. Anne refused to give up her friend, and when the Queen subsequently demanded her obedience more forcefully, dashed off a note to Sarah: 'I have just now received such an arbitrary letter from the Queen as I am sure she nor the King durst not have writ to any other of their subjects and which if I had any inclination to part with dear Mrs Freeman would make me keep her in spite of their teeth and which by the grace of God I will and go to the utmost verge of the earth rather than live with such monsters.'[7]

With Sarah to keep her firm to her purpose, Anne withstood all pressure from the throne, withdrawing from the capital to Syon House on the Thames, unabashed at the Court's ostracism of her receptions.

For almost two years the two Stuart sisters kept their distance from each other, and Queen Mary died without the consolation of a reconciliation.

The Marlboroughs survived that testing year of 1692, when, in May, John was arrested for High Treason – only to be acquitted.

In the King's mood of self-examination after his wife's death, he made overtures to his sister-in-law, and, with their mutual interest in Anne's only surviving son, William, Duke of Gloucester, and later in their shared grief at his early death, the brother and sister-in-law remained on reasonably good terms for the rest of William III's life. But the years of trial had shown Anne who her friends were: she clung to Sarah, even to the point of tolerating Lady Marlborough's continuing friendship with Lady Fitzharding (albeit warning her 'Remember none of that family [the Villiers] were ever good for anything'[8]), despite that lady's fidelity to the Queen. Lady Bathurst (Frances Apsley), however, was a casualty of the quarrel. Her husband, Anne's Treasurer, had compounded his wife's crime of friendship with Mary II by himself defrauding the Princess of a good deal of her savings and income.

Then, in 1702, came Anne's 'sunshine day', when as Queen at last she could settle her account with the Marlboroughs. William III had given John high command in the army; now, under Anne, he won supreme control, his position bolstered in Parliament by the supremacy there of his old friend Godolphin, the beloved 'Mr Montgomery' of Anne's correspondence with Sarah. And Sarah herself? She became Mistress of the Robes, Groom of the Stole (an obsolete but prestigious post) and Keeper of the Privy Purse, while her daughters Anne and Harriet were named among the Ladies of the Bedchamber.

For five years Sarah – 'Queen Zarah' as scandal-mongers named her – was the prime influence on Queen Anne. She had no rival in Prince George, the Queen's husband, whose stodgy, placid acceptance of panoply without power still bowed to Lady Marlborough's quicksilver but adamantine will. It was she, Sarah affirmed, who had made Anne what she was, who had created a dignified, dutiful Queen out of the unpromising material of an uneducated, indolent, frivolous Princess:

> I used to pass many hours in a day with her [Sarah wrote in her old age], and always endeavoured to give her notions of loving her country, of justice and governing by the laws and making herself be beloved rather than feared, and I always showed her how easy that was to do when she had so much in her power to do good; and I ever told her that nothing was so great and honourable as to govern upon the conditions that a crown was taken, nor no way so certain that to keep it as long as she lived.[9]

Many cavilled at Sarah's influence over Anne, and surely many more would have done so had not John Churchill justified his family's royal favour by proving to be the most glorious general England had ever produced. With his victory at Blenheim in 1704, in the War of the Spanish Succession, he won glory, renown and the title of Duke. Queen Anne and Duchess Sarah rode together to give thanksgiving at St Paul's amid the plaudits of all England.

But Sarah had already sown the seeds of her own downfall. In her eagerness to use her position to the benefit of her family, she had placed two impoverished cousins in the royal household. Alice Hill became laundress to the young Duke of Gloucester shortly before the boy's death in 1700, and her sister Abigail had become a serving-maid about the Queen.

Having reached the zenith of her power, and having long since tired of the inane companionship of her royal mistress, Sarah spent less and less time at Court, preferring country relaxation. She left her daughters with Anne, but neither was of an age or had the temperament to become all-in-all to the Queen in their mother's place. Abigail Hill, however, with her insinuating solicitude, applied her gentle, soothing hands to the Queen's gout and, perhaps as a humble contrast to the domineering Sarah, gradually won the Queen's affections.

Anne was hurt at what she regarded as her oldest friend's neglect of her. She begged Sarah repeatedly to return to residence at Windsor, or at least to pay protracted visits, but without success. Feeling hard-done-by, and prompted by Abigail Hill, who had an eye to her own promotion, a gradual change entered Anne's feelings towards Sarah. When Abigail decided to marry (a nonentity called Samuel Masham, who occupied a lowly royal post), she begged Anne not to tell the Duchess for fear of her meddling against her interests – besides, there is no stronger bond between women than a secret shared.

In the end, in the summer of 1707, some months after the wedding, Sarah discovered that her cousin Abigail was now Mrs Masham. Not knowing that Anne had been a party to the match, she offered to tell her on Abigail's behalf. It was only then that Anne revealed the extent of Mrs Masham's ingratiation: 'I have a hundred times bid Mrs Masham tell it you and she would not.'[10] Sarah was appalled. Not only had the Queen, who had always confided in her, kept back such news, but she had been on such terms with Abigail as to be so free with her.

Sarah's probings uncovered the work of the past months, and the full extent of her cousin's duplicity. What she did not realize until later, however, was Abigail's commitment to her paternal cousin Robert Harley, an up-and-coming politician who was a thorn in the flesh of the Duke of Marlborough and his colleague Godolphin. For years Abigail kept Harley *au fait* with the tenor of the Queen's political leanings and of her changing attitude to the Churchills. She spoke of Harley to the Queen and, since Anne had always had Tory sympathies, was of immense influence in wooing her from the avowedly Whig Sarah and the middle-of-the-road Marlborough and Godolphin. Without royal support for Marlborough personally, Parliamentary commitment to the war which he was so brilliantly prosecuting dwindled. For all the victories at Oudenarde and Malplaquet, the Commons were loath to grant the funds necessary to keep an army in the field.

Sarah, meanwhile, had been growing more and more angry with Anne, to whom she now imputed ingratitude and whom she suspected of loving Abigail Masham more than herself. Never a woman to hold her temper, the Duchess indulged in a few uncontrollable scenes which no friend, let alone a Queen who stood so upon her dignity in a tight spot, could tolerate. How Anne must have suffered to have to write to the Duke of Marlborough in such a vein as this:

> You know I have often had the misfortune of falling under the Duchess of Marlborough's displeasure and now, after several reconciliations, she is again relapsed into her cold unkind way and ... has taken a resolution not to come to me when I am alone, and fancies nobody will take notice of the change. She may impose upon some poor simple people, but how can she imagine she can on any that have a grain of sense? Can she think that the Duchess of Somerset and my Lady Fitzharding, who are two of the most observing, prying ladies in England, won't find out that she never comes near me nor looks on me as she used to do, that the tattling voice will not in a little time make us the jest of the town? Some people will blame her, others me, and a great many both. What a disagreeable noise she will be the occasion of making in the world besides, God knows what ill consequences it may be of. Therefore for God Almighty's sake, for the Duchess of Marlborough's, your own and my poor sake, endeavour all you can to persuade Mrs Freeman out of this strange unreasonable resolution. I have not as yet ventured to make any answer to her letter, nor dare not, for till this violent humour be over all I can say, though never so reasonable, will but inflame her more.[11]

Refusing to consider the harm she was doing, Sarah became increasingly open with her feeling against Anne and her new favourite. The worst moment occurred at the thanksgiving for John's victory at Oudenarde, in August 1708. Sarah, who always took her duties seriously and never allowed her own feelings to mar her performance of them, had exercised her usual taste and flair in choosing jewels for Anne to wear to the service at St Paul's. Her anger was thus commensurate with her surprise when she met the Queen on the cathedral steps and discovered that her efforts had been ignored. Then and there, in the public gaze, she stormed at Anne and, when the poor woman tried to reply, told her to keep quiet. 'When I had taken so much pains to put your jewels in a way I thought you would like,' the Duchess railed in a letter to Anne written after the service, 'Mrs Masham could make you refuse to wear them, in so unkind a manner, because that was a power she had not thought fit to exercise before. I will make no reflections upon it, only that I must needs observe that your Majesty chose a very wrong day to mortify me, when you were just going to return thanks for a victory obtained by Lord Marlborough.'[12]

This might have been the end of Sarah, but, two months later, Prince George died. He had been the perfect husband for Anne, one who appreciated her domesticity and looked for no more beauty and intelligence in his wife than he possessed himself – which was little enough. He was well-conducted and faithful, a tiresome and tedious companion to those of more imagination and comprehension than himself but a throughly well-principled man. Anne was heart-broken. Now, with her father and his second family abroad, and an immense chasm open between them since 1688, she was alone, the last of the Stuarts in England.

For all the former quarrel, Sarah descended on Windsor to take the Queen in hand. She was annoyed when Anne made a point of speaking with Mrs Masham, when she herself, the Duchess, claimed the place of the Queen's only comforter, and she took steps, by playing on Anne's grief, to keep her in seclusion and away from Abigail. The latter wrote to her cousin Harley (using her customary aliases):

> There is care taken she [the Queen] shall not be alone, for since the misfortune the Lady Pye [Sarah] has hardly left her so long as to let her say her private prayers but stays constantly with her. My Lady's friends say it is fit she should (and they

hope she always will) to keep that jade my cousin Kate [Abigail herself] from her. Oh my poor aunt [Anne] is in a very deplorable condition, for now her ready money [independent will] is all gone; because I will not trouble you with a melancholy story ... she has shut and bolted the door upon herself. Oh what can one say to all these things when I know what wise and good advice you have given her and yet she rejects it to satisfy those monsters who she knows will ruin her.[13]

But Sarah could not remain closeted with Anne forever, and it soon became apparent that a permanent breach would occur. It was a strange situation. Each woman swore affection for the other, each recalled old times to the other as a reminder of what they had been to each other, neither seemed willing to make the break but then neither would give up her own way. While Anne refused to give up her Abigail, Sarah refused to give up her independence. As Duchess of Marlborough, with a great palace being built in the country and the affairs of her numerous daughters to keep in train, Sarah had more than enough to satisfy her lively mind. But she hated to see her influence overcome by that of Abigail. By 1710 all England knew the meaning of the satirist's rhyme:

Bright Masham's the whirlwind that turns us about,
One whiff of whose breath can bring in or put out.

It was one thing for Sarah to have her protégée refused a place as Woman of the Bedchamber, in favour of Abigail's, but another to see her beloved John, with all his military glory, despised and thwarted because Abigail worked on Anne for the Tory cause against him.

After months of bitterness and patched-up quarrels, the end came in April 1710. Sarah sought a formal interview with the Queen, in which she poured out all her rage and unhappiness. Anne, with that stubbornness which was impenetrable, refused to discuss their differences and reduced the Duchess to frustrated tears. The two women never met again.

Anne saw John Churchill in January 1711 and asked him to persuade Sarah to return her gold key of office. When he tried to make his wife comply, she flung the key on the floor, and the unhappy man had to take it to the Queen himself.

Anne had just over three years to live. She continued to favour Abigail, now Lady Masham, but at the same time she was intimate with a much more suitable lady, Elizabeth, Duchess of Somerset, Sarah's successor in office, for all that she was the most staunch of Whigs. There was now no Churchill at Court for, when Marlborough was dismissed at the turn of the year 1711, his daughters gave the Queen their resignation from her bedchamber. John and Sarah lived happily enough in retirement, watching Blenheim Palace, begun as the gift of a grateful Queen, rise to splendour. John died in 1722, but Sarah lived to an active old age, dying in 1744, the bane of her family and servants, as ever.

At Anne's death, and with the return of a Whig government under the new, Hanoverian, King George I, Abigail realized that her day was done. She and her husband, like the Churchills, took to country life, and lived prosperously on their savings from the Secret Service Funds which they had plundered.

But Abigail, for all her 'backstairs" political influence, had never been the great character, the dominant figure of her age, which Sarah Churchill had been. Here, then, was the apogee of the lady-in-waiting. Not even those alluring ladies of the sixteenth century who had risen from a menial place in the queen's bedchamber to possession of the king's bed by legal wedlock could claim such power as Sarah had wielded in her heyday – nor perhaps such devotion from their king as Queen Anne awarded to her 'Mrs Freeman'.

8

At the accession of George of Hanover to the throne of England as the successor to Queen Anne, the ladies among his subjects who sought Court places were disappointed to find that their new monarch had no consort whom they might serve.

George I was not a bachelor, nor was he a widower. Indced, he had a wife who could still well claim the title of queen. But the Electress Sophia Dorothea was left behind in Germany when George arrived to take possession of his realm – left behind in captivity at the castle of Ahlden, convicted of adultery and discarded by her husband.

The ladies of England had only narrowly missed the joy of greeting another Queen Regnant. George's mother, Sophia, would have become Queen of England in her own right had she not predeceased Queen Anne by a mere two months. She was the youngest daughter of Elizabeth of Bohemia, only daughter of England's King James I, and had married Ernest Augustus, Elector of Hanover (having spurned, in her youth, the half-hearted advances of her cousin Charles II).

The Hanoverian Court of the past half-century had been, in many ways, like that of England. There were princes and princesses of easy virtue – and there were maids-of-honour with no virtue at all. Indeed, there was a dynasty of princes' mistresses who doubled in the role of ladies-in-waiting to those princes' wives. Sophia's husband Ernest Augustus had laid his lascivious gaze on the teenaged Clara von Meisenbug in the 1660s, and had brought her and her sister Maria to Court, as his wife's maids-of-honour, to have her conveniently to hand. Clara was married off to the complaisant Freiherr von Platen, and continued for many years as the Elector's mistress. Her sister Maria, having twice married, became the mistress of Ernest Augustus's son George, he who later became King of England. But another of George's mistresses was Sophia von Platen, the daughter of Ernest Augustus and Clara von Platen and thus his own half-sister.

Ernest Augustus's brother George William had taken a more honourable course. His fancy was a young Frenchwoman, Eléonore d'Olbreuse, the daugher of an impoverished noble Huguenot, who was maid-of-honour to the Princess de Tarente, a family connection. He had actually married Eléonore, though it had to be a morganatic marriage, which deprived their line of of its claim to both Hanoverian Electorate and English kingdom. Their daughter, Sophia Dorothea, married the Elector George and countered his infidelities with her own.

When Sophia Dorothea took as her lover the superbly attractive Count Philip von Königsmarck, meeting him clandestinely whenever she could, she had an able and devoted co-conspirator in her lady-in-waiting Eleanora von dem Knesebeck but a no less able enemy in the former maid-of-honour Countess Platen. Whether the Countess wanted Königsmarck for her own daughter, or whether she had deeper motives, she certainly had a hand in uncovering the *liaison* to George. After Sophia Dorothea's banishment, Sophia von Platen (Baroness von Kielmansegg by a convenient marriage) shared George's strange heart and the leading place at his Court with her by-no-means-unfriendly rival Ehrengarde Melusine von der Schulenberg. The latter, inevitably, had been a maid-of-honour too, in this case in the household of George's mother Sophia. She was tall and thin, where Sophia von Kielmansegg was short and fat, and the

English nicknamed the two royal mistresses 'the Maypole and the Elephant'. The old Electress Sophia herself led the jibes against her son's younger mistress: 'Do you see that mawkin?' she remarked of the Schulenburg to a visitor, 'You would scarcely believe that she has captivated my son.'[1]

This then was the *ménage à trois* which settled in England after the death of Queen Anne. Power these ladies had, in dispensing patronage to their flatterers, and titles enough (Schulenburg became Duchess of Kendal and Munster, and Kielmansegg Countess of Darlington) but they could never have legal title to the splendid entourage that a queen would have demanded from England.

However, George I did provide England with a Prince and Princess of Wales, who followed him to England not long after the accession. Caroline of Anspach, Princess of Wales, and later Queen to King George II, was thus the first lady in the kingdom and, fortunately for the ladies of England, kept a regal establishment.

This was the last great era of the maids-of-honour, before respectability and even sincere virtue robbed that name of its age-old jokes. 'Maids-of-honour Row', in Richmond, a line of houses built in 1723 when the Prince and Princess of Wales were making their home in the then village, still bears witness to the days of their conviviality. At the nearby baker's shop, small sweet cheese tartlets known as 'Maids-of-Honour' made a unique comment on their habits.

Bellenden, Lepel, Howe and their fellows were the liveliest bevy of girls ever to misbehave themselves in royal service. Their high spirits could not be curbed even in church:

> Bishop Burnet perceived that the beautiful dames
> Who flocked to the Chapel of hilly St James
> On their lovers alone their kind looks did bestow,
> And smiled not on him who bellowed below.

As this verse by the Earl of Peterborough tells, Burnet begged their mistress to put a stop to their preening and ogling by building up the sides of their pew:

And now Britain's nymphs in a Protestant reign
Are boxed up at prayers like the virgins of Spain.[2]

Yet still the sprightly Sophia Howe (a grand-daughter of the gallant Prince Rupert of the Rhine) could not control her giggles in the Chapel Royal. 'You could not do a worse thing,' the Duchess of St Alban's reproved her. 'I beg your Grace's pardon,' replied the saucy girl, 'I can do many worse things.' And so she could. She was seduced – if that is not too passive a word for so gleeful a participation – by the rake 'Nanty' Lowther, but died in 1726 with a 'blemished' reputation and a broken heart.

There were, of course, maids-of-honour who had happier fortunes. One was 'Plain Jane' Warburton, who had been in Queen Anne's service before the arrival of the Hanoverians. A raw country girl, newly come to Court, at a party for the Queen's birthday, when everyone was giving toasts and with her more sophisticated friends prudently raising their glasses to old men and staid *patrifamilias*, Jane ingenuously called the health of the (absent) Duke of Argyll, the idol of the Court. Told of the occurrence, and of Jane's mortification at the jeers which followed, the Duke singled her out at a ball. When his Duchess died in 1716, he asked her to marry him – so 'Plain Jane' had the last laugh.

Mary Lepel was not plain at all. When she first appeared among the ladies of the Princess of Wales, she immediately became the reigning belle. She was the protégée of old Duchess Sarah Marlborough, who had noted that 'Molly' was 'forward and pert' but who had recognized in her the qualities of a first-rate charmer. There were many hearts broken when, in 1720, she married Lord Hervey, her complement in looks:

Venus had never seen bedded
So perfect a beau and belle
As when Hervey the handsome was wedded
To the beautiful Molly Lepel.[3]

She gave him eight children, bore with his infidelities and outlived him by a quarter of a century.

> Nature took great care of her person [wrote a friend in later years], but quite forgot her mind, which had this effect, that she was of the same mind with every person she talked to. If she did not understand 'em, she still assented with a smile. ... She affected to be lively, which was expressed by a smile and opening her eyes a little wider than ordinary, which ended generally in an exclamation of some things being charming.[4]

Not many, however, saw through Molly Hervey's affectations. Even the great Voltaire was moved to verse by her:

> Hervey, would you know the passion
> You have kindled in my heart?
> Trifling is the inclination
> That by words can be expressed.
> In my silence, see the lover;
> True love is by silence known;
> In my eyes you'll best discover
> All the power of your own.[5]

She had her tribute from Alexander Pope, too. In a verse written to her fellow-maid Mary Howe (a sister of the imprudent Sophia), he voiced the maids' private grievances against such as their 'mother', the dragon Miss Meadows:

> What is prudery?
> 'Tis a beldam
> Seen with wit and beauty seldom.
> 'Tis a fear that starts at shadows.
> 'Tis – no 'tisn't – like Miss Meadows.
> 'Tis a virgin, hard of feature,
> Old and void of all good nature,
> Lean and fretful, would seem wise,
> Yet plays the fool before she dies.
> 'Tis an ugly, envious shrew
> That rails at dear Lepel and you.[6]

Mary Lepel shared the honours of the leadership of Court mirth with Mary Bellenden. In the poet Gay's words, which he imputes to Cupid:

So well I'm known at Court,
None ask where Cupid dwells
But readily resort
To Bellenden's or Lepel's.[7]

Again, there was no want of spirits in this one. A popular ballad:

Bellenden we needs must praise,
Who as down stairs she jumps,
Sings 'over the hills and far away',
Despising doleful dumps.[8]

Mary Lepel's husband described Mary Bellenden as 'incomparably the most insinuating and the most likeable woman of her time, made up of every ingredient likely to engage or attach a lover'.[9] And Horace Walpole: 'Her face and person were charming – lively she was almost to *étourderie*, and so agreeable that she was never mentioned by her contemporaries but as the most perfect creature they had ever known.'[10]

Mary Bellenden did not wait long to find her lover. It was the Prince of Wales himself. It was soon bruited about that she had become his mistress – though without any substance, for she knew the worth of virtue in the marriage-market. Nevertheless, Mary was not averse to the fame she attracted as the first Englishwoman to catch the German prince's fancy.

> But [according to Hervey], as she had to do with a man incapable of being engaged by any charm but habit, or attached to any woman but his wife – a man better pleased with the air of an intrigue than any other part of it and who did not care to pay a valuable consideration even for that – she began to find out that her situation was only having the scandal of being the Prince's mistress without the pleasure, and the confinement without the profit.[11]

Each evening Mary would have to put up with the company of the Prince, a notoriously dull man, while her friends disported themselves more gaily. One night, when the Prince sat counting out the change from his pocket for want of anything more absorbing to do, Mary flung the money on the floor and ran away.

She soon afterwards married Colonel Campbell, who later became Duke of Argyll, and left the way clear for another, more enterprising and patient woman to take her place with the Prince. This successor was one Henrietta Howard – not one of that fascinating tribe by birth but the wife of a lazy, ineffectual young Howard who found his true vocation in reaping the benefits of his wife's position at Court. The couple had been among the scavengers who had settled on Hanover in the months prior to the death of Queen Anne, in hopes of winning the favour of the future King George and gaining their recompense when he had more tangible rewards to dispense. Henrietta had even sacrificed her hair to a fashionable wig-maker to earn the fare. Caroline made her one of her Women of the Bedchamber.

In the weeks after Mary Bellenden's renunciation of her claims to be the Prince's favourite, Mrs Howard successfully took over her role, adding to it by becoming the Prince's mistress in fact. The Princess of Wales, a strong-minded, shrewd woman who was certainly a match for the wily Henrietta, showed no resentment of the arrangement, but, according to Hervey who later shared many of Caroline's confidences, 'knowing the vanity of her husband's temper, and that he must have some woman for the world to believe he lay with, wisely suffered one to remain in that situation whom she despised and had got the better of for fear of making room for a successor whom he might really love, and that might get the better of her'.[12]

Caroline had her own favourite among her ladies, one Mrs Charlotte Clayton, *née* Dyves, whose husband was a Treasury clerk and who had got her place as Woman of the Bedchamber through the extensive influence of the Duchess of Marlborough. Hervey again:

> Mrs Clayton had a head fitter for a Court than her temper, her passions being to the full as strong as her understanding, and as the one hindered her from being blind to people's

faults, the other often hindered her from seeming so. She had sense enough to perceive what black and dirty company, by living in a Court, she was forced to keep; had honour enough to despise them, and goodness enough to hate them, and not hypocrisy enough at the same time to tell them they were white and clean.

I knew her intimately, and think she had really a warm, honest, noble, generous, benevolent, friendly heart, and if she had the common weakness of letting those she wished ill to see it, she had in recompense the uncommon merit of letting those she wished well to not only see but feel it. She had so great a pleasure in doing real good that she frequently employed the interest she had at Court in favour of people who could no way repay her, and often for such as had not even solicited it; and by this conduct reversed the manners and maxims of most courtiers and politicians, as she seemed generally in the obligations she conferred to consider who wanted her than whom she wanted, a way of thinking very different from that of her master and mistress. ...[13]

Later, as Lady Sundon, she was one of the most powerful influences on Caroline, as Queen, in ecclesiastical patronage. The Prime Minister Robert Walpole loathed her but could do nothing to break her friendship with Caroline, which had strong undertones of shared religious beliefs.

Another of her enemies was Henrietta Howard, a natural enough situation, since Mrs Clayton was the favourite of the Princess and Mrs Howard that of the Prince, each jealous of the other's power and overrating it, for neither had the supreme political patronage which she craved.

Mrs Howard was more restrained in her temper than Mrs Clayton, perhaps even placid: 'She is made up of negatives,' wrote the Earl of Peterborough who admired her beauty more than her mind, 'and had not character enough to say a downright No.'[14] Part of her dignified, somewhat aloof bearing was due to the fact that she was very deaf. Everyone agreed that a woman so handsome, so civil and so astute deserved better than a man who, in Hervey's words, 'seemed to look upon a mistress rather as a necessary appurtenance to his grandeur as a prince than as an addition to his pleasures as a man, and that pretended to distinguish what it was evident he overlooked and affected to caress what it was manifest he did not love'.[15]

In this too, Caroline had the upper hand over her 'rival'. She was always able to attract her husband physically and had a very happy domestic life with him. With her lay the real power over the Prince, so that though many at first courted Mrs Howard for favours from her supposed lover, she 'never had power enough to do good to those to whom she wished well, though, by working on the susceptible passions of him whom she often endeavoured to irritate, she had just influence enough, by watching her opportunity, to distress those sometimes to whom she wished ill'.[16]

It was not until 1728 that Mr Howard became too greedy for his own good. He had been living apart from his wife for some time, though he certainly had a share in her perquisites, but in that year he chose to make a claim at law for restoration of his conjugal rights. But he overplayed his hand. When Henrietta refused to return to him, he took out a warrant to seize her on sight. For weeks the hounded woman remained in the Palace, not daring to set foot out of doors. Caroline, aware of the danger of her husband's losing his mistress, took pity on her and drove out with her in her own carriage for an airing. Inevitably, Howard was lurking outside the Palace. He actually dared to wrench open the door of the royal carriage, but before he could lay hands on his wife, Caroline had treated him to a display of *majesté* which daunted even his *insouciance.*

In the end, George II agreed to pay Howard £1,200 *per annum* during the lifetime of his brother the Earl of Suffolk. That lifetime was not of long duration: it was as Lady Suffolk and Mistress of the Queen's Robes from 1731, as well as mistress of the King, that Henrietta swanned through much of the reign.

By 1734, however, George had really tired of her. Lady Suffolk had made herself too well-known for her friendships with the politicians Bolingbroke and Pulteney, and with the poet Pope, none of them to the taste of the King, to retain his passive attachment to her. When he heard that she had been perpetually with Bolingbroke during the six weeks she had spent at Bath that summer, he was furious.

Henrietta felt it necessary to go to Caroline to resign her official post. Hervey was very curious as to what had passed between the two women. Had Lady Suffolk said to the Queen that, as her husband had tired of her, she could no longer serve her? After all, the Queen and her lady had never been enemies. Once there had been a few hasty words, when Henrietta had rebelled at a menial task in the Queen's *levée*; but Caroline, telling her story to Hervey, said that 'I made her no answer in anger, but calmly, as I would to a naughty child.'[17] Later, Henrietta had given in. Apart from that small incident, each had retained a remarkable dignity in her difficult situation.

Now Caroline remonstrated that there was no need for Lady Suffolk to leave her service. But for once Henrietta knew her own mind.

Fortunately for Queen Caroline, none of George's several mistresses after the fall of Henrietta Howard proved in any way a rival to herself, either in power or in physical attraction to the King. And when, on her deathbed in 1737, she begged her husband to marry again, he sobbed out: 'No, I shall have mistresses.' It was a remarkable tribute to her.

Not long after the Queen's death, the King brought over from Hanover one Amelia von Walmoden, who had given him pleasure during several of his visits to Germany. He created her Countess of Yarmouth. But this did not stop his looking elsewhere for a little occasional dalliance. At the age of sixty-seven, his fancy was taken by the teenaged Elizabeth Chudleigh, a maid-of-honour to his daughter-in-law, Augusta, Princess of Wales.

Elizabeth was outrageous, far more daring than ever Sophia Howe had been. She appeared at a Court masquerade dressed as Iphigenia – perhaps 'dressed' is the wrong word, for all that she wore was a thin robe of flesh-coloured silk which hid very little of the real flesh. As Elizabeth made her appearance, everyone gasped. The quick-witted Princess of Wales threw her veil over the girl, but not quickly enough for the whole Court to have had an impression of complete nudity. (A few years later, Elizabeth Chudleigh became the mistress, then secretly the wife, of one of Mary Lepel's sons. Subsequently she became the mistress of the Duke of Kingston, denied having married Hervey and married her lover; several years later, she was charged with bigamy, found guilty and fined heavily – escaping corporal punishment only by her rank as a peeress.)

George II's heir, Frederick Lewis, Prince of Wales, showed the usual family propensities from his youth. He had found, in Walpole's words, 'a maid-of-honour who was willing to cease to be so – at the first opportunity'.[18] She was Anne Vane, a clever young woman who managed to be the mistress of both the Prince of Wales and Lord Hervey, Mary's husband, without each other's knowledge, for some time. That situation could not go on indefinitely, of course, since Hervey was a great friend of the Prince's. There were triangular quarrels which resulted in Hervey's temporary withdrawal, and for a time Anne devoted herself entirely to Frederick. She gave him a child, named Cornwell fitzFrederick, and lived in some style in a house in Soho Square which her lover had provided. Hervey was full of resentment against Anne for having caused a breach between himself and the Prince. At one point he threatened to tell Frederick the whole unsavoury story of Anne's past, but Anne turned the tables on him by revealing his perfidy to the Prince. Later, however, Anne and Hervey were reconciled. Their relationship continued to have the ups and downs inevitable to their wayward temperaments, but it proved quite permanent.

Frederick decided to break with Anne in 1735. Ostensibly he did so because he was planning to marry; more probably, it was because he had become infatuated with another woman, Lady Archibald Hamilton. Anne was furious. Encouraged by Hervey, who still bore a grudge against the Prince, she published what she claimed to be Frederick's terms for ending their liaison; she claimed that he had offered her a pension in return for her going abroad and leaving her son in his care. In fact, Frederick had been far more generous and had made no such stipulations. The whole business became public. There were lampoons on 'Vanella' which were unpleasant to all concerned. In the end, she retired gracefully to Bath and died within the year.

When Frederick took a wife, the Princess Augusta of Saxe-Gotha, he insisted that his new love, Lady Archibald Hamilton, should figure among her ladies-in-waiting. His mother would not allow it, and it was only after Augusta had been in England some time, that she herself obtained permission from the King to employ the lady, who had made herself very agreeable to the Princess. Lady Archibald became the Princess's Lady of the Bedchamber, Keeper of the Privy Purse and Mistress of the Robes at the generous salary of £900 *per annum*. She was middle-aged, having been married very young to an old husband and given him ten children. A good deal of scandal had been attached to her name but she behaved in an exemplary manner to Augusta and never importuned and annoyed Frederick as Anne Vane had.

In true Hanoverian fashion, there was constant friction between George II and his son and daughter-in-law, on both political and domestic issues. But the Prince of Wales, 'Poor Fred', predeceased his father, leaving his eldest son, another George, to become King. Princess Augusta's tutelage of her son, when he became King in 1760, was conducted largely with the help of her confidant and supposed lover, Lord Bute. This gave Elizabeth Chudleigh, then still a maid-of-honour, though she was secretly the wife of Hervey, the opportunity to speak the famous line: '*Votre Altesse Royale sait que chacune a son Bute.*'[19] Not even the witty Catherine Sedley had made so apposite a pun.

While Caroline of Anspach was still Princess of Wales, the poet Alexander Pope one day sat down and wrote a letter to a friend which gives a splendid picture of the lives of her ladies-in-waiting:

I met the Prince, with all his ladies on horseback, coming

> from hunting. Mrs [Mistress] Bellenden and Mrs Lepel took me under their protection. We all agreed that the life of a maid-of-honour was of all things the most miserable, and wished that every woman who envied it had a specimen of it. To eat Westphalian ham in a morning, ride over hedges and ditches on borrowed hacks, come home in the heat of the day with a fever and (what is a hundred times worse) with a red mark on the forehead from an uneasy hat; all this may qualify them to make excellent wives for fox-hunters, and bear abundance of ruddy-complexioned children. As soon as they can wipe off the heat of the day, they must simper for an hour and catch cold in the Princess's apartments, from thence to dinner with what appetite they may, and after that, walk, work or think, which they please.[20]

The name 'ladies-in-waiting' had always meant both waiting on and waiting for a royal mistress. The perpetual sitting around expecting a call for service was one of the trials the ladies bemoaned even to the beginning of this century; the actual service, however, was diminishing.

When Caroline of Anspach arrived in England there was some doubt as to the duties which her ladies should perform and the etiquette which should govern them. It fell to Mrs Howard to write to that favoured servant of Queen Anne, Lady Masham, to elicit from her the customs of the last reign. Lady Masham was detailed in her reply:

> When the Queen washed her hands, the page of the back-stairs brought and set down on a side table the basin and ewer; then the Bedchamber Woman set it before the Queen, and knelt on the other side of the table over-against the Queen, the Bedchamber Lady only looking on. The Bedchamber Woman poured the water out of the ewer upon the Queen's hands.
>
> The Bedchamber Woman pulled on the Queen's gloves, when she could not do it herself.
>
> The page of the back-stairs was called in to put on the Queen's shoes.

When the Queen dined in public, the page reached the glass to the Bedchamber Woman and she to the lady-in-waiting.

The Bedchamber Woman brought the chocolate [to drink] and gave it without kneeling.[21]

If this etiquette seems elaborate, how much more so was that in the household of the French Queen. Since the days of Louis XIV, the Palace of Versailles had been governed by a thousand finicking rules of etiquette. When Louis XVI came to the throne, his impatient, unconventional wife Marie Antoinette had still to bear with many age-old customs which were as tiresome to her as they were to her ladies. Madame Campan, one of her Ladies of the Bedchamber, recalled in later years:

[Her] toilette was a masterpiece of etiquette; everything done on the occasion was in a prescribed form. Both the lady of honour and the tire-woman usually attended and officiated, assisted by the first *femme de chambre* and two inferior attendants. The tire-woman put on the petticoat and handed the gown to the Queen. The lady of honour poured out the water for her hands and put on her body linen. When a princess of the royal family happened to be present, while the Queen was dressing, the lady of honour yielded to her the latter act of dressing, but still did not yield it directly to the Princess of the Blood; in such a case, the lady of honour was accustomed to present the linen to the chief lady-in-waiting who, in her turn, handed it to the Princess of the Blood. Each of these ladies observed these rules scrupulously, as affecting her rights.

One winter's day, it happened that the Queen, who was entirely undressed, was just going to put on her body linen; I held it ready unfolded for her; the lady of honour came in, slipped off her gloves and took it. A rustling was heard at the door – it was opened, and in came the Duchess of Orleans; she took off her gloves and came forward to take the garment; but as it would have been wrong in the lady of honour to hand it to her, she gave it to me, and I handed it to the Princess. A further noise: it was the Countess of Provence [the Queen's sister-in-law]; the Duchess of Orleans handed her the linen.

All this while, the Queen kept her arms crossed upon her bosom, and appeared to feel cold. Madame observed her uncomfortable situation and, merely laying down her handkerchief, without taking off her gloves, she put on the linen, and in doing so, knocked the Queen's cap off. The Queen laughed to conceal her impatience, but not until she had muttered several times: 'How disagreeable! How tiresome!'

All this etiquette, however inconvenient, was suitable to the royal dignity, which expects to find servants in all classes of persons, beginning even with the brothers and sisters of the monarch.[22]

The ladies-in-waiting at the Court of England had never been so tried, nor indeed had ladies of the highest rank ever had to perform tasks so menial. Nevertheless, until the middle of the eighteenth century, it was still common for peeresses and their daughters to find themselves performing for a queen those tasks which in private life were allotted to ordinary serving-girls.

When the young bride of George III, Charlotte of Mecklenburg-Strelitz, arrived in England, application was made to Lady Suffolk to supply details of the ladies-in-waiting's duties (such as she had once solicited of Lady Masham). Women of the Bedchamber were no longer required to assist at the Queen's toilette, as they had in the days of Queen Anne; their duties now devolved on a 'wardrobe woman' and on the two German dressers whom Charlotte brought with her from her home. The Bedchamber Woman would be summoned only to tie on the Queen's necklace, to hand her her fan and gloves and to carry her train as far as the ante-room where the higher-ranking Lady of the Bechamber would take the train, to proceed into the public gaze.

An invaluable picture of Court life is provided by Fanny Burney, who served Queen Charlotte as her dresser in the 1780s. A commoner, with no pretensions to grandeur, she carried out the duties which a century or less before would have been the task of peeresses. In 1786 Fanny Burney wrote:

> I rise at six o'clock, dress in a morning gown and cap, and wait my first summons, which is at all times from seven to near eight, but commonly in the exact half hour between them.
>
> The Queen never sends for me till her hair is dressed. This, in a morning, is always done by her wardrobe woman, Mrs Thielky, a German, but who speaks English perfectly well.
>
> Mrs Schwellenberg [the senior 'dresser'], since the first week, has never come down in the morning at all. The Queen's dress is finished by Mrs Thielky and myself. No maid ever enters the room while the Queen is in it. Mrs Thielky hands the things to me, and I put them on. 'Tis fortunate for me I have not the handing of them! I should never know which to take first, embarrassed as I am, and should run the prodigious risk of giving the gown before the hoop, and the fan before the neckerchief.
>
> By eight o'clock, or a little after, for she is extremely expeditious, she is dressed. She then goes out to join the King, and to be joined by the Princesses, and they all proceed to the King's chapel in the Castle, to prayers, attended by the governesses of the Princesses, and the King's equerry. Various others at times attend; but only these indispensably.
>
> I then return to my own room to breakfast. I make this meal the most pleasant part of the day; I have a book for my companion, and I allow myself an hour for it. ...
>
> At nine o'clock, I send off my breakfast things and relinquish my book, to make a serious and steady examination of everything I have upon my hands in the way of business – in which preparations for dress are always included, not for the present day alone but for the Court days, which require a particular dress. ...
>
> That over, I have my time at my disposal till a quarter before twelve, except on Wednesdays and Saturdays, when I

have it only to a quarter before eleven . . . The hour advanced on Wednesdays and Saturdays is for curling and craping the hair, which it now requires twice a week.

A quarter before one is the usual time for the Queen to begin dressing for the day. Mrs Schwellenberg then constantly attends; so do I and Mrs Thielky, of course, at all times. We help her off with her gown, and on with her powdering things, and then the hairdresser is admitted. She generally reads the newspapers during that operation.

When she observes that I have run to her but half dressed, she constantly gives me leave to return and finish as soon as she is seated. ... I find her then always removed to her state dressing-room, if any room in this private mansion [Queen's Lodge, Windsor] can have the epithet of state. There, in a very short time, her dress is finished. She then says she won't detain me, and I hear and see no more of her till bedtime. It is commonly three o'clock when I am thus set at large. ...

Between eleven and twelve my last summons usually takes place, earlier and later occasionally. Twenty minutes is the customary time then spent with the Queen: half an hour, I believe, is seldom exceeded.

I then come back, and after doing whatever I can to forward my dress for the next morning, I go to bed – and to sleep, too, believe me. ...[23]

For all that the English etiquette in no way approached that of France in rigour, vestiges of the old manners remained when Fanny Burney arrived at Court. She wrote to her sister Esther in December 1785:

You would never believe – you, who, distant from Courts and courtiers, know nothing of their ways – the many things to be studied, for appearing with a proper propriety before crowned heads. Heads without crowns are quite other sort of rotundas.

Now, then, to the etiquette. I enquired into every particular, that no error might be committed. And as there is no saying what may happen in this mortal life, I shall give you those instructions I have received myself, that, should you find yourself in the royal presence, you may know how to comport yourself. ...

In the first place, you must not cough. If you find a cough tickling in your throat, you must arrest it from making any sound; if you find yourself choking with the forbearance, you must choke – but not cough.

In the second place, you must not sneeze. If you have a vehement cold, you must take no notice of it; if your nose membranes feel a great irritation, you must hold your breath; if a sneeze still insists upon making its way, you must oppose it, by keeping your teeth grinding together; if the violence of the repulse breaks some blood-vessel, you must break the blood-vessel – but not sneeze.

In the third place, you must not, upon any account, stir either hand or foot. If, by any chance, a black pin [in a lace cap] runs through your head, you must not take it out. If the pain is very great, you must be sure to bear it without wincing; if it brings tears into your eyes, you must not wipe them off; if they give you a tingling by running down your cheeks, you must look as if nothing was the matter. If the blood should gush from your head by means of the black pin, you must let it gush; if you are uneasy to think of making such a blurred appearance, you must be uneasy, but you must say nothing about it. If, however, the agony is very great, you may, privately, bite the inside of your cheek, or of your lips, for a little relief; taking care, meanwhile, to do it so cautiously as to make no apparent dent outwardly. And, with that precaution, if you even gnaw a piece out, it will not be minded, only be sure either to swallow it, or commit it to a corner of the inside of your mouth till they are gone – for you must not spit.[24]

As her term of service continued, Fanny Burney made other discoveries in etiquette; for example, one must leave the presence of the King by walking backwards to the door. On one occasion, on a visit to an Oxford college, the Queen left the room, leaving the King to talk to a professor. Those of her ladies who stood near the door had no difficulty in following her, but one of them, Lady Charlotte Bury, was far from the door, near the King. Fanny recorded the scene:

> She therefore faced the King, and began a march backwards – her ankle already sprained, and to walk forward and even leaning upon an arm was painful to her: nevertheless, back she went, perfectly upright, without one stumble, without even looking once behind to see what she might encounter; and with as graceful a motion, and as easy an air as I ever saw anybody enter a long room, she retreated, I am sure, full twenty yards backwards out of one.[25]

Such was the discipline gained through years at Court.

Later, the members of the royal household were lined up in their ranks facing the 'royal collationers' at their state meal at Christ Church. Fanny wrote to her sister Susan:

> It was agreed that we must all be absolutely famished unless we could partake of some refreshment, as we had breakfasted early, and had no chance of dining before six or seven o'clock. A whisper was soon buzzed through the semi-circle, of the deplorable state of our appetite apprehensions, and presently it reached the ears of some of the worthy Doctors. Immediately a new whisper was circulated, which made its progress with great vivacity, to offer us whatever we would wish, and to beg us to name what we chose. . . .
>
> The method of producing, and the means of swallowing them, were much more difficult to settle than the choice of what was acceptable. Major Price and Colonel Fairly, however, seeing a very large table close to the wainscot behind us, desired our refreshments might be privately conveyed there, behind the semi-circle, and that, while all the group backed very near it, one at a time might feed, screened by all the rest from observation.
>
> I suppose I need not inform you, my dear Susan, that to

eat in presence of any of the royal family is as much *hors d'usage* as to be seated.[26]

The Queen whom Fanny Burney served, and whom she came so much to admire, was the wife of George III. Charlotte of Mecklenburg-Strelitz was one of the most well-conducted of English queens, never involved in personal scandal, never meddling in politics, the mother of a large family, perhaps more at home with the few middle-class women who came her way than with the great aristocrats. There was no trace in her of the *hauteur*, frivolity and political intrigue which made her contemporary the French Queen Marie Antoinette so hated.

Charlotte arrived in England an unformed girl, very much in awe of her bridegroom, who was not much older than herself, and of his mother, who still had a good deal of power over him. It had been stipulated that she was to bring only two German ladies with her, but in the end the English envoy allowed Charlotte to travel from her home with four ladies-in-waiting (trusted servants of her mother) and two *femmes de chambre*, Juliana Schwellenberg and Johanna Hagerdorn, both aged about thirty, who were destined to spend the rest of their life in Charlotte's service.

Her English ladies were the choice of her mother-in-law. There were six Ladies of the Bedchamber, six Women of the Bedchamber and six maids-of-honour, each to be in waiting two months in the year. At their head was Mary Bertie, Duchess of Ancaster, as Mistress of the Robes. The Duchess of Ancester and her immediate junior, the Dowager Duchess of Hamilton, were sent to meet the new Queen, with one woman of the Bedchamber, Catherine Dashwood, who was, in effect, the 'mother of the maids' according to old usage. The English envoy, Graeme, warned Charlotte not to become too fond of her English ladies, advising her that that would only lead to suspicions of favouritism, and consequently jealousy and back-biting in her Court.

Fortunately, Charlotte was extremely docile, even submitting to an almost unbearable isolation imposed by her husband, who feared that her youth would make her a prey to unscrupulous manipulators. Thus, it was 'Mrs' Schwellenberg, the German dresser who never aspired to political influence and whom no great lady could see as a real threat to her dignity, who was closest to the Queen, especially in her friendless early years. Only once did she interfere in the affairs of the royal family: when George III was taken ill in 1765, and his mother tried to hide the seriousness of his condition from Charlotte, Mrs Schwellenberg protested that her mistress was making herself ill with worry and uncertainty. On his recovery, the King threatened to send her home if she made any more trouble.

As with most strong characters, Mrs Schwellenberg managed to make herself something of a personage at Court. She was mildly eccentric and had a nasty temper when crossed, but she had a deep well of generosity. Fanny Burney might complain bitterly that Mrs Schwellenberg insisted on driving with her carriage windows wide open in winter weather, but she also appreciated her senior's unwarranted generosity in bestowing on her a sedan chair which had come to her as a bequest, in 1788.

Inevitably, she was the butt of many jokes. There were the more serious sort, such as political lampoons and cartoons which attributed to her more power than she had; there were family jibes at the woman who was forever at the Queen's elbow: 'Hold your potato jaw, my dear,' roared Charlotte's son William at the garrulous German woman, when he was in his cups; even the gentle Fanny Burney could laugh when her own brother made a ridiculous poem about Mrs Schwellenberg. It was written on the occasion of Fanny's sending a copy of a play she had written (she was the popular author of the novels *Evelina* and *Camilla*) to the Queen through Mrs Schwellenberg, and part of it ran:

> To the Queen's House I went, when I'd powder'd my hair,
>   and put on my very best coat;
> That coat, which so oft made the Bath Belles declare
> That I look'd like a person of note!
> High ho! the dear Schwell – 'twas for sweet little Schwell!

– With a nod and a smirk,
To her damsel – By Jove, a fine creature!
Like Schwelly, a piece of Dame Nature's best work, and as
soft in her voice, air and feature –
High ho![27]

But never, surely, was so harmless a woman in such a position of trust.

The staid, respectable Court which George III and his wife created was in stark contrast to the ramshackle establishment, overcrowded with rakes and fading belles, kept by their eldest son and heir. The Prince of Wales, from his youth, determined to follow a life of hedonism as shocking to his parents as was his political opposition. He was already in his thirties before he could be induced to marry, and then the bride chosen for him was disastrous. She was his cousin Caroline of Brunswick-Wolfenbuttel, a hoydenish girl with only a high colour and sprightly movements to give her any appearance of charm, and whose uncontrolled vulgarity appalled the Prince, accustomed as he was to the ultra-sophistication of his mistresses. (Needless to say, he was no prize himself.)

The death-blow to the marriage was dealt even before the wedding: the Prince obtained his father's permission to appoint his current mistress, Frances Villiers, Lady Jersey, as first lady to his bride. This was no unique situation, of course: the case of Catherine of Braganza and Barbara Villiers is partly a parallel; but only partly, for Lady Jersey was a middle-aged woman, Caroline a mentally, if not physically, immature seventeen, powerless against her. Charles II shielded his wife against his mistress's vanity; George, Prince of Wales, supported it.

When Caroline landed at Greenwich on Easter Sunday 1795, Lady Jersey was not there to meet her, as had been arranged. Arriving impertinently late, she took one look at the Princess, in her plain travelling gown, exclaimed in horror and set about tricking her out in the height of fashionable Court dress. What charms Caroline had (once she had had a thorough wash, at the request of the English envoy to Brunswick) lay in her youth and freshness; the formal Court dress reduced her to nothing more than a stiff doll.

Even before the entourage had left Greenwich, Lady Jersey had made her attitude to Caroline obvious. She refused to take a backward-facing seat in the Princess's carriage, insisting on sharing the forward seat with Caroline. Here Lord Malmesbury, who had brought Caroline over to England, drew the line. He remarked acidly that surely Lady Jersey had known when she accepted her post as Lady of the Princess's Bedchamber that she would have to take the inferior seat. He suggested that she might prefer to travel in another carriage, where she might face forwards in comfort, rather than be sick facing backwards. This was not to her taste either, for she would then lose time on her campaign of thoroughly demoralizing Caroline before she even saw her bridegroom. Lady Jersey took her seat.

That night George and Caroline met for the first time. Many, perhaps even most, arranged marriages in royal families began with goodwill on either side; this one was damned from the first moment of the couple's meeting. George looked at Caroline and staggered away, calling for brandy. After the wedding (on honeymoon with Lady Jersey in attendance), the Prince and Princess shared a bed for the first two or three weeks – sufficient time, as it proved, for Caroline to conceive – and then separated by mutual consent.

Those ladies who had taken service with the Princess of Wales expecting to have a good share in the brilliant frivolities at the Prince's Carlton House and in the more formal entertainments of the King and Queen's establishment, were destined to disappointment. Not long after her marriage, Caroline set up a household separate from that of her husband, and, though she managed to enjoy herself in her own way, her backwater existence was no temptation to ambitious ladies-in-waiting.

In all the years that followed, as the scandals attached to Caroline's name increased, leaving all Europe gasping at her indiscretions, there were, nevertheless, virtuous ladies who were willing to swear that the Princess was as pure as the driven snow. Lady Charlotte Bury, no prude but certainly no libertine, bemoaned her mistress's follies but admired her fortitude in the face of united hostility in the royal family; Lady Charlotte Lindsay, who was with the Princess during that Continental tour when a certain Italian 'courier', Bergami, was very 'close' to Caroline, always asserted that the Princess had never misconducted herself. But then, there is so much contradictory evidence about Caroline that, though the ladies may have believed firmly in their own impressions of her, they could as well have been mistaken.

The child of the ill-fated marriage, another Charlotte, stood, from the moment of her birth, as second in line to the throne, eventual Heiress Presumptive. Once she had passed through her childhood perplexity at the appalling relationship between her parents, and having realized the loneliness of her situation as the only (legitimate) child in a family of ancient grandparents and middle-aged, waspish aunts and uncles, Charlotte proved the typical product of a broken marriage. She inclined to her mother, though she found time and again that she could not rely on either Caroline's word or her disinterested affection; her father, who had little interest in her as a child, she resented for his power over her. In herself, she had a great fund of cheerfulness, shrewdness if not intellectual intelligence and a tendency to enter passionate friendships with anyone who would give her a little affection.

The Princess's main governess was herself a product of the *mores* of the Court: Lady George Murray, a bride at sixteen, the mother of ten children, a widow at thirty, had already attended two of George III's daughters (themselves no saints in their youth) before she came to Charlotte. But when she retired, in 1812, the teenaged Princess felt herself beyond further tutelage. She demanded from her father her own ladies-in-waiting instead. Inevitably she was refused, but George allowed that the former position of 'under-governesses' might be retitled 'lady companions'. One of Charlotte's main aims was to have with her her friend Margaret Mercer Elphinstone, some years her senior, to whom she had been devoted for many years. Miss Elphinstone generally gave Charlotte good advice, but she was mistaken when she presumed that the fact that Charlotte was seventeen years old in January 1813 would warrant her some degree of freedom.

In July 1814, Charlotte at last began to rebel seriously. She had no love for the Prince of Orange to whom her father had engaged her, dreaded the prospect of living with him abroad and could rely only on her own wits to find release from such an intolerable situation. But she made the mistake of running to her mother and had to be forced to return home. The Prince of Wales (by then Regent for the supposedly mad George III) allowed Charlotte to break her engagement (though with many remonstrances) but put her under close restraint in the country. And when a new marriage was arranged, this time more to her taste, with Prince Leopold of Saxe-Coburg-Saalfeld, Charlotte's father insisted on choosing her new ladies for her.

In 1812, Charlotte had written to her friend Margaret: 'You have *everything requisite* for *anything* and *everything* you undertake. ... *You are mine then*, dearest M, from this moment, from your own words. *Remember you are* and that I shall lose no time to *claim* the *prize* from your hands when I have gained the victory.'[28] That victory, comparative freedom in marriage, and the power to claim the 'prize' of her friend's company as her lady-in-waiting, came in 1816, but by then there was already a breach between the two. Margaret had fallen in love with a Frenchman, Charles de Flahault, the illegitimate son of the great Talleyrand and the former lover of Napoleon's stepdaughter Hortense; while Charlotte mistrusted him as a libertine, her husband, Prince Leopold (who had fought the French in the recent wars), loathed him as a Bonapartist.

Princess Charlotte died in childbirth in November 1817, leaving her heirship to the throne to a series of elderly uncles and aunts, who between them had produced no legitimate offspring to stand in the line of succession. There followed a spate of royal marriages as the brothers of the Prince Regent sought to establish the claim to the throne of their own blood-line.

In 1820 George III died (two years after his wife), and for ten years England had a King (George IV) but no Queen Consort.

Having played out her tragi-comedy, having been refused admittance to her husband's coronation and any honours as rightful Queen, Caroline of Brunswick died in 1821.

George IV never remarried and so, at his death in 1830, it was his brother William who became King. William, as Duke of Clarence, had been one of the royal brothers who raced in so undignified a manner to the altar in 1818. But for all the haphazard nature of his choice of a bride (he had been refused by several English ladies, including Margaret Mercer Elphinstone, now Comtesse de Flahault), he had won a great prize. His bride, Adelaide of Saxe-Meiningen, had been neither young nor beautiful when she arrived in England to meet William, and to marry him swiftly. Nor was she able to produce children strong enough to survive infancy. But she had a great store of dignity and patience – sufficient even to allow her to take to her heart her husband's large brood of children by his late actress mistress. Only their rumbustious presence could diminish the innate respectability of the Queen's Court.

Adelaide was mistrusted deeply in the country, as the supposed inciter of the King to stand firmly against Parliamentary reform (she even had nightmares in which she figured as a latter-day Marie Antoinette at the guillotine). But those who knew Adelaide warmly appreciated her quiet qualities and her successful reformation of her husband, a former sailor with all the vices that profession implied in that age, into a cheerful, sober, courteous old gentleman. Her choice of ladies may not have been orthodox (one of them was the American-born Marianne, Lady Wellesley, formerly a sister-in-law of Jerome Bonaparte; another Lady Bedingfeld, a devout Catholic – at a time when memories of the 1812 war with America and the Napoleonic wars were still ripe, and when there was raging controversy over the 'emancipation' of Catholics), but Queen Adelaide could have had a no more dutiful and well-behaved set of friends about her.

At long last, there were no more 'maids-of-dishonour', eager to use their position to gain access to a susceptible king, no ladies-in-waiting anxious to win a share of political power or patronage. Both Queen Charlotte and Queen Adelaide had set the tone for a well-conducted Court, and passed on to Victoria, whose very name has become a by-word for respectability, traditions which allowed mothers to send their daughters, and husbands their wives, to Court without fear of their corruption.

9

TOWARDS the end of the second year of Queen Victoria's reign, a scandal in the royal household, involving the ladies-in-waiting, led indirectly to a crisis in politics and the constitution. What started as a purely domestic matter, built on feuds and intrigues, culminated in a national furore damaging to the Crown. The 'Bedchamber Crisis', as this episode was named, arose basically from the Queen's refusal to part with her Whig ladies-in-waiting when the Whig party fell from power in Parliament, but it was bound up with the publicity given to the part played by the Queen's ladies in a tragic drama within the household, with one Lady Flora Hastings as their victim.

The whole affair had its origins in the recent past. As a child, Victoria was brought up by her mother the Duchess of Kent. At Kensington Palace, Victoire of Kent, the German-born widow of George III's fourth son, Edward, Duke of Kent, kept her child secluded from the influence of other members of the royal family. Ostensibly, she refused to have her daughter sullied by the rakes and *mondaines* of George IV's Court or to have her associated with the unpopular political policies of William IV, both kings being the girl's uncles. On closer inspection, however, it becomes apparent that the Duchess was afraid that the young

Victoria would become attached to her royal uncles and aunts to the detriment of her own authority over her.

In this the Duchess of Kent was prompted and abetted by the Comptroller of her Household, Sir John Conroy. He had been an *aide-de-camp* to the late Duke and had proved himself the paramount influence over the Duchess in the 1820s, the first years of her widowhood. Ambitious on his own account and relying on his position for further advancement when the young Victoria should inherit the crown, Conroy used every means in his power to maintain the estrangement between the Kents and the royal family. Only thus could he hope to retain his hold over the Duchess and her daughter.

It has frequently been asserted that Conroy was the Duchess of Kent's lover. This was not so. There was a strong attraction between them and, indeed, the child Victoria once witnessed an embrace, but the Duchess was too firmly religious to allow herself to enter an adulterous relationship with Conroy (whose wife, in any case, was an *habituée* of her household). At the same time, both would realize how dangerous the discovery of such a relationship could be to their plans. William IV, only too eager to adopt his niece, would certainly not have scrupled to use any hint of her mother's unfitness to care for her to have Victoria removed from her charge. The Duchess never gave him that chance. Nevertheless, Conroy's power over Victoire of Kent was complete and extremely damaging to her long-term relations with her daughter.

From early childhood, Princess Victoria hated Conroy. She realized she owed the whole 'Kensington system' which kept her isolated and lonely, to his intriguing. When she entered her teens and Conroy stepped up his pressure to make her acknowledge his sway, she made the firm resolve never to give in. Right up to the days before her accession to the throne, at the age of eighteen, in 1837, she had to withstand his threats and tricks to make her agree either to a regency on her behalf operated nominally by her mother but really by himself, or to his becoming her private secretary with all the opportunities for influence which that post entailed.

Victoria's one staunch friend in these trying years was her governess Baroness Lehzen. At first Conroy had tolerated her, reckoning that, as a German, dependent for her place on the goodwill of the Duchess, she was powerless to oppose him. Later, he found out his mistake. Lehzen never openly opposed the Duchess and her 'adviser', but she did everything in her power to aid her charge to stand out against them. And the fact that she enjoyed a good measure of William IV's favour rendered her safe from dismissal by the Duchess.

Conroy and his dupe Victoire of Kent had few allies. They included the Duchess's brother-in-law the Duke of Sussex and her sister-in-law the Princess Sophia (another victim of Conroy, though a willing one, who financed him for many years). In 1831 they brought into the Kensington enclave Lady Flora Hastings, a young woman in her twenties who was to become the Duchess's lady-in-waiting and supposedly a companion to Princess Victoria to counter-balance her total reliance on Lehzen. But by making plain her allegiance to the Duchess and by her siding with Conroy in taunting Lehzen, Lady Flora earned the thorough dislike of the Princess.

When Victoria at last became Queen, she determined to pay Conroy for all his threats and torments. She accorded him scarcely even the most common courtesy in the first days of her reign and, after moving into Buckingham Palace, gave orders that he was never to be admitted to her apartments. The Duchess, who sincerely loved Victoria and who had always believed that Conroy's plans for her were for her own good, was accorded similarly cold treatment. She would appear at Victoria's dining-table and in her drawing-room of an evening, but the Queen refused to give her mother her confidence in any personal or political matter. And she merely tolerated the presence of Lady Flora, whom she had long since recognized as one of Conroy's pawns.

The Queen's ladies followed her lead. They avoided Sir John Conroy and his family, who haunted the Court, and were wary of Lady Flora. 'Scotty' as they called her from her origins, was by now in her early thirties, sophisticated and aloof from the common round of the maids-of-honour's cosy society, and held rather in awe by them as a published poet in her own right. Her fellows offered no confidences to her, and though they were always in and out of each others' rooms, they shunned hers: 'we never think of going to her rooms,' wrote one of the maids-of-honour, 'she does not wish it, and I should be afraid of meeting *Sir John* who is there a good deal'.[1] Lady Flora also made herself unpopular by continuing those jibes at Lehzen at which she and Sir John had become so adept in recent years. But nothing she could say could hurt the former governess now. If Lord Melbourne became to the young Queen the father-figure which Conroy had intended to be, so Lehzen was now her substitute mother, one whom Victoria could trust more than her own weak, misguided mother who was still in Conroy's power. And Lehzen was so popular with the ladies of the new Court that the slights cast at her by Sir John Conroy and Lady Flora Hastings only increased their estrangement from the Queen's staff.

In January 1839, when she had been on the throne only a year and a half, Victoria believed that she had discovered her enemy Conroy's paramount infamy. Lady Flora appeared to be in an advancing state of pregnancy. With Lehzen, and with her senior ladies-in-waiting, Lady Tavistock and Lady Portman, Queen Victoria went over the shreds of evidence which she had against Conroy and Lady Flora Hastings. The latter had always been an ally in Conroy's plans, they were much in each other's company in the Duchess's isolated apartments, and, the final charge, when Lady Flora had returned to Court from a holiday at home in Scotland recently, she had travelled *alone* in a coach with Conroy, sure evidence of improper familiarity. Thus Victoria, from the witness of Lady Flora's expanding waist-line, presumed that she had become pregnant by 'that monster and demon incarnate'.[2]

In fact, Lady Flora had been feeling unwell ever since her return to London, and was consulting Sir James Clark, the royal physician, twice a week. But when he was canvassed by Lord Melbourne on behalf of the Queen and her ladies, he could give no certain opinion as to the cause of Lady Flora's pains and increasing girth – after all, propriety demanded that he examine a lady over her dress, petticoats and corset, not without them.

From this point, motives become confused and dubious. It is certain that the ladies of the Queen's household were genuinely shocked by the whole affair; on the other hand, by throwing such discredit on the Duchess of Kent's household, Victoria had an almost certain lever to oust Conroy once and for all.

Lady Portman now took the initiative, demanding of Sir James Clark that he tell Lady Flora of everyone's suspicions and insist on a thorough examination. Clark was not ignorant of the under-currents of antagonism in the Palace; he thoroughly understood the implications of what was asked of him. Accordingly, he confronted Lady Flora, suggesting discreetly that perhaps she was secretly married. At first she did not understand; when she did, she was horrified. 'He became excited,' she later wrote, 'urged me to "confess" as the only thing to save me – stated his own conviction to agree with that of the "ladies", that it had occurred to him at first that "no one could look at me and doubt it", and remarks even more coarse.'[3]

Sir James reported to Lady Portman, Lady Portman to the Queen. The result was that Victoria refused Lady Flora admittance to the Court until she was proved innocent. Apart from the personal aspects of the case, Victoria had no wish to have her Court branded as loose in its morals as had been that of her notoriously profligate uncle George IV.

It was only now that the Duchess of Kent was told what had been going on. In her refusal to credit the charges against her lady-in-waiting and in her staunch championship of Lady Flora then and in the following, trying months lies yet more proof that the Duchess was not Conroy's mistress: in such a case, surely seeds of doubt would have been sown in her mind, and jealousy, born of suspicion, would have clouded her relationship with her two closest friends. But it was not the case; Victoire never swerved from her loyalty to Lady Flora and invariably backed her in her denials of her pregnancy.

Only Lady Flora and those few willing to credit her word believed that the reputed signs of pregnancy were false. What no one, even the poor lady herself, could know at that time was that she was suffering from a tumour on her liver which was making her body protrude as in pregnancy. The examination to which she finally submitted, performed by Sir James Clark and Sir Charles Clarke, in the presence of Lady Portman, should have ended the affair.

For a time, at least, it did so. Both Lady Portman and the Queen made abject apologies to Lady Flora for having doubted her word and her integrity.

Had Lady Flora herself acted discreetly, the matter might have been over. But she remained indignant at the unkind treatment she had received, and poured out all her pent-up wrath to her brother the Marquess of Hastings. Finding out for the first time, he was appalled. His first reaction was to challenge Lord Melbourne to a duel, for having imputed dishonour to his sister, but he was calmed down by the Prime Minister himself, who tried to shed a softer light on his part in the affair. But Melbourne was adamant in refusing to allow that young man, in the fire of his anger, to confront the Queen. Hastings, however, would not be put off. He made his appearance before Victoria, demanding the names of those who had maligned Lady Flora. Again, however, he was not satisfied.

It was now March 1839, two months after the first suspicions mongering of the Palace, and the noisy protestations and enquiries of Lord Hastings, should bring the whole affair to public attention. It was exacerbated by the appearance of a letter in the newspaper *The Examiner* – a letter written by Lady Flora, retailing the whole story to her uncle Hamilton Fitzgerald, who had seen fit to instigate its publication.

It was now March 1839, two months after the first suspicions had been aroused. Lord Hastings was conducting a vituperative correspondence with Lords Portman and Tavistock, on the parts their wives had taken in the persecution of his sister. Lady Hastings, his mother, was writing to the Queen, pleading 'the anguish of a mother's heart' at 'the atrocious calumnies and unblushing falsehoods against my daughter's reputation'.[4]

Victoria was still ready to apologise for her mistake, but she was becoming extremely angry at the adverse publicity which the Hastings family was raising against her. There were demands placed daily before her for the removal of Sir James Clark, of her ladies Portman and Tavistock and, above all, of 'that *baneful influence* which surrounds the throne',[5] Lehzen – whom all Lady Flora's family and friends believed to have been the originator of the proceedings against her.

Conroy had gone to ground. But he directed operations none the less. Here was his one chance of hitting back at the Queen who had so slighted him. He might never have his chance to rule through her now, but he could hurt her, and he could hurt his old enemy Lehzen. It was probably he who advised Lady Flora's mother to publish her already voluminous correspondence on her daughter's case in *The Morning Post*.

Those who loved Lady Flora might have stayed their hands from adding to her troubles had they known that she was dying from her liver tumour and that the excitement of the past months was rapidly sapping her strength. It was no compensation to be cheered by an anti-Victoria, anti-Melbourne populace in the streets when one had no moment of peace, or free from pain, at home.

Another inevitable aspect of the domestic crisis of the spring of 1839 was that it should become a matter of politics. The Queen's ladies-in-waiting, on whom so much public fury redounded for their treatment of the current heroine Lady Flora, were of the great Whig families. With Melbourne's Whig government in office and these Whig ladies surrounding the Queen, Tories averred that it was obvious that the Queen was herself a whole-hearted Whig partisan, contrary to the theoretical interpretation of the constitution that she should be above political partiality. But Melbourne's government was tottering. His majorities in Parliamentary divisions were, for many reasons, narrowing.

Victoria went in daily dread of losing her Prime Minister, the man to whom she had given all her confidence, who had helped her through the difficult early days of her reign to accustom herself to business and to understand the complexities of her career, who had given himself up to becoming her constant companion despite the tedium of such a 'nursery' Court. The Queen had been frightened by the uproar of the past months over Lady Flora, but now she was terrified that she might be delivered into the hands of the Tories.

Thus, when confronted by the Tory leader Peel, when it became apparent that he would have to undertake to form a new government, Victoria was in no amenable humour. He insisted that she give up her Whig ladies, all Melbourne nominees, and compose a new household of Tories as 'a proof that he enjoyed the entire confidence of Her Majesty'.

Victoria, claiming with perfect truth that her ladies were nothing to do with her role in government, refused to part with them. The thought was uppermost in her mind that should she relent in this, Peel might require the dismissal of the precious Lehzen also. Even when Peel claimed, however, that his demands affected only the Mistress of the Robes and the Ladies of the Bedchamber, not all Victoria's ladies, she would not give in.

Peel backed down. He needed this proof of the Queen's confidence, he said, in the dismissal of the Whigs around her, before he could form a ministry. Without such proof, he must decline the honour. Victoria was triumphant – and relieved. Melbourne's problems in pulling the Whigs together to build a government where the last had failed, was not her concern. She had her Melbourne, and she was satisfied. Many years later, in reviewing her decision of May 1839, Victoria said: 'I was very young, and perhaps I should act differently if it was all to be done again.'[6] She had been right, however, in claiming that there was neither precedent nor law to make her change her ladies with a change of government; but she had surely been wrong in using such a tool to force in her own favour the machinery of politics.

The 'Bedchamber Crisis' and the affair of Lady Flora Hastings were undeniably linked. Victoria firmly believed that there was malice against her ladies for their treatment of Lady

Flora in the Tories' determination to have them dismissed. Indeed, there had been so much feeling stirred up against her and her ladies in the Press that, at the time of the political crisis, it was Peel rather than the Queen who excited most of the nation's sympathy. Victoria's reign had begun with a flood of enthusiasm in the country for the young girl who faced so difficult a career, and public interest in the monarchy had not been so great for centuries. Had it not been for the Lady Flora affair, Victoria might have reckoned for national support in the face of political 'bullying', but the events of the past months had precluded much sympathy for her predicament.

Recent events had made the Queen forget her guilt at having so hounded Lady Flora, and now she was angry at the hounding she was herself suffering in the Press. She refused to send any kind word to the suffering Lady Flora, and her relations with the Duchess of Kent were deteriorating even further.

Lord Melbourne and the long-time 'trouble-shooter' of royal problems the Duke of Wellington did, however, contrive one lightening of the Queen's troubles. They finally engineered the resignation of Conroy. At his door they laid all the intrigues and ill-feeling in the royal household, and they determined that he should no longer have the chance to spoil Victoria's temper and jeopardize her very rule. By bribery and flattery they brought him round to the point of resignation. It was an expensive business – though not as expensive as Sir John tried to make it, with his demands for pensions and rank. He continued to pester later governments for the fulfilment of his demands, but at least his influence was removed from the Duchess of Kent as was his irritating proximity to the Queen.

Relations between mother and daughter also improved with the death of Lady Flora in July. From early June she had given up the struggle and finally left Court. Victoria sent kind messages to her, and on 27 June actually paid Lady Flora a visit. The Queen subsequently wrote in her journal:

> I found poor Lady Flora stretched on a couch looking as thin as anybody can be who is still alive; literally a skeleton, but

> the body *very* much swollen like a person who is with child; a searching look in her eyes, rather like a person who is dying; her voice like usual, a good deal of strength in her hands; she was very friendly, said she was very comfortable, and was very grateful for all I had done for her; and that she was glad to see me look well. I said to her, I hoped to see her again when she was better – upon which she grasped my hand as if to say 'I shall not see you again.'[7]

On 5 July the Queen learned that Lady Flora Hastings had died. A post-mortem showed that she was suffering from a tumour on the liver – but it was put about by the family that she died as the result of the months of persecution which she had suffered. Everywhere the attacks on the Queen's good name continued, and when Victoria sent a carriage to Lady Flora's funeral, stones were thrown at it.

But the worst was over. Even while Lord Hastings continued to publish documents relevant to his sister's case, intended to enflame public opinion further against the Queen, interest in the affair died down. Without the victim, the tragedy was stale.

Both Victoria and the Duchess of Kent made honest intentions to effect a mutual reconciliation. It made slow progress and it was many years before they enjoyed the proper relations of mother and daughter. But three months after the death of Lady Flora, the Queen's cousin Prince Albert of Saxe-Coburg-Gotha arrived in England. Victoria suddenly found herself in love. Four months later she married Albert. It was he who did the most to bring the Duchess of Kent back into her daughter's favour, just as he brought a new regularity and balance into Victoria's emotions and made her Court and household a haven of sober, pleasant peace.

10

It is said that a Victorian lady, after seeing the Shakespearian antics of the Egyptian Queen Cleopatra, remarked: 'So different from the home life of our own dear Queen!' The royal household had become, even a decade after the beginning of Victoria's reign, a byword for respectability.

In retrospect, and in comparison with other contemporary Courts, it might seem to have been a dull existence for Queen Victoria's ladies. After all, while she sang duets with her Albert and took sedate walks in flowery gardens, the Queen Regnant of Portugal was enduring national rebellion, *coup d'état* and assorted catastrophes, and the Queen Consort of France suffered violent dismissal from the kingdom and the humiliation of exile. And what must have been the sufferings and discomforts of ladies-in-waiting at these Courts! While Victoria's ladies seldom endured more than cold bedrooms, tedious hours of 'waiting' and the horror of having to sing or play the piano before crowned heads. ('Does not your daughter "shake"?' the Queen once asked a maid-of-honour's mother, as they listened to the girl render a song featuring a *vibrato* passage. 'Yes, Ma'am, she is shaking all over,'[1] was the reply.)

In the early years of Victoria's reign, before her marriage, the Court was as gay as any young woman could wish, and even in the years of Victoria's marriage, there were treats galore, though the English Court never reached the heights of brilliance ascribed to France's Second Empire. It is customary to look back on the forty years of Victoria's widowhood as the nadir of tedium in Court life, with black-garbed attendants whispering comfort to an ever grieving Queen. Yet, from the evidence of many of her ladies, after the first few years of mourning, though the Queen insisted on wearing 'weeds' herself and on dark toned clothes for her elder ladies, there was amusement enough for even the liveliest young maid-of-honour. And whatever tribulations there were, every lady whose words remain to testify to her years of service bears witness to loving the Queen and to finding her ways endearing.

When Victoria came to the throne, she was only eighteen years old. After years of seclusion in Kensington Palace, with only her summer tours to enliven her round, she was delighted with her independence. The fact of having her own Court and ladies with whom she could chat, sing and make outings was at first an overwhelming pleasure.

Her first choices were generally dictated by prudence and made by the advice of Lord Melbourne. (Notably her contemporary Victoire Conroy, daughter of her mother's detested Comptroller, was not among Victoria's first maids-of-honour, though she did choose Mary Davys, a daughter of her admired tutor to figure in their number.) When her first ladies came into waiting, Victoria exclaimed in delight in her journal: Miss Pitt was 'a *very* elegant nice girl', Miss Spring-Rice 'a clever-looking girl' and Mary Davys 'a very nice girl (although not at all pretty)'.[2] Lord Melbourne might carp at playing his part in such a 'nursery' Court, full of playful young ladies, but to Victoria it was a happy dream.

The 'Bedchamber Crisis' of 1839 put a damper on Victoria's spirits, but by the time that she was faced again with the prospect of a change in ministry, she had Albert to help her and to smooth the way for the incoming Prime Minister, so that all Peel demanded of Victoria in the way of household changes was that she should retain no lady whose husband was a member of the Opposition. Never again would any of Victoria's ladies figure in a political context, and it seems from all the evidence that no lady ever had the slightest political influence on the Queen.

The role of the lady-in-waiting had undergone slow, often untraceable changes over the centuries. No longer did any lady perform any menial task: now there were dressers (such as Victoria's beloved Annie Macdonald) to arrange her toilette and take care of her clothes. No longer were there petitions for commissions and benefices and pensions whispered into the royal ear by ladies well-paid to be patrons of the ambitious. No longer were there aspiring 'maids-of-dishonour' arriving at Court in the hopes of ensnaring a royal lover. The lady-in-waiting was now merely a companion to the Queen, a handsome appendage on State occasions, a confiding gossip in private, a subsidiary hostess to visitors and the penman of innumerable notes and memoranda on the Queen's behalf.

Victoria's ladies were always part of the family. They played with the children, wrote descriptions of fine dresses and interesting entertainments for Victoria to send abroad to her relations, painted china and glass to stand among royal *bric-à-brac* in already-overcrowded parlours and hovered solicitously at moments of crisis. And in return, they could always be assured of Victoria's unfailing interest in their own families and their own problems. 'She asked after Uncle Johnnie, Aunt Edie and Aunt G.B. the other day,' wrote a maid-of-honour Marie Adeane to her mother in 1889, 'and frequently refers to Aunt Nety, and every few days she asks of the news I have of you. It sounds trivial but these are the little things that make one love the Queen. Her interest is real and not the least put on.'[2] The smallest gift from Marie's family was always appreciated: Victoria ate and drank with relish various gifts of apples or pomagne. The Queen never made the slightest difficulty over 'time off' for family weddings or funerals, and if any of her ladies had small children at home, she would issue an open invitation for them to visit their mother in waiting.

Marie Adeane, like many of Victoria's ladies, came of a

family long accustomed to royal service. Her maternal grandfather, the Earl of Hardwicke, had been a Lord-in-Waiting, her mother had been a Woman of the Bedchamber and her uncle, Alick Yorke, having been equerry to two of the Queen's sons, was now, when Marie came into waiting in 1887, a Gentleman-in-Waiting to Victoria. In addition, she could count among her cousins such of the Queen's ladies as Edith, Lady Lytton and the Honourable Harriet Phipps. Like Elizabeth I, by the end of her long reign, Victoria could count several generations of ladies in various families.

At first, the greatest care was taken that no maid-of-honour should bring the Court into disrepute (which made Lady Flora Hasting's supposed fall from grace such a blow to Victoria). 'Not that they are disorderly inclined, poor little things', wrote Lady Lyttelton who, as a senior lady, was in some measure responsible for the maids, 'but there is a painful recollection of doing things in the last reigns, which makes everybody *over*-careful now almost.'[4] It was Lady Lyttelton to whom the maids-of-honour would apply for permission for exemption from the minor rules of the Windsor regime in 1838:

> The maids-of-honour (Miss Lister and Miss Paget) are very coaxy and wheedly with me, and nice creatures both of them. 'Lady L., *mayn't* I walk *just for once* by myself on the slopes? I know it's against the rules, but what harm *can* it do? We used to be allowed, but now Lord Melbourne won't let us. I'm sure we *never* have met anybody there, except once only Mr van der Weyer [the drawing-master], and what could that signify? *Pray* let me.' (Says Lady L.: 'No, no.') Then another time a gentle knock: 'Lady L., *may* I go out? My feet are so cold, poking up in my room all the morning! I will only go on the Terrace, and keep quite in sight. *Pray* let me.' (Says Lady L.: 'Yes, yes.')[5]

The maids-of-honour were fortunate in having the mild, good humoured surveillance of such as Lady Lyttelton. She approached her formidable task, as Lady of the Bedchamber, in 1838, with a wonderful sense of humour:

> ... the character of an adviser, a woman of influence, a probable preserver or improver of the *national morals*, is exactly *the very last* I could fill decently. ... If I am able (which I dread and tremble to think I may not prove) to conduct myself tolerably well, to keep out of incessant scrapes from indiscreet words and irresolute blunderings, so that I can return from Windsor to my quiet and cross-stitch at Hagley with a tolerably easy conscience, I shall be thankful and surprised. I am afraid that knowing all this I ought to have refused entirely – but I trust I may be helped in my new trials.[6]

She was. Lady Lyttelton was never implicated in the unhappy 'Bedchamber' affair, and so well did she prove her merits and abilities, so easily win affections, that she was put in charge of the royal nurseries in 1841, becoming the most successful of all Victoria's children's governesses.

But as far as the morals of the maids-of-honour were concerned, there was never any cause for worry in the whole course of Victoria's long reign. Indeed, of the dozens of maids at Court between 1837 and 1901 nothing more scandalous that the comparatively mild conduct of one Miss Lambart could be found: this young lady (whose home-made toffee cakes were a favourite delicacy of Victoria's) was once so bold as to throw a piece of apple-peel over her shoulder in the hope of seeing it fall in the shape of the initial of the man she hoped to marry, to be twice reproved for wearing make-up and, having danced for the Queen, to ask for Gladstone's head on a charger. (The Queen refused her request, though not with the severity perhaps warranted, for it could not be denied that Victoria had no love for the sententious statesman who, she said, always addressed her as if she were a public meeting.)

Nevertheless, the maids-of-honour did not go to Court lacking in good advice any more than had Bridget Manners three centuries earlier. In September 1839 Lady Anne Maria Dawson went to Court as a lady to the Queen's mother, the Duchess of Kent, and was solemnly charged by Lady Louisa Stuart:

... You must positively resolve never to let your maid, whether English or foreign, say a single word to you about any thing or passage or person or character within the palace walls. You must resolve never to ask her a single question, and make her understand that she is to tell you nothing that passes, not even if the house should be on fire. If you can also seal up her lips to all others, it will be best; recommend it towards her fellows, but peremptorily insist upon it towards yourself. Never ask who is coming or going except from your equals. You have no notion what a safeguard you will find this, a prescriptive against getting into any *tracasserie* or scrape; for at Court mischief of every sort very often has no higher origin. ...

At a Court, amongst other necessary cautions, people should be on their guard never to say a careless word that can injure another, or throw ridicule of any sort on their neighbours. It is really a *Christian* duty because if once a prejudice gets into a royal head, it can never be got out again to the end of time. Princes form a class apart; they do not, like us, mingle with the world and hear different opinions; nor does anybody venture to contradict theirs; so impressions upon them, once made, are indelible. I have heard, and do believe, that at this present hour, the personal dislike to one (Sir Robert Peel) comes in a great measure from the ladies on the other side having laughed at him, and pointed out the little awkwardnesses in his manner; mighty important objections to a statesman! If it be so, it shows what serious consequences the most contemptible trifles may produce![7]

So strict were the rules about ladies' discretion that each maid and lady was requested not to keep a diary of the events of her terms of waiting. Fortunately for this study, Lady Lytton did, and her fellows wrote such interesting letters home, under dire warnings of secrecy to their correspondents, that there is a great deal of material on the duties, trials and pleasures of royal service in Victoria's reign.

Discretion was strongly emphasized again in the advice given to a young lady (later Georgiana, Baroness Bloomfield) by her mother, when she became a maid-of-honour in 1841:

> In the first place, your first study should be to please the Queen, not by base flattery or servile cringing but by the most assiduous attention even in the merest trifles; the most rigid punctuality and obedience; not only to orders, but in being always ready at the proper time, and in the proper place.
>
> Your natural good sense will also show you that the least *brusquerie* or appearance of *ennui* is incompatible with high breeding and the respect due to the Sovereign, and that you must accustom yourself rather to sit or stand for hours without any amusement save the resources of your own thoughts. . . .
>
> The next piece of advice I wish to impress on your mind is, that whatever you see, hear or think must be kept to yourself. It is almost needless to add that in whatever concerns your royal mistress, your lips should be sealed; but you must likewise repulse all vain enquiries and impertinent questions, not rudely but decidedly, either by silence or by pleading ignorance. . . .
>
> I need hardly warn my modest, quiet child against intimacy or flirtation with any of the gentlemen about the Court; for you cannot be too cautious where so many eyes are turned upon you, and where, under the specious garb of civility, much envy and ill-will are often concealed, and those that flatter most are least to be trusted.[8]

By the time that Marie Adeane arrived at Court, in the 1880s, the Queen had found a formula to test the suitability of her prospective maids. Marie received a questionnaire as to her ability to speak and write in French and German, to play the piano and to ride. The Queen also enquired if she was likely to be married in the near future; this was of great importance, for Victoria much disliked settling in comfortably with a new lady only to find her whisked off to the altar and a new lady brought in to replace her.

But once settled in the royal household, no maid-of-honour

need find her duties arduous. Indeed, many of them complained more of lack of occupation than of over-work. In Victoria's youth, they would go horse-riding with her, and later they were expected to drive in her carriage or walk beside her to engage in conversation; they were to make themselves pleasant to guests, especially at the dinner-table where there was a duty to make general conversation, bringing in their neighbours but not entering into any exclusive *tête-à-tête*; sometimes there was a good deal of copying to be done – passages of description from the Queen's holiday journals for example, which were to be despatched to far-away royal cousins. But mainly, the maids-of-honour were for ceremonial decoration.

'Our chief duty', wrote the future Lady Bloomfield, in 1842, 'seems to consist in giving the Queen her bouquet before dinner, which is certainly very hard work! and even this happens only every other day.'[9] 'Putting grumbling aside,' wrote Marie Adeane to her mother nearly fifty years later, 'the life here [at Balmoral] is utterly dull; we see nothing of the Queen except at dinner on alternate nights, we have *no* duties to perform to occupy our minds and the weather is horribly cold and wet. At the same time, it is impossible to settle to anything on account of interruptions. We just exist from meal to meal and do our best to kill time.'[10]

The watershed in the lives of the Queen's ladies came with the death of the Prince Consort in 1861. Immediately the royal household was plunged into deep mourning – both emotionally and in appearance. At first Victoria shut herself away, refusing to see anyone but her half-sister, her youngest child Princess Beatrice and her confidante Lady Augusta Bruce. Lady Augusta had been fifteen years a lady-in-waiting to the Queen's mother and had given up the whole of her youth to her service. When the Duchess of Kent died, in March 1861, Lady Augusta had been offered a resident place with the Queen, not on the usual terms of the ladies, with set terms of waiting, but with year-round duties and a permanent home with the royal family. The comfort which Lady Augusta had given Victoria after her mother's death ensured her one of the closest places next to the

Queen when the Prince Consort died only nine months later.

By 1863 the Queen was over the worst, but she was still furious when she found that her favourite lady, without even youth as an excuse, had decided to marry: 'My dear Lady Augusta, at forty-one', wrote Victoria in her journal, '... has most unnecessarily decided to *marry* (! !) ... I thought she *never* would leave me.'[11]

Like Elizabeth I, Victoria hated the changes in her retinue consequent on marriages, but apart from sighing wistfully and making her ladies feel as guilty as she could, she did nothing to stop them. Several of the maids-of-honour made matches of which Victoria thoroughly approved, especially when they would stay near her, as when Mary Bulteel married Henry Ponsonby, himself a royal equerry (and later the Queen's Private Secretary). She could not *quite* approve the marriage of her maid-of-honour Sylvia Edwardes to her own great-nephew Count Gleichen in 1897 (any more than she had that of Gleichen's naval officer father to his admiral's daughter a generation earlier); and she was quite shocked when, in July 1895, Ina McNeil married the seventy-two year old Duke of Argyll as his third wife (Argyll's heir was the husband of Victoria's daughter Louise). But the marriage which most provoked the Queen was that of Susan Baring to the royal physician Sir James Reid. Victoria could not rid herself of the idea that such an alliance was *infra dig.* for one of her ladies: 'If I had been younger I wld have let him go rather – but at my age it wld be hazardous and disagreeable and so he remains living in my House wherever we are! and she quite consents to it. But it is too tiresome and I can't conceal my annoyance. I have never said a word to her yet.'[12]

However, when Sir James begged an audience of Victoria and promised 'never to do it again', she could not help but smile, and thereafter all paths were smoothed for the couple.

But on the whole Victoria preferred widows as her companions. She liked to feel that they could share her own grief and understand her need for occasional tears at happy memories of past days. In 1895, hearing that Lady Lytton, the recent widow of the Viceroy of India (and, incidentally, a latter-day member of the fascinating Villiers family) had emerged from seclusion after three and a half years' mourning, the Queen offered her a post. At first Lady Lytton was reluctant, even thinking that perhaps she might send her daughter Emily as a maid-of-honour in her place (Emily staunchly refused, claiming to be a red-hot republican); then, having pondered deeply as to what her late husband would have advised, accepted.

Thus Lady Lytton joined the widows who formed a phalanx round the Queen. There was Lady Ely, charming but of a passive character, and Lady Churchill, a genuine toady. The Queen bullied both these ladies terribly, giving them the most unpleasant tasks of administering rebukes to Cabinet ministers and royal children alike – but both adored her. Lady Ely, who often wailed out her tribulations to her friends against all rules of discretions, made a great show of her place close to the Queen, speaking to Victoria in a 'mysterious whisper' on even the most mundane subjects, to enhance her own importance with those who were watching.

Yet for all her querulous whims which she inflicted on these two ladies, Victoria genuinely loved them. When Lady Churchill died at Osborne House on Christmas Eve 1900, Victoria was at her side, and the festivities were quite blighted by her grief.

Obviously, many aspects of the ladies' duties changed with the times. In the last years of the nineteenth century there was less dancing at Court and more musical concerts than had been the case in the early years. And it was a different matter to chat gaily to keep an old lady awake on a cold carriage-drive than to 'speak when you are spoken to' with a young Queen. But then, in 1839, Lady Lyttelton had written: 'If Her Majesty would wear less than *four* different wraps (all to be taken off and put on), and go [to the theatre] without a bouquet *and* a bag *and* an opera-glass, there would be no difficulty at all';[13] sixty years later, ladies-in-waiting would still be plagued by the Queen's frequent insistence on changing a light shawl for a heavy one, or a plaid rug for a dust-wrap, on her outings.

In Victoria's prime, holidays in the Highlands or at Osborne on the Isle of Wight had been quite active affairs, with long walks or rides, swimming and games with the children – all of which the younger ladies at least were expected to share; in the later years tea on the lawn was the most strenuous exercise apart from a gentle carriage-run. Victoria and Albert had made several Continental excursions, sometimes to the family home at Coburg, sometimes to the French or Belgian royal families. Voyages in the royal yacht were more comfortable by far than those endured by ladies-in-waiting in centuries past, but the horrors of foreign cooking, service and habits had still their power. On a State Visit to France in 1855, Lady Charlemont was terrorized by a French footman; there was no lock on her bedroom door, and the man would keep entering unannounced:

> By dint of the greatest watchfulness and constantly starting out of her bath [recorded Lady Augusta Bruce, who heard the tale first-hand], and shouldering the door of which he was always turning the handle whenever he proceeded further than mere fidgetting with it, she contrived to baffle him during the bathing moments, but at all other times, he made good his entrance, despite her shrieks and remonstrances. ...[14]

In later years, Victoria made annual visits to the South of France, but on these occasions no Englishwoman was expected to put herself at the mercy of the French. Irish stew, in stone jars wrapped up in flannel, was stowed in the royal train for consumption on the journey; the royal bed-linen was in evidence on all beds used by the party; a chef and minor domestics as well as her courtiers accompanied the Queen to the sun of the south.

Just as the Queen had an immense network of family relationships spreading through the royal Houses of Europe, so her ladies-in-waiting came to have acquaintances the length and width of the Continent. There was a vast sorority of ladies-in-waiting, built up through the numerous visits of foreign kings and queens, princes and princesses, dukes and duchesses to 'the Grandmother of Europe'. For wherever a royal lady went, there also were her own ladies, and scarcely a month went by without some visitor to Windsor, Balmoral, Buckingham Palace or

Osborne. These visiting ladies, with their foreign ways and their foreign ideas of discretion (which was mainly, it seems, no idea at all) were the natural guests of Victoria's ladies, their teatime companions in tower rooms through long evenings when no formal service was required. While in the royal armchairs diplomatic links were forged between cousinly monarchs, their ladies in the background could compare notes on international gossip. If those secrets could be told!

Queen Victoria died in January 1901 at Osborne. Lady Lytton was due to go into waiting on the very day of her death but a few days previously received warning not to go, as the house was full of the royal family. Then, on 28 January, she received a note from Miss Harriet Phipps, a Bedchamber Woman who had served the Queen as confidential secretary: 'You and I have the great privilege of attending our most beloved Queen on her last journey,'[15] she wrote. And so these two ladies-in-waiting did their last service to the Queen by walking with her family in the procession to Cowes Pier, then crossing to the mainland and attending the coffin to the mausoleum at Windsor.

It is customary to regard the reign of Edward VII, the son and successor of Queen Victoria, as a latter-day golden age of aristocratic life centred on the monarch. Under the tutelage of Prince Albert, the late Queen had early come to appreciate the pleasures of domesticity, preferring family gatherings and, later, life among her close household staff, to the mêlée of fashionable 'society', but her son, sophisticated and cosmopolitan, relished the extravaganza of the *Belle Epoque* to the full.

However, the Court of Edward VII did not entirely reflect the new King's own predilections for the company of noble rakes and *coquettes*. Court assemblies of 1901–10 were far more staid, and far more traditionally managed, than the informal parties in which the King so delighted. When Edward was at Sandringham (the setting for so many nocturnal wanderings from the royal bed and for incessant practical joking), the Court as such almost ceased to exist, and the royal party became practically indistinguishable from any other contemporary country-house gathering.

So the Court in London retained much of the procedure and stability of Victoria's reign. Besides, though in her youth the new Queen, Alexandra, had joined in her husband's revelries, in middle age the couple's amusements were more disparate. The Queen made no complaint against her husband's always discreet infidelities, and in return he never demanded from her that she should receive any lady whom convention would not anyway have put before her. Edward VII was no Charles II or George IV to force a favourite into his wife's service as lady-in-waiting.

Legend has it that a visiting Shah of Persia, regarding Alexandra's ladies-in-waiting and mistaking them for Edward's harem, exclaimed: 'These are your wives? They are old and ugly. Have them beheaded and take new and pretty ones.' On two counts that Shah was wrong: in the first place, Alexandra delighted in showing herself off among handsome women and pretty girls, so he must have seen them on an 'off' day; secondly, the King never approached any of his wife's ladies for their favours. He dismissed her maids-of-honour as 'bread-and-butter misses', preferring the more experienced charms of such 'women of the world' as Lady Randolph Churchill and Mrs Lillie Langtry. Indeed, the English royal family had been singularly immune to the charms of ladies-in-waiting for some century by then.

Abroad, there had been many scandals linking princes with ladies-in-waiting. The closest to home had involved Queen Victoria's half-brother in the 1820s. He had become enamoured of one Marie Klebelsberg, one of his grandmother's ladies, and even, in 1828, married her, to the horror of the family. True to all predictions, the couple were unhappy together. Charles, Prince of Leiningen, who might have made a grand match through his connection with the 'Coburg stud' which provided so many illustrious matches for its scions, found himself tied to a woman who brought no advantage of rank or wealth to his House. Inevitably, they parted – she to go off with her own 'cavalier', who subsequently eloped with her maid.

In later years, there were whispers and sniggers in Courts and Chancelleries when Queen Victoria allowed her daughter Beatrice to marry Prince Henry of Battenberg, whose grandfather had married a lady-in-waiting of his sister the Tsarina, Julia von Hauke. But this was nothing in comparison with three notorious scandals in Continental dynasties. First, the heir to the Romanian throne, Prince Ferdinand, had taken as his mistress Elena Vacarescu, a maid-of-honour to his aunt Queen Elizabeth. The latter was the romantic eccentric 'Carmen Sylva' of literary fame, and she thoroughly approved the 'all for love' sacrifice of her nephew; her husband the King was less liberal, and he demanded the end of the liaison. Ferdinand was married off suitably to one of Victoria's grand-daughters.

Then there was beautiful Draga Mashin, a lady-in-waiting to the Queen of Serbia. She actually became queen by marrying the Serbian King Alexander in 1900 – to be murdered in the revolution of 1903. But the most famous *mésalliance* of the age was that of the Archduke Franz Ferdinand, heir to the Austrian Empire. He gave up his claim to the throne by marrying his sister's lady, Sophie Chotek, to the horror of the whole House of Habsburg. When the couple were so dramatically and fatefully assassinated at Sarajevo in 1914, Sophie's coffin at the lying-in-state was placed noticeably lower than her husband's, to denote her rank – and on the coffin were placed the fan and gloves which were the traditional symbols of the lady-in-waiting, rather than an imperial tiara. Even to the grave high birth was all in all to the bitter family.

Back in England, Queen Alexandra was the most 'stylish' consort for centuries. Herself tall and beautiful, she liked to be seen surrounded by beauties who themselves had a graceful height. It was noticeable that she took the most attractive of her ladies to such public events as Ascot week and to support her in visits to foreign royalty, while those who were short in stature or plain of feature were relegated to such dreary duties as attendance at the family memorial services. 'Mausoleum waiting' was the nadir of boredom.

To the very time of her death, Queen Alexandra retained her wonderful good looks and even in old age could inspire devotion in the men she met. At the head of her list of admirers was Sir Dighton Probyn, a lifelong royal servant, though there was never a breath of scandal in their relations. But she also had the knack of drawing the loyalty of women and of forming lasting friendships. When Alexandra was first in England as a young bride, Lady Macclesfield, one of her Ladies of the Bedchamber, was her chief friend. It was she who helped the then Princess of Wales with the premature birth of her first child. So early was the birth that no layette had been gathered, and the presumptive heir to the English crown was delivered into Lady Macclesfield's flannel petticoat. 'Dearest old Mac', herself the mother of thirteen children, was the Princess's strengh in her hard days: 'As long as I see your face,' wrote the Princess, 'I am comfortable.'[16]

Lady Macclesfield's successor in Alexandra's affections was Miss Charlotte Knollys. She came to Court in 1873, the sister of Sir Francis Knollys (later Secretary to Edward VII), as a Woman of the Bedchamber. She remained unmarried (though there were rumours that Sir Dighton Probyn, a widower, might marry her, they were never realized), and devoted herself entirely to Alexandra. 'The inevitable Charlotte', as the family came to call her, was always hovering, dowdy and graceless, in the wake of the Queen.

Charlotte's great moment came in 1900, when she was on a state visit to Brussels with Edward and Alexandra. As she sat with the royal couple in their train at the city's Gare du Nord station, a fifteen-year-old anarchist named Sipido aimed a shot at the Prince. The bullet missed, lodging itself in the 'bun' of hair on Charlotte's head. It was treasured for years afterwards and is still preserved in the Windsor Archives.

The First World War, in the reign of King George V, saw the onset of decline in English Court life. Queen Mary, his consort, was the most regally inclined of ladies; when asked once what she most wanted for a birthday present, she replied: 'A Court ball.' But she, who could so ably and gracefully carry off a State occasion, reigned in an era of increasing democratization and through periods of national austerity. During the First World War, the Queen made a courageous visit to battle-scarred France to meet wounded soldiers, but for the most part she was left deposited in the quiet safety of Sandringham. Her ladies would follow her round the grounds in her never-ceasing pursuit of seasonal horse-chestnuts which were of some, scarcely imaginable, use, in munitions factories. In the Second War, at Badminton, the Queen would plague her household with her daily forays for timber and scrap metal (occasionally dragging home farm equipment which had to be returned surreptitiously and tactfully to its owner). It was no rare sight to see the stately old lady marching down a country lane followed by a lady-in-waiting bearing her mistress's muddy trophies of a morning's scavenging.

On one occasion Queen Mary and her Lady of the Bedchamber, Lady Desborough, were driving from Badminton to Oxford, for lunch with the University's Chancellor, when their car broke down. In conditions of wartime shortages there was little traffic on the country road. The first vehicle to pass was a small car in which sat a farmer, his wife and a load of onions. Readily agreeing to transport the Queen to her engagement, the farmer moved his onions into the back seat: while the Queen joined him in the front, his wife and Lady Desborough spent the rest of the journey atop a mound of high-smelling onions in the back.

With the reign of George VI, the end of the old custom of Court life was in sight. His queen, Elizabeth Bowes-Lyon, retained no maids-of-honour, and, with war breaking out only three years into the reign, the formal 'waiting' duties of her ladies almost ceased. In recent years, the Lady of the Bedchamber had not lived in the Palace, during her period of waiting, though transport was always available for her to travel between her own London house and the Palace. Now, in wartime, the Lady remained at home, with only the Woman of the Bedchamber in service on most occasions. And during the London air-raids, Queen, lady-in-waiting and housemaid could all be found crouching together in a cupboard waiting for the siren's 'all-clear'.

From those years dates the precedent of the Lady of the Bedchamber's coming into waiting only when specifically needed for a special duty. Today the Woman of the Bedchamber to Her Majesty the Queen is the only resident royal attendant. At present there are five Women of the Bedchamber, who go into waiting at fortnightly intervals. Apart from appearing at State functions, the leader of the ladies-in-waiting, the Mistress of the Robes, is responsible only for arranging their rota.

Most of the present ladies-in-waiting owe their appointments to their being personally known to the Queen. Lady Abel Smith, for example, one of the Women of the Bedchamber, is distantly related to the royal family. When the young Duchess of Gloucester, then the bride Princess Richard of Gloucester, sought her first lady-in-waiting, she chose Mrs Louise Wigley, formerly a secretary on the staff of her mother-in-law, the then Duchess.

The duties of a lady-in-waiting today follow traditional patterns. The ladies attend the Queen on public occasions, holding bouquets and carrying type-written speeches. There are the occasional mixed blessings of fascinating but strenuous royal tours abroad, but more usually a day in the shires opening hospitals, touring old peoples' homes and laying foundation stones. Gone are the days of formal *débutantes'* presentations; in their place are the immense garden parties at Buckingham Palace where men and women are entertained to tea who in the old days of rigid class distinction would themselves have carried tea-trays and washed up afterwards for their sovereign.

Nor are the ladies-in-waiting of today the grand, selfish aristocrats of the past, waited on hand and foot. Annabel Hoyer-Millar, lady-in-waiting to Princess Anne, worked in a Chelsea boutique before her royal appointment; Lady Jean Rankin rears blue snow geese in Scotland when she is not in waiting on the Queen Mother.

Entirely divorced from politics and patronage, rarely on display in satin gown and tiara, the ladies-in-waiting of today are surely far from the glamorous figures of past centuries who intrigued in national politics and reigned in royal bedrooms. But there are more links with the past than meet the eye: Miss Mary

Dawnay, a lady-in-waiting to Princess Anne, is the great-granddaughter of one of Queen Victoria's ladies, and Lady Mary Fitzalan Howard, a lady to Princess Alexandra, can count among her ancestors generations of royal servants, including both Anne Boleyn and Catherine Howard.

The royal household has shrunk; the role of the lady-in-waiting has been minimized; there are now few State occasions at which ladies can appear in 'bright array'; but as long as there is a queen, regnant or consort, there will surely be ladies-in-waiting. Duke's daughter or dustman's, the future lady-in-waiting will still stand in full glare of television arc-lights and within shot of the assassin's bullet, a pace behind the Queen.

Bibliography and Notes

Chapter 1

This chapter, of them all, was the hardest to compile because of the paucity of direct sources and the multiplicity of fragmentary references to ladies-in-waiting in primary sources. The best place to start is, however, with the excellent *English Government at Work, 1327–36*, volume I, edited by J. F. Williard and W. A. Morris (Medieval Academy of America, 1940) and *Chapters in Medieval Administrative History*, T. F. Tout (Manchester University Press, volume V, 1930) – the chapters in both works by Hilda Johnstone on the Queens' Household. These refer in several instances to papers in the Public Record Office inaccessible to the general reader and to Exchequer and Household papers of the medieval kings, many of which were published in the nineteenth century.

Of the many medieval chronicles consulted for this chapter, those of Thomas Walsingham, Henry of Knighton, Thomas Rymer (the *Foedera*), Leland (the *Collectanea*), Higden and Monstrelet were the most interesting – most of them collected and published in the nineteenth century. The most helpful edition of Froissart's chronicle is the Berners translation of the sixteenth century, edited by W. Paton Ker (David Nutt: Tudor Translations, 1901–3). Froissart was a member of the household of Philippa of Hainault, Edward III's wife; as such, he was eyewitness to many of the notable events of the era and picked up a good deal of Court gossip, for what it was worth.

From Froissart's time, sources become easier to find, and there are many fascinating works which are available to the general reader. Such is B. C. Hardy, *Phillippa of Hainault and her times* (John Long, 1910), a book compiled, with painstaking detail, from contemporary documents. Another is F. J. Furnivall, *Life Records of Chaucer* (1876) which collects the various documents relevant to Chaucer's life, which was spent largely at Court. It is unsatisfactory, however, on the identification of 'Philippa Chaucer'.

F. G. Kay's *Lady of the Sun* (Muller, 1966) is the best work available on Alice Perrers and could be profitably read in conjunction with G. Mathew's *Court of Richard II* (John Murray, 1968).

Agnes Strickland's *Lives of the Queens of England* (written in the nineteenth century but recently reprinted by Portway of Bath) details, with fascinating but not always accurate anecdote, the life-histories of the queens from Matilda of Flanders to Queen Anne. The first two volumes (of eight) are relevant to this chapter. More recent works, which include, of course, matter on the queens' ladies-in-waiting, are: J. J. Bagley, *Margaret of Anjou, Queen of England* (Herbert Jenkins, 1948); D. MacGibbon, *Elizabeth Woodville* (Arthur Barker, 1948) and N. L. Harvey, *Elizabeth of York* (Arthur Barker, 1973).

There are several minor works on royal households of various medieval periods, notably those by A. R. Myers, including 'The captivity of a royal witch' – Joanna of Navarre (*Bulletin of John Rylands Library*, 1940, volume XXIV); 'The Household of Queen Margaret of Anjou' (*ibid*, 1957, volume XL); also N. H. Nicholas, *Privy Purse Expenses of Elizabeth of York* (1830).

Various miscellaneous works should be added here: G. Smith, *The Coronation of Elizabeth Woodville* (Ellis, 1935); T. Wright, *Political Songs and Poems* (1861) – for the verses on Eleanor

Cobham; C. L. Kingsford, *English Historical Literature of the fifteenth century* (Oxford University Press, 1913) – mainly for the document by Bluemantle Pursuivant on the visit to the Court of Edward IV of Louis de Gruthuyse. Finally, in 1790 the Society of Antiquaries published a *Collection of Ordinances ...* which covers the royal household of the Middle Ages, but which also includes the ordinances for the Lady Cecily's household described in this chapter.

It is extremely rare for works of fiction to be included in a bibliography to a work of historical non-fiction, but two novels are so outstanding as to merit inclusion. Anya Seton's *Catherine* (Swynford) (Hodder & Stoughton, 1954) and Hilda Lewis's *Gentle Falcon* (Oxford Children's Library, 1952) are both based on their authors' excellent research among contemporary documents, from which they build up a credible picture of Court life in the late fourteenth and early fifteenth centuries.

1 Berners, ed. W. Paton Ker, *Froissart's Chronicle*, volume I, p. 316
2 *Collection of Ordinances* ..., p. 39.
3 Kingsford, *English Historical Literature* ..., p. 383.
4 Strickland, *Lives of the Queens of England*, volume I, p. 161.
5 *Ibid.*, p. 588.
6 *Ibid.*, p. 589.
7 Berners, *op. cit.*, volume V, p. 22.
8 *Ibid.*, volume VI, p. 191.
9 Strickland, *op. cit.*, volume II, p. 14.
10 *Ibid.*, p. 34.
11 *Monstrelet's Chronicle* (1840), volume I, pp. 535–6.
12 Wright, *Political Songs* ..., volume II, p. 208.
13 *Hall's Chronicle* (1809), p. 264.

Chapter 2

The main documentary sources for the reign of Henry VIII, which throw much light on the affairs of his family and Court, are comprised in the abstracts of the royal correspondence and state papers published in the nineteenth century: *State Papers of the Reign of Henry VIII*; *Calendar of Letters and Papers, Foreign and Domestic, Henry VIII*; and the *Calendar of State Papers* of Venice and Spain, all published by the State Paper Commission. The most important chronicles of the period are those of Hall, Vergil, Stow and Holinshed, with Leland's *Collectanea.*

An invaluable picture of Henry's household is given in *Four Years at the Court of Henry VIII: Selections from Despatches written by Sebastian Giustiniano*, ed. L. Rawdon Brown (1854). Of the many secondary sources on Henry's Court, the most interesting are N. Williams, *Henry VIII and his Court* (Weidenfeld & Nicolson, 1971) and D. Mathew, *The Courtiers of Henry VIII* (Eyre & Spottiswoode, 1970).

For the Queens themselves: again, Agnes Strickland, *Lives of the Queens of England*, volumes II and III; the biographies of Catherine of Aragon by Francesca Claremont (Robert Hale, 1939) and G. Mattingly (Jonathan Cape, 1942); of Anne Boleyn by H. W. Chapman (Jonathan Cape, 1974) and M. L. Bruce (Collins, 1972); of Catherine Howard by L. B. Smith, *A Tudor Tragedy* (Jonathan Cape, 1961); and of Catherine Parr by A. Martienssen (Secker & Warburg, 1973).

The Basset letters quoted in this chapter are to be found in M. A. E. Wood, *Letters of Royal and Illustrious Ladies* (1846) and H. Ellis, *Original Letters Illustrative of Englih History*, (1824–46).

1 *Letters and Papers ...*, volume I, part ii, p. 1403.
2 *Ibid.*, p. 1413.
3 *Ibid.*
4 *Ibid.*, p. 1421.
5 *Ibid.*, p. 1433.
6 Strickland, *op. cit.*, volume II, pp. 571–2.
7 Williams, *Henry VIII and his Court*, p. 50.
8 *Lettres de Henri VIII à Anne Boleyn* (1826), pp. 112-13.
9 *Letters and Papers ...*, volume x, p. 373.
10 Wood, *Letters ...*, volume II, pp. 296–7.
11 *Ibid.*, pp. 312–3.

12 *Ibid.*, volume III, p. 145.
13 *Ibid.*, pp. 145–6.
14 *Chronicle of Calais*, ed. J. G. Nichols (Camden Society, 1846), no. 179, p. 151.
15 Strickland, *op. cit.*, volume III, p. 62.
16 Wood, *op. cit.*, volume III, p. 150.
17 *Ibid.*, pp. 151–2.
18 *Collection of Ordinances*, p. 164.
19 Strickland, *op. cit.*, volume III, p. 145.
20 *Ibid.*, p. 147.

Chapter 3

The State Papers, foreign and domestic, published by the State Papers Commission in the last century, together with the *Calendar of Letters, Despatches and State Papers relating to the negotiations between England and Spain*, volume XI, provide most of the documentary sources for Mary's reign, and for the last part of this chapter should be supplemented by the *Calendar of Letters and Papers relating to English affairs in the reign of Elizabeth I*. Again the letters edited by Ellis and Wood, already cited, are useful. *Privy Purse Expenses of Princess Mary*, edited by F. Madden (1831) provides a list of the payments and gifts which passed between Mary Tudor and her friends and servants.

Apart from Agnes Strickland's life of the Queen (*op. cit.*, volume III), the only serious recent biography of the Queen is H. F. M. Prescott's *Spanish Tudor* (Constable, 1940).

H. Clifford's *Life of Jane Dormer, Duchess of Feria* is reproduced in the *Quarterly Series* of 1887, volume LXII, and R. Smith's *Life of Magdalen Dacre, Viscountess Montague* in *An Elizabethan Recusant House*, ed. A. C. Southern (Sands & Co, 1954). The only biography of Mary's cousin Margaret Douglas is by Agnes Strickland in volume II of her *Lives of the Queens of Scotland* (1854).

The intriguing story of Catherine Grey's courtship and marriage is told by H. W. Chapman in her *Two Tudor Portraits* (where references also to Mary Howard, Duchess of Richmond may be found, in the section on her brother the Earl of Surrey) (Jonathan Cape, 1960). The political significance of Catherine's marriage is well explained in M. Levine's *Early Elizabethan Succession Question, 1558–68* (Stanford University Press, USA, 1966).

1 Clifford, *Life of Jane Dormer ...*, p. 60.
2 Southern, *An Elizabethan Recusant House*, p. 12.
3 Clifford, *op. cit.*, pp. 168–9.
4 Southern, *op. cit.*, p. 26.
5 *Letters and Papers ...*, volume XXI, part ii, p. 285.
6 *Calendar of English Affairs*, volume I, no. 84.
7 British Museum: Harleian MS 6286.
8 *Ibid.*
9 *Ibid.*
10 Strickland, *op. cit.*, volume IV, p. 238.

Chapter 4

Even apart from the many invaluable State Papers of Elizabeth I's reign, the primary sources for the period are so numerous as to preclude their being listed here. The most valuable for this subject, however, are the works of Sir John Harington (son of Elizabeth's lady-in-waiting Isabella Markham): *Nugae Antiquae*, of 1779, and N. E. McClure's edition of *The Letters and Epigrams of Sir John Harington* (University of Pennsylvania Press, USA, 1930). J. G. Nicholls's *Progresses and Public Processions of Queen Elizabeth I* (1788–1821) was also useful for its quotations from many primary sources.

Of modern works on the Elizabethan Court, I. Dunlop's *Palaces and Progresses of Elizabeth I* (Jonathan Cape, 1962), N. Williams, *All the Queen's Men* (Weidenfeld & Nicolson, 1972) and A. L. Rowse, *The Elizabethan Renaissance: The Life of the Society* (Macmillan, 1971) were the main books consulted here.

Dozens of books, of varying worth, have been written on the

life and character of Elizabeth I: Agnes Strickland's life (*op. cit.*, volume IV) has some value – if only for its detail, but the best biographies are those by J. E. Neale (Jonathan Cape, 1934) and N. Williams (Weidenfeld & Nicolson, 1967).

Violet Wilson's *Queen Elizabeth's Maids of Honour* (Bodley Head, 1922) is the only comprehensive work on the subject, though it should be read with caution since several of the theories of motivation and character have been queried in more recent scholarship. In recent years A. L. Rowse has thrown considerable doubt on the identification of Mary Fitton as Shakespeare's 'Dark Lady of the Sonnets', but there is still a good deal of worthwhile matter in F. J. Furnivall's *Shakespeare and Mary Fitton* (1897).

C. A. Bradford has written excellent biographies of Blanche Parry (1935) and Helena, Marchioness of Northampton (George Allen & Unwin, 1936), and T. Lever's *The Herberts of Wilton* (John Murray, 1967) gives a good deal of information on Mary Sidney and her daughter the Countess of Pembroke.

1 *Calendar of State Papers, Domestic*, 1583, p. 98.
2 *Ibid.*, 1547–80, p. 494.
3 Bradford, *Helena, Marchioness of Northampton*, p. 49.
4 P. Hentzner, *Travels in England* (1889), pp. 50–1.
5 McClure, *Letters and Epigrams ...*, p. 95.
6 Strickland, *op. cit.*, volume IV, p. 471.
7 Historical Manuscripts Commission: Rutland MSS.
8 Thoms, *Anecdotes and Traditions* (1889), pp. 70–1.
9 Strickland, *op. cit.*, volume IV, p. 472.
10 Harington, *Nugae Antiquae*, volume I, p. 232.
11 *Ibid.*, p. 246.
12 Strickland, *op. cit.*, volume IV, p. 598.
13 Williams, *All the Queen's Men*, p. 147.
14 *Ibid.*, p. 21.
15 Strickland, *op. cit.*, volume IV, p. 412.
16 *Ibid.*
17. *Ibid.*, p. 690.
18 J. Aubrey, *Brief Lives* (Secker & Warburg, 1949), pp. 137–8.
19 E. Edwards, *Letters of Sir Walter Raleigh* (1868), pp. 255–6.

20 HMC: Rutland MSS.

21 N. E. McClure, *Letters of John Chamberlain* (American Philosophical Society, volume XII, 1939) i, p. 44.

22 Lady Newdegate-Newdigate, *Gossip from a Muniment Room* (1898), pp. 10–11.

23 *Ibid.*, pp. 15–6.

24 Strickland, *op. cit.*, volume IV, p. 429.

Chapter 5

The Stuart papers are of less interest for the researcher into the stories of ladies-in-waiting for this period than for others, since no one lady in the reign of James I made her mark, though they have some value for the early reign of Charles I. But there are glimpses of the ladies' duties in the Society of Antiquaries' *Collection of Ordinances* (1790) and in Thoms's *Book of the Court* (1838).

There is much valuable background material for this chapter in the *Nugae Antiquae* of Sir John Harington (1804), in Edmund Lodge's *Illustrations of British History* (1791) and in the following: J. G. Nichols, *The Progresses, Processions and Festivities of King James I ...* (1828); L. Aikin, *Memoirs of the Court of James I* (1822) and *Memoirs of the Court of Charles I* (1833); T. Birch, *The Court and Times of James I* (1849) and *The Court and Times of Charles I* (1848); G. Goodman, *The Court and Times of James I* (1839) and especially J. H. Jesse, *Memoirs of the Court of England during the reigns of the Stuarts*, volumes I and II (1855).

Of the many books on the Court masque, some of the most helpful are Enid Welsford's *The Court Masque* (Russell, USA, 1927), A. Nicoll's *Stuart Masques and the Renaissance Stage* (Harrap, 1937) and R. Strong's *Splendour at Court* (Weidenfeld & Nicolson, 1973).

For the first Stuart queens, again Agnes Strickland (volume V), with E. Carleton Williams, *Anne of Denmark* (Longman, 1970) and C. Oman, *Henrietta Maria* (Hodder & Stoughton, 1936).

Carola Oman was also the biographer of Elizabeth of Bohemia (Hodder & Stoughton, 1938). *The letters of Queen Henrietta Maria* were edited for publication by M. A. E. Green (1857) and L. M. Baker edited *The Letters of Elizabeth of Bohemia* (Bodley Head, 1953). There is also a biography of Elizabeth of Bohemia in volume VIII of Agnes Strickland's *Lives of the Queens of Scotland and English Princesses* (1859).

P. Handover has written the most recent biography of Arbella Stuart (Eyre & Spottiswoode, 1957). Unfortunately there is no life of the interesting Lucy, Countess of Carlisle, but her character is drawn in T. Matthew's *Collection of Letters* (1660) and in Jesse, *op. cit.*

1 J. Melville, *Memoirs of his own Life* (Bannantyne Club, Edinburgh, 1827), p. 370.
2 Aikin, *Memoirs of the Court of James I*, volume I, p. 45.
3 *Calendar of Domestic State Papers, 1603–10*, p. 43.
4 Strickland, *op. cit.*, volume IV, p. 735.
5 W. Kennet, *Complete History of England* (1706) p. 685.
6 Harington, *Nugae Antiquae*, volume I, p. 348.
7 *Ibid.*, pp. 348–9.
8 Lodge, *Illustrations of English History*, volume III, pp. 227–8.
9 Strickland, *Lives of the Queens of Scotland* ..., volume VIII, p. 83.
10 Oman, *Henrietta Maria*, p. 17.
11 *Ibid.*, p. 34.
12 *Ibid.*, p. 59.
13 Jesse, *Memoirs* . . ., volume II, p. 120.
14 Oman, *op. cit.*, p. 143.
15 *Ibid.*, p. 152.

Chapter 6

From the immense literature on the reigns of Charles II and James II and of their Courts, the Stuart Papers published by the Historical Manuscripts Commission and the State Papers provide the main documentary sources. The diaries of Pepys, edited by R. C. Latham and W. Matthews (G. Bell & Sons, 1970–) and Evelyn, edited by E. S. de Beer (Clarendon Press, 1955) are invaluable. *The Memoirs of Count Gramont* are best read in the C. H. Hartmann and P. Quennell edition (Routledge & Kegan Paul, 1930–2), but even with the editors' scholarly comments, they should be read warily since their colourful stories are often open to disproof. In addition there is J. J. Jusserand, *A French Ambassador at the Court of Charles II* (1892) and J. H. Jesse, *Memoirs of the Court of England during the reigns of the Stuarts*, volume III (1855).

The main biography of Anne Hyde is by J. R. Henslowe (T. Werner Laurie, 1915), useful despite its caution on sexual matters, supplemented by A. Fea, *James II and his wives* (Methuen, 1908). The Fairfax manuscripts in *Memorials of the Civil War*, edited by R. Bell (1849) have some points on Anne's early life, while Baroness S. van Z. van Nyevelt deals expertly with *Court Life in the Dutch Republic, 1633–89* (Dent, 1906). Additional information can be found in the works by and about Anne's father, Lord Chancellor Clarendon, *The Life of Edward Hyde, Earl of Clarendon*, (1827) and its *Continuation* (1828).

On Catherine of Braganza and Mary of Modena, Strickland (*op. cit.*, volumes V and VI) is updated by J. Mackay (John Long, 1937) and H. Elsna (Robert Hale, 1967) on the former, and C. Oman (Hodder & Stoughton, 1962) and M. Hopkirk, *Queen over the Water* (John Murray, 1953) on the latter.

M. Ashley's *Stuarts in Love* (Hodder & Stoughton, 1963) establishes a reasonable chronology for the love-affairs of Charles II and James II.

For the ladies-in-waiting themselves, the following books have been consulted: A. Andrews, *The Royal Whore* (Hutchinson, 1971) with P. W. Sergeant, *My Lady Castlemaine* (Hutchinson, 1912); C. H. Hartmann, *La Belle Stuart* (G. Routledge & Sons, 1924); John Evelyn's *Life of Mrs Godolphin* (1847), M. E. Tabor, *Four Margarets* (Sheldon Press, 1929) and W. G. Hiscock, *John Evelyn and Mrs Godolphin* (Macmillan, 1951); P. W. Sergeant, *Little Jennings and Fighting Dick Talbot*

(Hutchinson, 1913); and Anne Killigrew's *Poems, 1686* (Scholars' Facsmilies and Reprints, USA, 1967).

1 Strickland, *op. cit.*, volume V, p. 421.
2 Clarendon MSS, volume XXXIX, folio 70.
3 Hartmann and Quennell, *Memoirs of Count Gramont*, p. 161.
4 *Ibid.*, p. 162.
5 Jusserand, *A French Ambassador ...*, p. 107.
6 Evelyn, *Diary*, volume XIX, pp. 320–1.
7 Hartmann and Quennell, *op. cit.*, p. 102.
8 Clarendon, *Continuation*, para 357.
9 Historical Manuscripts Commission, 12, IX, p. 52.
10 Clarendon, *op. cit.*, para. 391.
11 *Ibid.*
12 *Ibid.*, para. 392.
13 Pepys, *Diary*, volume IV, p. 216.
14 E. Burnet, *History of his own Times* (1900), volume I, p. 476.
15 Hartmann and Quennell, *op. cit.*, p. 253.
16 Hartmann, *The King my Brother* (Heinemann, 1954), p. 38.
17 *Ibid.*, p. 201.
18 *Ibid.*, p. 216.
19 Hartmann and Quennell, *op. cit.*, p. 218.
20 Pepys, *op. cit.*, volume IV, p. 37.
21 Tabor, *Four Margarets*, p. 97.
22 *Ibid.*, p. 99.
23 *Ibid.*, p. 111.
24 Evelyn, *Life of Mrs Godolphin*, pp. 13–14.
25 Strickland, *op. cit.*, volume VI, p. 46.
26 Oman, *Mary of Modena*, p. 62.
27 *Ibid.*, p. 96.
28 F. Turner, *James II* (Eyre & Spottiswoode, 1948), p. 143.

Chapter 7

The State Papers and documents published by the Historical Manuscripts Commission cited for the previous chapter are relevant here also, with the secondary sources M. and S. Grew, *The Court of William III* (Mills & Boon, 1910) and J. H. Jesse, *Memoirs of the Court of England from 1688 ...* (1843).

The lives of Mary II and Anne appear in Strickland (*op. cit.*, volumes VII and VIII). R. Doebner edited *The Memoirs of Mary, Queen of England, 1689–93* (1886) and her recent biographers include W. H. Chapman, *Mary II, Queen of England* (Jonathan Cape, 1953) and E. Hamilton, *William's Mary* (Hamish Hamilton, 1972). The main biographer of Queen Anne is D. Green (Collins, 1970). B. C. Brown edited *The Letters of Queen Anne* (Cassell, 1935).

Inevitably, there have been numerous works on Sarah Churchill, but the best is undeniably D. Green, *Sarah, Duchess of Marlborough* (Collins, 1967). Mary's and Anne's letters to Frances Apsley appear in B. Bathurst, *Letters of Two Queens* (Robert Holden, 1924).

1 Historical Manuscripts Commission: Bath MSS 158–9.
2 *Ibid*: Stopford-Sackville MSS 29–30.
3 Doebner, *Memoirs of Mary, Queen of England, 1689–93*, p. 42.
4 Marlborough MSS at Althorp, Book A.
5 Sarah, Duchess of Marlborough, *Conduct* ... (1742), p. 14.
6 Blenheim MSS G–I–9.
7 *Ibid.*, E 17.
8 *Ibid.*, E 19.
9 *Ibid.*, E 17.
10 *Conduct* ..., p. 183.
11 Brown, *Letters of Queen Anne*, pp. 244–5.
12 *Conduct* ..., p. 219.
13 HMC: Portland MSS IV 510–1.

Chapter 8

Besides the biographies of the individual Hanoverian queens of England listed below, two books provide a good resumé of the queens and their Courts in the eighteenth century: J. Doran,

Lives of the Queens of England under the House of Hanover (1855) and A. P. Greenwood, *Lives of the Hanoverian Queens of England* (G. Bell & Sons, 1911). They are well supplemented by J. H. Jesse, *Memoirs of the Court of England from 1688 ... to George II* (1843). A superbly illustrated book on the Courts of Europe in the eighteenth century is *The Princes* by H. V. Molesworth (Weidenfeld & Nicolson, 1969).

The House of Hanover before its arrival in England is chronicled in many recent works, but the two most relevant here are F. E. Baily, *Sophia of Hanover and her times* (Hutchinson, 1936) and M. Kroll, *Sophie, Electress of Hanover* (Gollancz, 1973).

There is no recent biography of Caroline of Anspach, but two excellent works are W. H. Wilkins, *Caroline the Illustrious* (Longmans, 1901) and R. L. Arkell, *Caroline of Anspach* (Oxford University Press, 1939). However, there are ample primary sources of the period to provide colourful background material: *Lord Hervey's Memoirs* (William Kimber, 1952) and *Some Materials towards Memoirs of the reign of George II* (Eyre & Spottiswoode, 1931) both edited by R. Sedgwick; Horace Walpole's *Reminiscences* (Clarendon Press, 1924) and his *Letters* (Clarendon Press, 1903–18) both edited by E. Paget Toynbee; *The Letters and Journals of Lady Mary Coke* (Kingsmead Reprints, 1970); a rather vituperative verse against some of Caroline's ladies in Lady Mary Wortley Montague's *Six Town Eclogues* (1747).

Of Caroline's ladies themselves, there are *The Memoirs of Viscountess Sundon*, edited by K. Thompson (1847); *Letters to and from Henrietta Howard, Countess of Suffolk*, edited by J. W. Croker (1824); the *Letters* of Mary Lepel (1821) and her biography, *Mary Lepel, Lady Hervey*, by D. M. Stuart (Harrap, 1936).

There is unfortunately no biography of Augusta, Princess of Wales, but the *affaire* between her husband and Anne Vane is told in full in *Poor Fred, the People's Prince*, by G. Young (Oxford University Press, 1937) and M. Marples, *Poor Fred and the Butcher* (Michael Joseph, 1970). *The Diary of Mary,*

Countess Cowper, 1714–20 (1864) gives some background to Augusta's Court.

Olwen Hedley's *Queen Charlotte* (John Murray, 1975) is the best sort of biography, full of information and anecdote. The affairs of her lady-in-waiting Lady Harcourt are amply covered in her 'Diary of the Court of George III' in *Miscellanies of the Philobiblion Society,* volume XIII (1871) and in the fourteen volumes of *Harcourt Papers*, edited by E. W. Harcourt (1895). Mrs Papendiek was the wife of one of the royal pages, and her observations of Court life appear in her *Court and Private Life of the Time of Queen Charlotte*, edited by V. D. Broughton (1887). Queen Charlotte's private life is chronicled in *Letters from Mrs Delany* (1820) and in C. Geary, *Royal Friendships* (1898). There have been several editions of Fanny Burney's diary, most notably her *Diary and Letters, 1768–1840*, edited by A. Dobson (1904), who also wrote her biography (1903), though perhaps J. Hemlow, *The History of Fanny Burney* (Clarendon Press, 1958) makes better reading.

The extract from Madame Campan about the etiquette of the contemporary French Court appears in her *Memoirs of Marie Antoinette* (Hutchinson).

The life of Caroline of Brunswick is told by Lord Russell of Liverpool in his *Caroline, the Unhappy Queen* (Robert Hale, 1967) and that of her daughter Charlotte in D. M. Stuart, *Daughter of England* (Macmillan, 1951) and D. Creston, *The Regent and his daughter* (Eyre & Spottiswoode, 1932). *The Letters of Princess Charlotte* were edited by A. Aspinall (Home & van Thal, 1949) and the memoirs of her lady companion by R. Fulford, *Autobiography of Miss Knight* (William Kimber, 1960).

The best biography of Queen Adelaide is that by Mary Hopkirk (John Murray, 1946), and contemporary sources on her Court include E. S. Cust, Countess Brownlow, *Eve of Victorianism* (John Murray, 1940) and the *Jerningham Letters, 1780–1843*, edited by E. Castle (1896).

1 Jesse, *Memoirs* ..., volume II, p. 322.

2 Wilkins, *Caroline the Illustrious*, volume I, p. 204.

3 Sedgwick, *Some Materials ...*, volume I, p. xvi.
4 *Ibid.*, p. xvii.
5 Jesse, *op. cit.*, volume II, p. 389.
6 Alexander Pope, 'An answer to a question from Mrs Howe'.
7 Jesse, *op. cit.*, volume II, p. 436.
8 *Ibid.*, p. 437.
9 Sedgwick, *op. cit.*, volume I, p. 41.
10 Walpole, *Reminiscences*, p. 60.
11 Sedgwick, *op. cit.*, volume I, p. 41.
12 *Ibid.*, p. 43.
13 *Ibid.*, p, 67.
14 *A Memoir of Charles Mordaunt, Earl of Peterborough* (1853), volume II, p. 209.
15 Sedgwick, *op. cit.*, volume I, p. 42.
16 *Ibid.*, volume II, p. 385.
17 *Ibid.*, p. 474.
18 Young, *Poor Fred ...*, p. 47.
19 Jesse, *op. cit.*, volume III, p. 328.
20 Wilkins, *op. cit.*, volume I, pp. 313–4.
21 Croker, *Letters to ... Henrietta Howard ...*, volume I, pp. 292–3.
22 Campan, *Memoirs ...*, pp. 70–1.
23 Burney, *Diary and Letters ...*, volume II, pp. 396–400.
24 *Ibid.*, pp. 352-3.
25 *Ibid.*, pp. 472–3.
26 *Ibid.*, pp. 468–9.
27 Hedley, *Queen Charlotte*, p. 195.
28 Aspinall, *Letters ...*, pp. 47–8.

Chapter 9

Queen Victoria's own journals and letters are the best source for her early Court, despite early twentieth-century editing which removed her frank remarks about the Lady Flora Hastings affair and Conroy's intrigues. The journals are comprised in *The Girlhood of Queen Victoria*, edited by Viscount Esher (John

Murray, 1912) and her letters, 1826–61, were edited by Viscount Esher and A. C. Benson (John Murray, 1907). C. C. F. Greville tapped the scandals of the Court in his *Memoirs*, edited by R. Fulford and L. Strachey (Macmillan, 1938).

The events leading up to the Lady Flora Hastings affair and the 'Bedchamber Crisis' are traced in Lady Longford's *Victoria RI* (Weidenfeld & Nicolson, 1964), D. Creston, *The Youthful Queen Victoria* (Macmillan, 1952) and D. M. Ashdown, *Queen Victoria's Mother* (Robert Hale, 1974).

Several pamphlets were issued by Lady Flora's partisans in 1839, including *Victim of Scandal* and *The Palace Martyr!*

1 Creston, *The Youthful Queen Victoria*, p. 307.
2 Longford, *Victoria RI*, p. 121.
3 Creston, *op. cit.*, p. 361.
4 *Ibid.*, p. 377.
5 *Ibid.*, p. 368.
6 Longford, *op. cit.*, p. 142.
7 Longford, *op. cit.*, p. 151.

Chapter 10

The background sources for Queen Victoria's reign are mainly comprised in the list for Chapter 9, to be supplemented with V. Watson, *A Queen at Home* (W. H. Allen, 1952) and E. E. P. Tisdell, *Queen Victoria's Private Life* (Jarrolds, 1961) from a very long list of works on the Queen and her reign.

Specific works on the Queen's ladies-in-waiting include *Lady Lytton's Court Diary*, edited by M. Lutyens (Rupert Hart-Davis, 1961); *Letters of Lady Augusta Stanley, 1849–63*, edited by H. Bolitho and W. Baillie (Howe, 1927); *Correspondence of Sarah Spencer, Lady Lyttelton, 1787–1870*, edited by H. Wyndham (John Murray, 1912); *Life with Queen Victoria*, edited by V. Mallet (John Murray, 1968); *Twenty Years at Court*, edited by Mrs Steuart Erskine (Nisbet & Co, 1916); *The Diary of Lady Frederick Cavendish*, edited by J. Bailey (John Murray, 1927); M. Ponsonby, *Mary Ponsonby* (John Murray, 1927), and

Georgiana, Baroness Bloomfield *Reminiscences of Court and Diplomatic Life* (1883).

Biographers of Queen Alexandra have been hampered by the fact that her friend Charlotte Knollys, obedient to the Queen's wishes, destroyed most of her mistress's private correspondence. However, there is much valuable information in H. G. Madol, *The Private Life of Queen Alexandra* (Hutchinson, 1940) and E. E. P. Tisdall, *Unpredictable Queen* (Stanley Paul, 1953), with the more recent G. Battiscombe, *Queen Alexandra* (Constable, 1969). Daily bulletins of the Court Circular for 1906 were edited, with valuable lists of royal attendants, by A. C. F. Davies, *Their Majesties' Court* (Caxton Publishing Company, 1907.

The best biography of Queen Mary is that by J. Pope-Hennessey (George Allen & Unwin, 1959), and fascinating side-lights on her character and eccentricities are provided by O. Sitwell, *Queen Mary and Others* (Michael Joseph, 1974). Two of the Queen's ladies-in-waiting wrote memoirs: Lady Cynthia Colville, *Crowded Life* (Evans, 1963) and Mabel, Countess of Airlie, *Thatched with Gold* (Hutchinson, 1962).

Inevitably, there is little material on ladies-in-waiting of recent years, but some is provided in D. Laird, *Queen Elizabeth the Queen Mother* (Hodder & Stoughton, 1966) and in three books by Helen Cathcart: *Her Majesty, The Queen Mother* and *The Duchess of Kent* (W. H. Allen, 1962, 1965 and 1971 respectively). An article by Helen Cathcart on ladies-in-waiting appeared in the magazine *Woman's Weekly*, on 9 June 1973, to which the author of this present work is particularly indebted.

1 Mallet, *Life with Queen Victoria*, p. 6.
2 Watson, *A Queen at Home*, p. 17.
3 Mallet, *op. cit.*, p. 35.
4 Wyndham, *Correspondence of Sarah Spencer* ..., pp. 283–4.
5 *Ibid.*, p. 282.
6 *Ibid.*, p. 278.
7 Steuart Erskine, *Twenty Years at Court*, pp. 23–4.
8 Bloomfield, *Reminiscences* ..., volume 1, pp. 21–5.
9 *Ibid.*, p. 29.

10 Mallet, *op. cit.*, p. 37.
11 Longford, *Victoria RI*, p. 383.
12 *Ibid.*, p. 719.
13 Wyndham, *op. cit.*, p. 286.
14 Bolitho and Baillie, *Letters of Lady Augusta Stanley, 1849–63*, pp. 68–9.
15 Lutyens, *Lady Lytton's Court Diary*, p. 152.
16 Battiscombe, *Queen Alexandra*, p. 62.

Index

This index does not include the names of every character mentioned in this book. Rather, here may be found the most notable ladies-in-waiting, their queens, lovers and husbands, and those politicians who figured largely in their lives.

Some ladies are entered under their maiden names, others under their various titles: the general principle used has been that of entering them under the name by which they are best known and cross-referencing where there may be confusion (e.g. Hill and Masham).

Q1